WHY I AM NOT A SECULARIST

Also by William E. Connolly

WHY I AM NOT A SECULARIST

William E. Connolly

UNIVERSITY OF MINNESOTA PRESS
Minneapolis
London

The publication of this book was assisted by a bequest from Josiah H. Chase to honor his parents, Ellen Rankin Chase and Josiah Hook Chase, Minnesota territorial pioneers.

The University of Minnesota Press gratefully acknowledges permission to reprint the following. An earlier version of chapter 2 originally appeared as "Suffering, Justice, and the Politics of Becoming," *Culture, Medicine, and Psychiatry* 20 (3, September 1996): 251–77, copyright Kluwer Academic Publishers; reprinted with kind permission of Kluwer Academic Publishers. Chapter 2 also appeared under the same title in *Moral Spaces: Rethinking Ethics and World Politics,* edited by David Campbell and Michael J. Shapiro (Minneapolis: University of Minnesota Press, 1999). An earlier version of chapter 4 originally appeared as "Freelancing the Nation: The Moral Universe of William Bennett," *Theory and Event* (1997), copyright The Johns Hopkins University Press, used by permission of the publisher. An earlier version of chapter 7 originally appeared as "A Critique of Pure Politics," *Philosophy and Social Criticism* (September 1997), copyright 1997, Sage Ltd., UK; reprinted by permission of Sage Publications Ltd.

Published by the University of Minnesota Press
111 Third Avenue South, Suite 290
Minneapolis, MN 55401-2520
http://www.upress.umn.edu

Library of Congress Cataloging-in-Publication Data

Connolly, William E.
    Why I am not a secularist / William E. Connolly.
        p.   cm.
    Includes bibliographical references and index.
    ISBN 0-8166-3331-2 (hc : acid-free paper). — ISBN 0-8166-3332-0
(pb : acid-free paper)
    1. Religion and politics.   2. Secularism.   I. Title.
    BL65.P7C66   1999
    291.1'77—dc21   98-43815

Printed in the United States of America on acid-free paper

The University of Minnesota is an equal-opportunity educator and employer.

11 10 09 08 07   10 9 8 7 6 5 4 3

For Jane

Contents

Acknowledgments

I have been fortunate to have the opportunity to present several chapters in this book to very stimulating groups. I am particularly grateful to Arthur Kleinman for inviting me to present the Roger Allen Moore Lecture at the Harvard Medical School in the spring of 1995 and for his very thoughtful commentary on the lecture that eventually became chapter 2 of this book. I also thank the organizers of the 1998 Program of The English Institute at Harvard University, particularly Judith Butler, for inviting me to speak on "refashioning the secular." It was during the summer of 1997, when I was a visitor at the Research School for the Social Sciences at Australian National University, that it became clear to me just what my thesis was and how much more work was needed to articulate it. Responses to papers I gave at ANU, the University of Sydney, and the University of Melbourne were inordinately helpful. That may be in part because Australia is both the most secular country I have yet to visit and the least haunted by religious wars. Many secularists there were very receptive to the need to refashion the secular. I must give special thanks to Ann Curthroy, John Docker, Carol Johnson, Christine Helliwell, Barry Hindess, Moira Gatens, Ian Hunter, Duncan Ivison, Brian Massumi, Paul Patton, Michael Peters, Sandi Buckley, James Tully (a fellow visitor), and Philip Pettit both for the rewarding conversations we had in general and for the very reflective comments they made on chapters in this book.

Closer to home, the wonderful atmosphere for theory at the Johns Hopkins University is very much due to the influence of my colleagues Dick Flathman and Kirstie McClure. Graduate students in two seminars have made major contributions to my thinking on this topic. I must mention in particular the contributions of Jason Frank, Davide Panagia, John Tambornino, Nicholas Tampio, and Kathy Trevenen. Above all, Paul Saurette took on the assignment of going over the entire manuscript in its penultimate draft. His suggestions have been extremely helpful.

Talal Asad, Romand Coles, Bonnie Honig, David Kettler, Mort Schoolman, Mike Shapiro, Michael Warner, Nathan Widder, and Linda Zerilli have made invaluable suggestions on particular chapters in this study. I am especially grateful to Tom Dumm, Barry Hindess, Wendy Brown, Kathy Ferguson, and Stephen White, who took time out from busy schedules to read and comment on the entire manuscript. Their commentaries have been particularly important to me in crafting the final version of this book. Finally, I am grateful beyond words to Jane Bennett, to whom this book is dedicated. Not only is she my favorite coteacher, gentle critic, and source of intellectual stimulation, she makes life enchanting by her mode of being in the world.

Introduction
Refashioning the Secular

Visceral Aptitudes and Secular Doctrine

To grow up in a factory town in the American Midwest is to get used to guttural things. On a hot summer's night in my town you could smell the Flint river several blocks away. On a clear day you could see the class struggle billowing from smokestacks down the street. More palpable yet was the religious fervor displayed by kids in the neighborhood, particularly when Negroes, Jews, or Italians came up for discussion. Many white parents had moved north in the 1940s and 1950s to find jobs, and they often carried the Southern Baptist faith with them. My parents were neither churchgoers nor believers, so my early experience with local Christianity was close to the ground and outside the house. "How do you *know* the Jews killed Jesus?" Billy would ask. "Because it's *in* the Bible," his friend would reply.

One winter, when he was twelve, Billy attended a Baptist church nearby with his friends. The church organized a contest to see who could learn the most verses in the Bible. The competition among the girls was fierce, with the eventual winner earning more than 400 points. The boys' contest was more composed. The day before it ended a Sunday school teacher pulled Billy aside. "You know," she said, "you have 93 points, and that puts you just 5 points behind Allen for first place." Billy pulled out the stops that night. He was declared winner the next day, with a measly 112 points.

The winner won a free week at the Unified Baptist Summer Camp, sixty miles away. The camp consisted of rules, obligations, and assignments, punctuated by enough regulated fun to discourage the inmates from plotting an escape. And there were also the daily salvation assemblies. Billy kept a low

1

profile at those. Nonetheless, one day he and two other boys were held over. "Do you want to give yourself to Jesus, Billy?" an adult hovering over him would repeat. Billy adopted a delinquent pose: don't look up, don't gaze off, just stare down, stupidly. Wait em out.

Finally, after letting loose a cascade of tears, he was released from interrogation. He ran to the ball field to join the game in progress. But the smear of old tears did him in this time. The coach and players gathered around. "Billy, you've been saved! It's all over your face." So he marched silently those last three days, an undocumented prisoner of cultural war.

A couple of years later, he confided to his parents that he had become an atheist. Within a few years Bill's conversion crystallized into a creed, particularly after he read Bertrand Russell's *Why I Am Not a Christian*. Atheism was now installed both in his (thought-imbued) gut feelings and in the arguments through which he represented himself.

As it turned out, the critique of Christianity had made Bertrand Russell the object of an American campaign of vilification a couple of decades earlier. He had been appointed to a one-year term at City College in New York City in 1940, but conservative Christian leaders launched a crusade to overturn the appointment. Bishop Manning from the Episcopal Church kicked the campaign off with a letter to all the New York newspapers:

> What is to be said of colleges and universities which hold up before our youth as a responsible teacher of philosophy...a man who is a recognized propagandist against both religion and morality, and who specifically defends adultery....Can anyone who cares for the welfare of the country be willing to see such teaching disseminated with the countenance of our colleges and universities....There are those who are so confused morally and mentally that they see nothing wrong in the appointment...of one who in his published writings said "outside of human desires there is no moral standard."[1]

Several Catholic and Protestant groups joined the crusade, with some city politicians chiming in. Russell's social views were roundly misrepresented in the process. Public support for him came from some liberals and secularists in the academy, several liberal religious leaders, and a few publishing houses. Rabbi Jonah Wise, E. S. Brightman, director of the National Council on Religion and Education, and the Reverend Guy Emery Shipler were prominent clerical supporters of the appointment. John Dewey and Sidney Hook were leading secular supporters. The judge, nonetheless, ruled against Russell and the college, basing his judgment on "norms and criteria...which are the laws of nature and nature's God."[2] Russell's greatest sins were support for cohabitation before marriage and tolerance of homosexual experimentation among schoolboys if it did not "interfere with the growth of normal sexual life later." The judge labeled the latter endorsement of "the damnable felony of homosexualism."[3]

Under the spell of his conversion to atheism it was quite a while before Bill called into question many things Russell endorsed. That included secularism. For Paul Edwards, in the introduction to *Why I Am Not a Christian,* had defined the fight over Russell's appointment as a cultural war between religious bigotry and secular tolerance:

> I have added as an appendix to this book, a very full account of how Bertrand Russell was prevented from becoming Professor of Philosophy at the College of the City University of New York. The facts of this case deserve to be more widely known, if only to show the incredible distortions and abuses of power which fanatics are willing to employ when they are out to vanquish an enemy. Those people who succeeded in nullifying Russell's appointment are the same ones who would destroy the secular character of the United States. They and their British counterparts are on the whole more powerful today than they were in 1940.[4]

I imagine that everyone — "believers" and "nonbelievers" alike — could tell stories comparable to the minor trauma recounted here. Indeed, today we are often invited to find a traumatic niche for ourselves. But perhaps we are less primed to explore what such events indicate more generally about the layered intricacy of thinking and judgment — and about the positive role they often play in life. Such contingencies become burned into your brain,[5] providing premonitions from which reflection proceeds and signposts to which it appeals. Ethical and political thinking could not gather the complexity they need unless they had such storehouses to draw upon. But the intensity of some of these experiences can also forestall critical thinking about defects and deficiencies in the judgments to which they are bonded. The visceral register of subjectivity and intersubjectivity, as I will call it, is at once part of thinking, indispensable to more conceptually refined thinking, a periodic spur to creative thinking, and a potential impediment to rethinking. The visceral register, moreover, can be drawn upon to thicken an intersubjective ethos of generous engagement between diverse constituencies or to harden strife between partisans. It can be and do all these things, and others besides. And yet modern secularism — in the main and for the most part — either ignores this register or disparages it. It does so in the name of a public sphere in which reason, morality, and tolerance flourish. By doing so it forfeits some of the very resources needed to foster a generous pluralism.

I continue to admire Russell's opposition to bullies on the Christian right who first advance profoundly contestable doctrines as the normative ground of life itself and then pull them above the reach of public debate because of their sacred character. I also accept his judgment that while each metaphysical or religious orientation makes a difference in politics, no such perspective suffices by itself to determine a political stance. But over the past few decades I have increasingly found secular conceptions of language, ethics, discourse, and politics in which Russell participated to be insufficiently alert to the layered density of political thinking and judgment, even as I oppose a religiously centered politics in which the state represents the dictates of a specific church or of a religious faith as general as Christianity. I am neither a secularist in my conception of public life nor the defender of a specific church. Are there, though, other spaces of possibility? Or am I merely conflicted about the possibilities that do exist? This study is an attempt to engage tensions within myself as well as to advance considerations worthy of the attention of others. My sense is that many people chafe under the constrictions of secular doctrine without being ready to accept one of the disturbing options its most fervent defenders present as the only alternative. The idea is to rework the secular problematic by exploring layered conceptions of thinking, ethos, and public life appropriate to a timely vision of multidimensional pluralism.

The historical modus vivendi of secularism, while seeking to chasten religious dogmatism, embodies unacknowledged elements of immodesty in itself. The very intensity of the struggle it wages against religious intolerance may induce blind spots with respect to itself. I also wonder whether the time of the secular modus vivendi is drawing to a close. We may need to fashion modifications in secular practices today, modifications that both honor debts to it and support more religious and nonreligious variety in public life than many traditional secularists and monotheists tend to appreciate.

This is a risky track to pursue. Many believe that the thin blue line of secularism, however frayed and tattered it has become, is still necessary to contain religious enthusiasm and dogmatism. While I harbor a few such anxieties myself, the strains of dogmatism in secularism may make a contribution to the effects secularists decry. People say that Communism kept virulent nationalisms alive in Eastern Europe by suppressing public engagement with them. Maybe secularism in democratic capitalist states has muffled the public ventilation of diverse religious and irreligious perspectives needed to adjust public life to the multidimensional pluralism of today. Or perhaps it is wise to remain agnostic about the past ambiguities of secularism while focusing upon the confining effects of that legacy on the present. There is little doubt that some compromise formation was needed with the breakup of the Catholic monopoly over religious belief in Christendom, and that the secular formation contained admirable features. But there is also a case to be made in favor of its reexamination under new conditions of being.

I am aware that several doctrines walk under the large umbrella of secularism, even if you limit yourself—as I do because of limitations in my grasp of the world—to Western conceptions of the secular. But there is also a discernible hierarchy among them. The shape of that hierarchy may be governed by a general secular wish to provide an authoritative and self-sufficient public space equipped to regulate and limit "religious" disputes in public life. The pursuit of a modified ideal of public life, then, may strengthen the hand of minority perspectives already circulating within secularism. Refashioning secularism might help to temper or disperse religious intolerance while honoring the desire of a variety of believers and nonbelievers to represent their faiths in public life. It might, thereby, help to render public life more pluralistic in shape and, particularly, more responsive to what I call the politics of becoming. These are big "ifs" and "maybes," but it seems timely to give them a hearing.

Several variants of secularism kill two birds with one stone: as they try to seal public life from religious doctrines they also cast out a set of nontheistic orientations to reverence, ethics, and public life that deserve to be heard. These two effects follow from the secular conceit to provide a single, authoritative basis of public reason and/or public ethics that governs all reasonable citizens regardless of "personal" or "private" faith. To invoke that principle against religious enthusiasts, secularists are also pressed to be pugnacious against asecular, nontheistic perspectives that call these very assumptions and prerogatives into question. That's one reason it rolls off the tongue rather easily to describe John Rawls, Jürgen Habermas, Amy Guttmann, and Hans Blumenberg as secularists and to think of Alasdair MacIntyre, Paul Ricoeur, and Charles Taylor as defenders of a larger role for theological concern in public life, while a diverse set of nontheistic thinkers such as Friedrich Nietzsche, Sigmund Freud, Michel Foucault, Gilles Deleuze, Judith Butler, Paul Patton, Thomas Dumm, Romand Coles, Barbara Herrnstein Smith, Wendy Brown, and Michael Shapiro do not fit comfortably on either side of that unstable line between secular and sacred orientations to public life. For to adhere to a separation of church and state is not automatically to concur in those conceptions of public life most widely bound up with secularism. To put the point briefly, the secular wish to *contain* religious and irreligious passions within private life helps to engender the immodest conceptions of public life peddled by so many secularists. The need today is to cultivate a public ethos of *engagement* in which a wider variety of perspectives than heretofore acknowledged inform and restrain one another.

Today reflective engagement is needed among a variety of religions and irreligions to support a more vibrant public pluralism. Bound up with these judgments is the conviction that secular models of thinking, discourse, and ethics are too constipated to sustain the diversity they seek to admire, while several theocratic models that do engage the density of culture do so in ways that are too highly centered. The division of labor that fell out of that historic compromise within predominantly Christian states may indeed have provided fragile protection against sectarian conflict and intolerance for a few centuries. But it also spawned practices of public life too dogmatic and terse to sustain the creative tension needed between democratic governance and critical responsiveness to the politics of becoming. And the destructive orientations it supported to non-Christian countries left a lot to be desired too. Limitations in the early organization of secularism leave fingerprints all over contemporary life. And yet, ironically, the precarious, multidimensional pluralization of life occurring before our eyes may create new conditions of possibility (I do not say probability) to renegotiate the old modus vivendi of secularism.

Is it, again, possible to refashion secularism as a model of thinking, discourse, and public life without lapsing into the "opposite" view that "Christianity" or "the Judeo-Christian tradition" must set the authoritative matrix of public life? Not if you think the world comes predesigned with these two options alone. Or even if your goal is to elevate the particular faith to which you are attached into the *new* center of gravity around which secularism and a couple of monotheisms rotate. Such a game plan recapitulates the historic objectives of secularism and Christianity, respectively. There is another way. *If* the objective is to project your own perspective into the fray while also decentering the political imagination of the ensconced contestants so that each becomes an honored participant in a pluralistic culture rather than the authoritative embodiment of it, *then* the positive possibilities expand. Now partisans of several types might negotiate a public ethos of engagement drawn from several moral sources. Here no constituency would be allowed to represent authoritatively the single source from which all others must draw in public life, even as each continued to articulate the strengths of the source it honors. For, again, secular and religious struggles to occupy the authoritative center help to manufacture those reciprocal recipes of dogmatism discernible in and around us.

Secularism is represented by some of its religious detractors to be a set of procedures that eventually drives virtue, morality, and faith out of culture. What if that charge is onto something, even in its false reduction of secularism to proceduralism, while the authoritative conceptions of virtue, morality, and faith prominent antisecularists often endorse are too stingy, exclusionary, and self-sanctifying? If that were so, the last thing needed would be the introduction of another perspective asserting its obligation to occupy the authoritative center. We need, rather, to renegotiate relations between interdependent partisans in a world in which no constituency's claim to *embody* the authoritative source of public reason is sanctified.

Sure, a few formalists will scream from the rooftops that any proposal to diversify the center constitutes—formally, as it were—a new center. But since they often advance such critiques on the way to supporting an old, narrow center, they reveal an ability to distinguish between a network of constituency relations modulated by a general ethos of generosity and forbearance drawn from multiple sources and a narrow practice of public life governed by one conception of reason or morality. The success of the formalist ruse, in this instance, depends upon the critic's and the target's both forgetting momentarily the care for the plurovocity of being that inspired the latter to support pluralization of the center in the first place. If the formalist recognizes no source of morality beyond the dictates of argument, it is all too easy to override a different *type* of element in the ethic of cultivation endorsed by the other. But when that discordant element is folded back into the engagement, the power of the formalist critique fades.

Such a result does not mean that either formalists or secularists must now endorse care for the plurovocity of being as a key element in their ethic—for one version of formalism may be set in a contestable metaphysic that promises the possibility of an intrinsic community while another is lodged in one that projects automatic harmonization between self-interested parties abiding by general principles of rationality in a market society. It means only that both formalists and secularists are now placed under ethical pressure to negotiate in good faith with those inspired by alternative faiths, doing so at least until they establish the *positive capacity* to fix their own moral practice as necessary and universal. Every such attempt to date has fallen far short of the mark.

There are several ruses of formalism. Those adopted by one type of secularist (for many secularists are not formalists) are prefigured in Augustine's critiques of heretics and pagans. But the faith that inspired Augustine's tactics against the heretics of his day was lifted to the forefront of his presentations, while contemporary formalists generally keep their own faith in what Gilles Deleuze calls "the good nature of thought" shrouded. Nonetheless, I have yet to meet a formalist who is simply one. There is always a sensibility moving below and within the argument, propelling the intensity with which a critique is advanced and the insistence through which the terms of the other are contracted.[6] Maybe it is timely, then, to place the question of ethical sensibility more actively onto the agenda of political reflection, for in matters such as these variations in sensibility make much of the difference. There may be expansive modes of persuasion, convincing, and inspiration that can alter the sensibility in which an argument is set and open up new lines of communication among partisans. At least the explorations to follow of the visceral register of subjectivity and intersubjectivity, an ethic of cultivation, relational arts of the self, freelancing and micropolitics, and a generous ethos of public engagement pursue these possibilities.

Condensations and Abbreviations

This book explores a possible world of intersecting publics, expressing a variety of religious and metaphysical orientations, interacting on several registers of being. No constituency gets everything it wants in such a world, particularly if it imagines itself—in its purity, neutrality, simplicity, faith, rationality, sanctity, or civilizational necessity—to be the one party to the case that must also be its final judge. If and when the immodest demands of transcendental narcissism are relaxed, the substance of your judgment can sometimes be separated from the character of the public decision you endorse, accept, or tolerate. The key is to acknowledge the comparative *contestability* of the fundamental perspectives you bring into public engagements while working hard not to convert that acknowledgment into a stolid or angry stance of existential resentment.[7] For those who resent the fragility of their own fundamentals are apt, eventually, to blame some other group or doctrine for this obdurate condition.

Appreciation of the profound contestability of the fundamentals you honor does not mean that you must forfeit faith in a loving or commanding god, give up secular faith in reason (or one of its surrogates), or adopt my nontheistic faith in the plurovocity of being. It means that you and I come to terms with our respective inabilities, so far at least, to secure our respective faiths so tightly that all reasonable humans must place either one at the center of public life. And it means that we do not follow this acknowledgment of modesty immediately with another doctrine of justice or constitutional correctness or public reason or truth or communicative rationality invested with the same certainty just called into question. Now the crystallization of agonistic respect between interdependent partisans can support attempts to build protections, exemptions, deferrals, individualities, or diversities into a variety of collective decisions. And in those cases where that proves impossible or seems destructive, acknowledgment of an element of tragedy, injustice, or uncertainty in the decision can now more readily be addressed: searches can be organized to find other ways to reduce or compensate for losses incurred. Moreover, when you acknowledge the *comparative* contestability of the fundamentals you endorse—for a new zone of contestability might be exposed at any time by the entrance of an unexpected party into the fray—you are in a better position to cultivate critical responsiveness to emerging constituencies who seek to modify the operative register of identity, justice, or constitutional legitimacy.

Another thing: to legitimate bringing fundamental orientations into the public realm does not mean it is either necessary or honorable to announce all the fundamentals you can marshal each time you address an issue. *A lot can be held back much of the time.* It means that when the issue is, say, the right to die, it is relevant to bring some dimensions of your theological or atheological perspective to the engagement, and when it is the just distribution of income another set may be pertinent. Forbearance and modesty are presumptive virtues in pluralist politics. They become even more important as the secular delineation between private life and public debate is rendered more fluid.

Let me, then, draw up a list of charges and lines of connection to other traditions as they find expression in the following chapters. In the first chapter, I begin by reviewing a few secular manifestoes. I then dig into the conceptions of thought, intersubjectivity, and ethics residing in them. The goal is first to disclose a connection between medieval practices of Christian ritual and Nietzschean arts of the self and then to bring both to bear upon Kantian and Habermasian conceptions of thinking and public discourse. What falls out when the latter conceptions prevail? How do these practices of reason block potential lines of communication between theistic and asecular, nontheistic dogmas? Chapter 1, then, explores the ethical implications of taking the visceral register of inter/subjectivity seriously. A host of historically contingent routines, traumas, joys, and conversion experiences leave imprints upon the visceral register of thinking and judgment, and these thought-imbued, often intersubjective intensities also exert effects on linguistically refined patterns of discourse and judgment. Moreover, attention to the fund of cultural inscriptions incorporated into those human brains less linguistically refined than the prefrontal cortex may be crucial to elaboration of a more generous ethos of engagement between multiple constituencies honoring different moral sources.

The next thing is to uncover the implications of secular conceptions of thinking for delineation of "the public sphere." Here Kant is taken as forerunner and Habermas as exemplar, for Kant developed a classic strategy through which to curtail the authority of Christian ecclesiology within both the university and the state, and Habermas bears crucial debts to Kant even as he tries to scrap the latter's practical metaphysic of the supersensible. Finally, an engagement among Kantian, Habermasian, Kierkegaardian, and Deleuzian perspectives is simulated to show how it is possible to refashion the secular. For once the hangman's noose of Habermasian theory (i.e., the performative self-contradiction) is lifted from the necks of those who dissent from its assumptions, the limits set by high secularism on public communication have been broken. Now it may be possible to uncover traces of other traditions in the substructure of your own, thereby opening up spaces for relations of partial indebtedness and agonistic respect between interdependent partisans. Since high secularism itself was crafted through a historic set of crossings between the organization of the university and the organization of public discourse, a contemporary simulation might aspire to exert modest effects in both domains.

Secularism and liberalism are connected, though neither is entirely reducible to the other. There are, for instance, theological liberalisms and nonliberal secularisms. Some neoconservatives, for instance, define themselves as secularists and resist pressures from theoconservatives. I myself aspire to a critical liberalism that both expands and thickens the range of secularism. Often, though, the differences between liberalism and secularism are those of inflection. Liberalism draws your attention to questions of rights, justice, tolerance, and the role of the state, whereas secularism draws it to the character of public discourse, the role of religion and nonreligion in public life, and so on. If you push against secularism very long you come up against the models of thinking it promotes and the limits it sets upon the politics of becoming. Chapter 2, then, examines John Rawls, a secularist who is also a liberal. I argue that Rawlsian theory engages conflicts between constituencies and claims already raised to the register of justice, but its rendering of the separation between the private and the public makes it tone-deaf to multiple modes of suffering and subordination currently subsisting below the public register of justice. Rawlsian theory, in short, is both invaluable once an identity is placed on the scales of justice and radically insufficient to the politics of becoming. The politics of becoming is that conflictual process by which new identities are propelled into being by moving the preexisting shape of diversity, justice, and legitimacy. Sure, Rawlsians often display an admirable ability to assimilate new constituencies and demands after much of the arduous, dangerous, and inventive work has been done. But the arid conceptions of persons, public reason, and justice sanctioned by Rawls disable him from listening receptively to such protean movements *at their dense points of inception* below the threshold at which the formal practice of justice kicks in. To come to terms with the paradoxical politics of becoming is to endorse a more complex public ethos, one in which the practice of justice exists in constitutive tension with critical responsiveness to the politics of becoming. No simple formula can dissolve this interdependence and tension between an ethos of critical responsiveness and the practice of justice. That means, though, that Kantian, neo-Kantian, and secular drives to simplicity and singularity in public life do not cope subtly enough with the complexity and multifaceted character of actually existing ethical issues. And it means that cultivation of an ethical sensibility appropriate to the complexity and ambiguity of cultural life is as important to a generous public ethos as commitment to the practice of justice.

In the first two chapters a series of resonances between Christianity and secularism emerges. In John Stuart Mill's image of the nation, these connections become even more apparent. In chapter 3, the idea is to excavate the Millian image of the nation and to explore an alternative to it. Mill himself helps with the second assignment, for existing in tension with his dominant image of the nation is a set of ideas about nonnational pluralism. I mine and rework this secondary theme to explore the emergent possibility of a rhizomatic or network pluralism ranging beyond the Tocqueville/ Mill legacies of national pluralism. The rhizome — as a network of diverse intersections between constituencies of numerous types — both already operates to some degree in societies marked by secularism and provides a model of aspiration for contemporary politics. The rhizome now assumes a place alongside other asecular conceptions elaborated to this point, such as the visceral register of intersubjectivity, an ethic of cultivation, and the politics of becoming.

The first three chapters play up differences between secular perspectives and the positions endorsed here, but they also identify some affinities and connections from which political connections can be forged across these differences in perspective. For the objective is not to eliminate secularism, but to convert it into one perspective among several in a pluralistic culture. Chapter 4 underlines some connections between secularism and the perspective advanced here. I first show how the American Republican moralist William Bennett reduces academic "secularists," "liberals," and "deconstructionists" to a common denominator and then examine how he deploys this trio to wage cultural war. Although Mill would gag on Bennett's tactics, Mill's nineteenth-century image of the nation stocks Bennett's arsenal in the different circumstances of the late twentieth century. Bennett dogmatizes the Millian image of the nation in circumstances even less conducive to its realization. Bennett is a master at working on the visceral register of subjectivity and intersubjectivity. If you contend, as I do, that it is impossible to shuffle the visceral register of intersubjectivity out of politics, if you think that its neglect in liberal and secular doctrines opens up opportunities for oligopolistic control of it by conservative forces, then it becomes very pertinent to understand how Bennett participates in what is here called micropolitics. And important to ask how critical intellectuals might work on these same registers in nonmanipulative ways. Chapter 4 continues to refashion secularism, but it also shows why people like me need to forge alliances with those who retain commitments to old-style secularism. That is not a concession, but a cardinal lesson of a perspective that prizes the ineliminable plurality of contestable perspectives in public life and the recurrent need to form collective assemblages of common action from this diversity.

If chapter 4 is organized around the role drug wars play in mobilizing disaffected constituencies to reinstate a nation that never was, the next chapter explores capital punishment along similar lines. Some secular critics of capital punishment believe it is possible to issue definitive arguments against it. I suggest in chapter 5 that an aggressive politics of forgetfulness about the long history of uncertainty and instability over "the will" forms a key part in campaigns on behalf of capital punishment. The idea is to disclose the constitutive experience of uncertainty and instability in the will, while identifying social pressures that press for cultural forgetfulness in this domain. This agenda is complicated by the fact that the state, as the official site of accountability to citizens and a crucial forum for the mobilization of national sentiments, has reasons of its own to nurture such forgetfulness. For when the state is both the highest site of electoral accountability and the paradigmatic target of electoral criticism for ineptness, it is tempting to convert its power to execute criminals into a theatrical politics of apparent accountability.

Chapter 6 clarifies the shape and character of a positive ethos of engagement among multiple constituencies in a culture where no single conception of public rationality or morality can hope to gain the free assent of a significant majority. I begin by addressing the individualism of George Kateb and the problem of evil recognized through it. There are several lines of connection between Kateb's position and mine. I participate, for instance, in his desire to think a nontheistic conception of evil. Nonetheless, differences persist. Because Kateb finds the worst evils to flow from collective politics, he supports an individualism of political minimalism. It seems to me, however, that a robust *politics* that addresses ambiguities in ethics, the paradoxical character of becoming, rhizomatic pluralism, and a positive ethos of engagement among diverse constituencies is better equipped than political minimalism to resist the evils he identifies.

Chapter 6 explores the indispensable role of relational arts and micropolitics in public ethics once the multiple registers of subjectivity and intersubjectivity have been acknowledged. It proceeds from there to explore an ethos of engagement between diverse constituencies honoring different moral sources. The work required is not all that arduous, since several elements in this imaginary already find some expression in existing practices.

Chapter 7 examines more closely admixtures, impurities, and instabilities secreted into Kantian conceptions of morality and the will. It joins the exploration in chapter 1 of thought-imbued *intensities* below the level of feeling and conceptual sophistication to thought-imbued *feelings* subsisting below the threshold of conceptual refinement. When you bring these two themes together the comparative contestability of the Kantian idea of pure morality drawn from an inscrutable supersensible source becomes apparent. One hinge in several secular models of justice and morality falls off the wall too. An ethic of cultivation emphasizing the positive possibilities in micropolitics now becomes more plausible to consider, as does the drive to negotiate a public ethos of engagement between multiple constituencies honoring different moral sources.

In chapter 7, I engage Kantian conceptions to challenge the exclusive authority of any morality anchored in the commands of a god, practical reason, or communicative competence; in doing so, I reopen thinking about the registers upon which subjectivity and intersubjectivity are organized. Kant is alert to the ethical import of arts of the self, even though his practical metaphysic of the supersensible limits their range. By placing the Kantian metaphysic of the inscrutable supersensible and the crude sensible into competition with the Deleuzian metaphysic of a protean infrasensible and a layered sensibility, we are in a better position to think about how the arts of the self work, what they work upon, and what role they might play in a public ethos.

This second encounter with Kant underlines something operative in the first. It is not just your agreements or disagreements with Kant that are important. It is sometimes profitable to squeeze through cracks he pries open but does not himself pass through. Such possibilities emerge in that brief moment of uncertainty between his critique of speculative theology and the defense of rational theology; in his experimentation with the thought that "radical evil" arises out of childhood duress before reason has had a chance to mature; in his appreciation of the opacity of the supersensible prior to insistence that it issues moral laws recognizable by any "ordinary man"; in his appreciation of arts of the self before placing the will and the supersensible above their reach; and in his exploration of the sublime just before hitching it to an imperative of inscrutable reason.

To resist one site of purification is sometimes to open up another. The case of Hannah Arendt is fascinating; she forms the second dialogical partner in chapter 7. Arendt attracts many who are dissatisfied with both secular models of politics and those governed by one or another religion of the Book. She explores how love for the world is fundamental to an ethical perspective worthy of admiration. She charts the paradoxical politics by which the new is brought into being. And she knows that these explorations carry her beyond the reach of Kantian and secular conceptions of morality. But Arendt may reinstate purity in "the political realm" after pulling it out of morality. It is not simply that she pushes out "the social question" and "the body" to render the world clean enough for political action. But, first, these expulsions bring back into play the reactive politics of the nation she resists. And, second, her tendency to reduce so much of the body to a set of automatisms and then to valorize "carefree" thinking, opinion, and engagement drains thinking and judgment of some of their richness and density. This drive draws her along one dimension toward forms of secular thinness she otherwise resists. And it pushes some significant sites of politics below the threshold of Arendtian nurturance. True, the visceral is a dangerous site of politics. But all sites are. And there is never a vacuum in this domain. An ethic of cultivation that supports and broadens Arendtian pluralism is blocked by the terms of her corporeal abstinence.

Several readers of Arendt interpret her to be a forerunner of "postmetaphysical thought," an orientation represented in the first chapter of this book by the recent work of Jürgen Habermas. I am uncertain whether Arendt actually belongs to that camp, even though her orientation resists the two or three perspectives commonly recognized by the crew of postmetaphysicians *as* metaphysical. But once contending renderings of the corporeal/cultural relation are brought into view that depart from the metaphysical tradition of Plato, Augustine, and Kant while being indebted to countertraditions of Epicurus, Lucretius, Spinoza, Nietzsche, and Deleuze, the claim to be postmetaphysical is seen to rest upon exposure to too small a sample of possibilities.

Cynicism and Enchantment

Is the desire to be postmetaphysical bonded to the secular attempt to protect a universal matrix of public discourse by thinning it out each time a new disturbance arises? The drive to *be* postmetaphysical contains many liabilities: it represses too many operative assumptions of its own carriers, it thins out the resources they can draw upon in making a case, and it opens them to charges of hypocrisy or innocence by other groups who quite happily bring their metaphysical and religious perspectives into public life. Today, the need is to draw a larger plurality of metaphysical/religious orientations into public life than heretofore, and to do so in ways that encourage more people to adjust more positively to the inevitable bouts of uncertainty, disruption, and surprise to which their own faiths are periodically subjected. For a positive ethos of public life requires more constituencies to respond graciously and generously to elements of comparative contestability in their own religious, secular, and asecular faiths. Again, I concur that this is a risky enterprise, but the risks must be compared to the losses and risks occasioned by the contemporary decline of secularism.

Nietzsche, Deleuze, Foucault, and Arendt, amid significant differences in their interpretations of thinking, corporeality, intersubjectivity, ethics, and democracy, inspire a lot in this book. That is partly because none is easily described as a secularist, even though none supports reinstatement of a theologically centered politics. I would not reduce my perspective to any of these thinkers. But the first three do insist upon the ethical importance of engaging the visceral register of subjectivity and intersubjectivity. And they do place a minority metaphysic into competition with the dominant metaphysical perspectives of the West. In expanding the range of available possibilities, they expose those delicate tactics by which secularists first purport to leave religious/metaphysical perspectives in the closet at home and then quietly draw upon a subset of them to elevate themselves into pillars of public authority.

Arendt joins the first three in cultivating that fugitive enchantment with being and becoming from which joy emanates and care for the plurovocity of existence might grow. Arendt, in her love of the world, and Nietzsche, in his gratitude for existence, both confound that dour division between the enchanted world of medieval Christianity and the disenchanted world of secular modernism. Such a temporal division not only exaggerates complex historical differences, it stifles distinctive possibilities of enchantment on each side of its fictive divide. Informed by the recent work of Jane Bennett, more of us might cultivate those fugitive spaces of enchantment lodged between theistic faith and secular abstinence.[8] For secular stories of disenchantment and theological nostalgia for a past when enchantment is alone thought to have been possible combine to squeeze out these alternative spaces of possibility. Bennett pluralizes the sites and sources of enchantment. She also shows how enchantment can be ethically significant even as it is irreducible to experiences of happiness or satisfaction, for its fascinations disturb as well as inspire, and limit as well as enable.

Nietzsche and Deleuze also inspire fugitive experiences of enchantment that exceed most secular representations and resist theological monopolization. Despite Nietzsche's aristocratic procliviities, his enchantment with the plurovocity of being is highly pertinent to a democratic ethos of generosity and forbearance. Such a source of ethical receptivity does not soar above the partisanships of identity, interest, and interpretation, nor does it subject them to transcendental command. It infiltrates into practices of partisanship, modulating them and opening partisans to more gracious engagements with differences within and without. As the discussion of an ethos of engagement between partisans in a world of multidimensional plurality contends, such dispositions can be cultivated inside religious traditions as well as outside them. Indeed, the formation of multiple lines of connection across these spaces of difference is crucial to a generous ethos of engagement in a post-secular society. I contend that nontheistic enchantment with the world provides one valuable source of such a temper, not the only one.

The four thinkers honored here come to terms with the tragic character of existence through the rubric of enchantment. On this reading a secular wish to master a disenchanted world too readily degenerates into cynicism if and when that world proves unsusceptible to mastery. Both the wish to master and the temptation to cynicism recede if you experience being as Nietzsche, Deleuze, Arendt, and Foucault do, in their different inflections. All four, in the moments I admire, find the most fervent secular representations of a disenchanted world to be almost as enervating to an ethos of reciprocal generosity as the demand that everyone adopt a singular theistic faith is destructive to human plurality.

A hardy minority of secularists today locate themselves on the democratic left. Perhaps the greatest risk faced by this band is a decline into cynicism. It is pertinent to be critical about the gap between the pretensions of democratic regimes and their performance in employment, income distribution, health care, race relations, education, housing, and cities. But generic cynicism is at risk of becoming the defining mark of the sophisticated left. Any expression of attachment to the world is thus chastized by being treated as incompatible with a commitment to social justice. But attachment to the world, it seems to me, provides an invaluable source for participation in the politics of social justice. Indeed, the mood of generic cynicism may express residual faith in the Kantian model of morality in which most democrats on the left purport to have lost effective faith. Such a residual faith is exhibited, first, by treating the ideal radicals officially renounce as the *operative standard* through which alternative orientations to political ethics are judged and, second, by failing to tap into alternative sources of energy rendered available by an ethic of cultivation.

The slide toward generic cynicism undercuts the nerve of critical action within radicalism, liberalism, and secularism. It may be wise, then, to cultivate little spaces of enchantment, both individually and collectively, partly for your own sake and partly to lend energy to political struggles against unnecessary suffering. An ethic of cultivation seeks both to expose its practitioners to voices and movements beyond their previous range of hearing and to mobilize energy to participate in the resulting campaigns.

Each of the thinkers discussed above, then, contributes something to an ethic of cultivation as well as to pursuit of a general ethos of engagement among adherents of divergent moral sources. None commandeers a universal moral source complete, automatic, or authoritative enough to generate a masterful response to every difficult issue. In drawing generosity and forbearance from that tropical undergrowth of life flourishing beneath the brittle trees of grand moral theory, each contributes something to an appreciation of the indispensability and constitutive fragility of ethics in political life.

1

The Conceits of Secularism

The Modus Vivendi of Secularism

The historical modus vivendi called secularism is coming apart at the seams. Secularism, in its Euro-American forms, was a shifting, somewhat unsettled, and yet reasonably efficacious organization of public space that opened up new possibilities of freedom and action. It shuffled some of its own preconditions of being into a newly crafted space of private religion, faith, and ritual. It requires cautious reconfiguration now when religious, metaphysical, ethnic, gender, and sexual differences both exceed those previously legitimate within European Christendom and challenge the immodest conceptions of ethics, public space, and theory secularism carved out of Christendom. I certainly do not suggest that a common religion needs to be reinstated in public life or that separation of church and state in some sense of that phrase needs to be reversed. Such attempts would intensify cultural wars already in motion. Secularism needs refashioning, not elimination.

The secular modus vivendi ignores or devalues some dimensions of being that need to be engaged more openly. On one level the secular is more bound up with generic characteristics of Christian culture than its most enthusiastic proponents acknowledge. On another level, the partial success of secularism in pushing specific Christian sects into private life has had the secondary effect of consolidating flat conceptions of theory, ethics, and public life.

Many academic secularists, following the lead of Kant, model public life upon an organization of university life they endorse. And vice versa. The field and authority divisions they project in the university among philoso-

19

phy, theology, arts, and the sciences marshal an ideal of thinking and discourse that is insufficient either to the university or to public life. The secular division of labor between "religious faith" and "secular argument," where faith and ritual are to be contained in a protected private preserve and rational argument is said to exhaust public life, suppresses complex registers of persuasion, judgment, and discourse operative in public life. Again, these registers continue to operate, even within secularism. But they do so largely below the threshold of appreciation by secularists. A cautious reconfiguration of secular conceptions of theory, thinking, discourse, subjectivity, and intersubjectivity is needed to come to terms more actively with these registers of being. Indeed, such a project might open up promising lines of connection between theistic orientations on the one hand and nontheistic, asecular orientations on the other blocked by the historic secular division between private and public life. For representatives of these two orientations often share important insights into the character of thought and intersubjectivity before they break over specific questions of faith and divinity.

Secularism, in its dominant expression, combines a distinctive organization of public space with a generic understanding of how discourse and ethical judgment proceed on that space. The historical narrative secularists commonly offer in support of this historical modus vivendi goes something like this:

> Once the universal Catholic Church was challenged and dispersed by various Protestant sects a unified public authority grounded in a common faith was drawn into a series of sectarian conflicts and wars. Because the sovereign's support of the right way to eternal life was said to hang in the balance, these conflicts were often horribly destructive and intractable. The best hope for a peaceful and just world under these new circumstances was institution of a public life in which the final meaning of life, the proper route to life after death, and the divine source of morality were pulled out of the public realm and deposited into private life. The secularization of public life is thus crucial to private freedom, pluralistic democracy, individual rights, public reason, and the primacy of the state. The key to its success is the separation of church and state and general acceptance of a conception of public reason (or some surrogate) through which to reach public agreement on nonreligious issues.

This is not the only story that could be told about the origins and legitimacy of secularism. You could tell one about the needs of capital and commercial society to increase the range and scope of monetary exchange in social relations. Here Adam Smith, Montesquieu, and Adam Ferguson would

take on great salience.[1] Or you could concentrate on the challenge that nom-
inalism posed within Christianity to enchanted conceptions of the world in
the medieval era, showing how the nominalist intensification of faith in an
omnipotent God presiding over a contingent world (rather than one obey-
ing the dictates of a teleological order) ironically opened the door to secularist conceptions of mastery over a disenchanted nature.[2] Or you could
treat secularism as the loss of organic connections that can be sustained
only by general participation in a common Christian faith. Or play up the
role of princely statecraft in supporting secular forces in order to strengthen
itself.[3] I want to suggest, however, that the story summarized above has become the dominant self-representation by secularists in several Western states.
This story prevails largely because it paints the picture of a self-sufficient
public realm fostering freedom and governance without recourse to a specific religious faith.

Evidence of the dominance of the first story can be found in the *Oxford
English Dictionary*. According to it, *Seculere,* in Christian Latin, means "the
world" as opposed to the One Church or heaven. The early (Christian) Church
treated the secular as a necessary but residual domain of its way of life. It
was, the *OED* says, mostly "a negative term," even though a restricted secular
domain of life was deemed essential. A sense of how it could be both lowly
and necessary is revealed in this statement by a priest in 1593 (quoted in
the *OED*): "The tongue is the Judge; the rest of our organs but the secular
executioners of his sentence." As you go down the list of *OED* meanings
and up the list of temporal references, the secular becomes a more positive
and independent domain. Thus Ben Franklin is moved to say, ironically,
that he speaks as "a mere secular man" in expressing his opinions. By the
modern period secularism, as a distinctive political perspective and social
movement, is represented positively as "the doctrine that morality should
be based solely in regard to the well-being of mankind in the present life
to the exclusion of all considerations drawn from the belief in God or in a
future state." Note, for later consideration, the reference to "the belief in
God," in which both a personal God and *beliefs* about it are treated as definitive of religious practice. And now to "secularize" is to "dissociate (say
art or educational studies) from religion or spiritual concerns." This language
of "solely," "exclusion," "dissociation" conceals the subterranean flow between the Christian sacred, which now becomes lodged in something called
the private domain, and secular discourse, which now becomes associated
with public authority, common sense, rational argument, justice, tolerance,
the public interest, publicity, and the like. The *OED* story, in fact, becomes

a partisan secular history of the sacred/secular division in the West, adopting as neutral terms of analysis several concepts and themes that became authoritative only through the hegemony of secularism.

John Rawls, too, participates in the dominant story of secularization. In *Political Liberalism,* for instance, he says that "Catholics and Protestants in the sixteenth century" lacked the ability or willingness to disconnect their divergent religious views from contending conceptions of public life. He then distills one cardinal point about the insufficiency of presecular regimes: "Both faiths held that it was the duty of the ruler to uphold the true religion and to repress the spread of heresy and false doctrines." Under such intense conditions either tolerance emerged as a precarious modus vivendi between contending groups or one side suppressed the others in the interests of truth or justice. Finally, Rawls insists upon the sanctity of an authoritative line of division between religion in private life and public political discourse, even while joining a list of modern predecessors in trying to redefine that line:

> We appeal (instead) to a political conception of justice to distinguish between those questions that can be reasonably removed from the political agenda and those that cannot. . . . To illustrate: from within a political conception of justice let us suppose we can account both for equal liberty of conscience, which takes the truths of religion off the agenda, and the equal political and civil liberties, which by ruling out serfdom and slavery take the possibility of those institutions off the agenda. But controversial issues remain: for example, how, more exactly, to draw the boundaries of the basic liberties when they conflict (where to set the "wall between church and state"); how to interpret requirements of distributive justice even when there is considerable agreement on general principles. . . . But by avoiding comprehensive doctrines [i.e., basic religious and metaphysical systems] we try to bypass religion and philosophy's profoundest controversies so as to have some hope of uncovering a stable overlapping consensus.[4]

So secularism strains metaphysics out of politics. But notice how fragile the specific discrimination between the secular public realm and private life has become amid insistence that such a line of discrimination provides *the* way to regulate "religious" disputes in public life: "Let us suppose"; "We try to bypass"; "avoiding"; "so as to have some hope of uncovering a basis for a stable, overlapping consensus." The word "avoid" is revealing because it mediates effortlessly between a demarcation *established* by some philosophical means and one commended because its political acceptance *prior* to introduction of an impartial philosophy of justice would reduce the intensity of cultural conflict. You also encounter in these lines a paradigmatic secular tactic for taming conflict: the idea is to dredge out of public life as much cultural density and depth as possible so that muddy "metaphysical" and "religious" differences don't flow into the pure water of public reason, procedure, and justice. Finally, the word "religion" now becomes treated as a universal term, as if "it" could always be distilled from a variety of cultures in a variety of times rather than representing a specific fashioning of spiritual life engendered by the secular public space carved out of Christendom.

The first quandary of secularism, then, is that its inability to draw a firm line between private life and public discourse creates opportunities for some Christian enthusiasts to call for the return to a theologically centered state, while the increasingly transparent favoritism of its "neutral" public space opens a window of opportunity for critics to accuse secularists of moral hypocrisy. Thus, in an issue of *First Things: A Journal of Religion and Public Life,* the editors assert that the American courts have lost cultural legitimacy because of their (secular) stands on abortion, homosexuality, and the right to die. The substantive positions the authors oppose are not too far from those many secularists say emerge out of the dictates of public reason itself. In a follow up the next month, the editors asserted:

> Almost all Americans claim adherence to an ethic and morality that transcends human invention, and for all but a relatively small minority, that adherence is expressed in terms of biblical religion. By the strange doctrine promulgated by the courts, Christians, Jews and others who adhere to a transcendent morality would, to the extent that their actions as citizens are influenced by that morality, be effectively disenfranchised.... It is a doctrine that ends up casting religious Americans, traditionally the most loyal of citizens, into the role of enemies of the public order.[5]

Secularism, its (primarily) Christian critics contend, lacks the ability to come to terms with the sources of morality most citizens endorse; therefore, secularism itself drifts toward public orientations that challenge the moral sensibilities of many of its citizens. Many such theological critics call upon secularists to return to the nineteenth century vision of public life registered by Tocqueville. Tocqueville contended that the separation of church and state was viable only because public life was already grounded in a larger Christian civilization. Tocqueville's version of church and state is both objectionable to contemporary secularists and revelatory of a subterranean component of contemporary life too often minimized in secular self-representations.

Consider two quotations from Tocqueville. The first deals with a network of internal relations among religion, mores, reason, and morals in American civilization:

> In the United States it is not only *mores* that are controlled by religion,
> but its sway extends over *reason*. . . . Among Anglo-Americans there are
> some who profess Christian dogmas because they believe them and
> others who do so because they are afraid to look as though they did
> not believe them. So Christianity reigns without obstacles, by universal
> consent; consequently . . . *everything in the moral field is certain and
> fixed,* although the world of politics seems given over to argument and
> experimentation.[6]

You might read this to say that while politics is *located* in a secular
realm, that realm remains safe for Christianity as long as the unconscious
mores that *organize* public reason, morality, and politics are Christian. Christianity does not need to be invoked that often because it is already inscribed in the prediscursive dispositions and cultural instincts of the civilization. Tocqueville defends a secularism contained within Christianity, while
modern secularists generally seek to contain Christianity within the private
realm. Tocqueville proceeds by invoking a conception of preconscious mores
eventually pushed out or debased by most secular self-representations. But
why, then, bother to support separation of church and state at all? Here is
part of the answer, for Tocqueville at least:

> There is an innumerable multitude of sects in the United States. . . .
> Each sect worships God in its own fashion, but all preach the same
> morality in the name of God. . . . America is still the place where the
> Christian religion has kept the greatest power over men's souls; and
> nothing better demonstrates how useful and natural it is to man, since
> the country where it now has widest sway is both the most enlightened
> and freest.[7]

Separation of church and state functions to soften sectarian divisions
between Christian sects while retaining the civilizational hegemony of Christianity in a larger sense. This is so because the instinctive register of intersubjective judgment to which Tocqueville appeals both embodies Christian
culture and helps to regulate public argumentation. Most contemporary secularists, unlike Tocqueville, either ignore this register of being or locate it beneath public deliberation. Indeed, at the very point where many secularists
and devotees of public religious faith meet in combat a space opens up occupied by neither. For most critics of secularism who recognize the visceral
register invoke it to deepen the quest for unity or community in public life,
while most secularists who eschew it act as if diversity can be fostered only
by leaving the guttural register of being out of public life. My suspicion,
contrary to one element in each view, is that elaboration of an expansive
pluralism appropriate to contemporary life requires cultural investments
in the visceral register of subjectivity and intersubjectivity. We must press

Tocqueville's appreciation of intersubjective mores beyond his colonization of them by a civilization of Christian containment. And we must press the (underdeveloped) secular appreciation of diversity into registers of being it tends to reserve to "religion."

Visceral Judgment and Represented Beliefs

Talal Asad, an anthropologist of Islamic heritage, has explored long-term shifts in the Christian experience of ritual, symbol, belief, faith, and doctrine. It is not simply that dominant Christian *beliefs* have changed over the centuries, as, say, the doctrine of original sin gives ground to that of individual choice. But the operative meanings of ritual and symbol have shifted too. With the emergence of secularism and Protestantism, a symbol, in its dominant valence, becomes the representation of an inner state of belief that precedes it; and ritual is now understood to be the primitive enactment of *beliefs* that could also be displayed through cognitive representation. Even sophisticated anthropologists such as Clifford Geertz, says Asad, tend to adopt these historically specific meanings of symbol and ritual as if they were pertinent to the universal experience of "religion." But in medieval Christianity, Asad asserts, a symbol was bound up with *enactment or perfection* of inner states and meanings it also represented; and ritual was practiced as a means of educating and constituting appropriate dispositions of appraisal and aptitudes of performance. In medieval monastic life,

> the liturgy is not a species of enacted symbolism to be classified separately from activities defined as technical but is a practice among others essential to the acquisition of Christian virtues.... Each thing done was not only to be done aptly in itself, but done in order to make the self approximate more and more to a predefined model of excellence. The things prescribed, including liturgical services, had a place in the overall scheme of training the Christian self. In this conception there could be no radical disjunction between outer behavior and inner motive, between social rituals and individual sentiments, between activities that are expressive and those that are technical.[8]

Asad draws upon Mauss's exploration of *habitus* as "embodied aptitude" to sharpen the sense of how intersubjective dispositions, instincts, and virtues can be constituted through ritual performance. If Asad is right, then secular understandings of discourse, analysis, and argument capture merely one dimension of thinking, intersubjective judgment, and doctrinal commitment in public life. You might say, then, that intersubjectivity operates on several registers (with significant subjective variations) and that each register exerts effects upon the organization of the others.

I would augment Asad modestly. First, as the reading of Kant to follow suggests, it would exaggerate to draw a sharp line between presecular and secular understandings. Some of these practices persist in Christian Protestantism as well as in some secular orientations to education and training in citizenship. Secularists sometimes address these practices, but seldom in ways that affect profoundly their presentations of how an ethos is to be fostered in public life. So Asad seems right in suggesting that the significance of such practices in contemporary life is underappreciated in secular discourse. Second, and connected to the above, it may be important to underline how representational discourse itself, including the public expression and defense of fundamental beliefs, affects and is affected by the visceral register of intersubjectivity. Public discourses do operate within dense linguistic fields that specify how beliefs are to be articulated and tested and how ethical claims are to be redeemed. But repetitions and defenses of these articulations also write scripts upon prerepresentational sites of appraisal. Although secular presentations of public reason and moral discourse remain tone-deaf to this second register of intersubjectivity, they nonetheless depend upon it to stabilize those practices.

Most pertinent for my purposes, however, is that in addition to the appreciation of this register by many theological thinkers, several nonsecular, a-theistic thinkers pay attention to it as well. This correspondence opens a line of potential communication between theistic and nonsecular, a-theistic agents deflected historically by the secular division between private faith and secular public argument. Indeed, as we shall soon see more closely, secularism as an authoritative model of public life is predicated upon a twofold strategy of containment: to secure the public realm as it construes it, it is almost as important to quarantine certain nontheistic patterns of thinking and technique as it is to monitor ecclesiastical intrusions into public life.

Consider, then, how Nietzsche makes contact with Christian practices of training and thinking. In *The Anti-Christ,* he distinguishes between Christian *doctrines* of original sin, free will, heaven, and damnation, which he attributes to Paul, and pre-Pauline *practices* of character formation, which he attributes to Jesus. He finds the latter infinitely preferable to the former:

> It is false to the point of absurdity to see in a "belief," perchance the belief in redemption through Christ, the distinguishing characteristic of the Christian: only Christian *practice,* a life such as he who died on the Cross *lived,* is Christian. . . . Not a belief but a doing, above all, a not doing of many things, a different *being.* . . . States of consciousness, beliefs of any kind, holding something to be true, for example — every psychologist knows this — are a matter of complete indifference and of fifth rank compared to the value of the instincts. . . . "Faith" has been at

all times, with Luther for instance, only a cloak, a pretext, a *screen,* behind which the instincts played their game — a shrewd blindness to the dominance of *certain* instincts.[9]

If you attend to what Nietzsche says elsewhere about the relations among culture, instinct, thinking, and language, it becomes apparent that instinct is more than a brutish, biologically fixed force. Instincts are proto-thoughts situated in culturally formed moods, affects, and situations. They are not even entirely reducible to implicit thoughts or tacit judgments, for the latter imply thoughts and judgments like those in explicit discourse that have not been raised to its level. In such a view a dialectical logic of rendering explicit what was implicit would be sufficient to the case, fitting the new entry into an emergent, coherent whole. But for Nietzsche thinking bounces in magical bumps and charges across several registers. Proto-thoughts undergo significant modification and refinement when bumped into a complex linguistic network of contrasts. Moreover, these visceral modes of appraisal are often invested with considerable *intensity,* carrying considerable energy and fervency with them into the other registers of being. This "invisible" set of intensive appraisals forms (as I will call it) an infrasensible subtext from which conscious thoughts, feelings, and discursive judgments draw part of their sustenance. Moreover, instincts that are culturally formed can sometimes be modified by cultural strategies applied by groups to themselves and by individual arts of the self. Hence Nietzsche's durable interest in polytheistic and monotheistic rituals and festivals, and the "misuses" to which Christianity has subjected them.

So Nietzsche says things like, "Our true experiences are not garrulous" and "Even one's thoughts one cannot reduce entirely to words," and "Our invisible moral qualities follow their own course — probably a wholly different course; and they might give pleasure to a god with a divine microscope." He says these things because instincts are thought-imbued intensities moving below linguistic sophistication, consciousness, and reflective judgment as well as through them.[10]

What Nietzsche shares with the medieval Christian perspective explored by Asad is the idea that thinking and intersubjectivity operate on more than one register and that to work on the instinctive register of intersubjective judgment can also be to introduce new possibilities of thinking and being into life. What the medieval and Nietzschean orientations have in common is an appreciation of the significant role the visceral register of intersubjectivity plays in moral and political life and a desire to do some of their ethical work on that register. Where they may differ is in the goals they set for such work, though it is not at all clear that such differences can be read off simply by knowing whether a thinker is a theist or a nontheist. Bertrand Russell and Nietzsche were both atheists, but they diverged significantly in their orientations to ethics and the registers of being they acknowledged.

When Nietzsche, again, speaks of "thoughts behind your thoughts and thoughts behind those thoughts," he is speaking of "concealed gardens and plantings" below the threshold of reflective surveillance.[11] Now ecclesiastical practices of ritual are translated by Nietzsche and Foucault into experimental arts of the self and by Deleuze into an experimental micropolitics of intersubjectivity. Each tries to shift ethical practices that impinge on the visceral register from their uses, say, in the Augustinian confessional or in state practices of discipline, but each also strives to make investments in this domain that exceed the scope of secular self-representations. Such strategies are experimental because they work on thought-imbued intensities behind conscious thoughts not readily or fully subject to conscious purview; they are important to thinking and theory because such work on oneself can sometimes untie knots in one's thinking; they are important to politics because such work can pave the way for new movement in the politics of becoming; and they are pertinent to the ethos of a pluralist culture because such work can help to install generosity and forbearance into ethical *sensibilities* in a world of multidimensional plurality. To change an intersubjective ethos significantly is to modify the instinctive subjectivities and intersubjectivities in which it is set. But this may sound like mumbo jumbo to many secularists.

The recent work by Joseph LeDoux, a neurophysiologist who maps complex intersections connecting the several human brains involved in our thought-imbued emotional life, may be pertinent here. His study not only confounds behaviorist and computer models of thinking, it may expose insufficiencies in linguistic models of thought and discourse. Let us focus on the relation between the amygdala, a small, almond-shaped brain located at the base of the cortex, and the prefrontal cortex, the large brain developed more extensively in humans than in other animals. The amygdala and the prefrontal cortex can receive messages from the same sources, but each registers them in a different way. When receiving, say, a sign it has stored as an indication of danger, the amygdala reacts quickly, relatively crudely, and with intense energy. Exposure to signs that resemble a past trauma, panic, or disturbance "pass like greased lightning over the potentiated pathways to the amygdala, unleashing the fear reaction."[12] The prefrontal cortex receives its version of the message more slowly, processing it through a sophisticated linguistic network in a more refined way and forming a more complex judgment. In a situation of stress, the amygdala also transmits its interpretation and much of its intensity to the prefrontal cortex; and

> the amygdala has a greater influence on the cortex than the cortex has on the amygdala, allowing emotional arousal to dominate and control thinking.... Although thoughts can easily trigger emotions (by activating the amygdala), we are not very effective at willfully turning off emotions (by deactivating the amygdala).[13]

The amygdala is a site of thought-imbued intensities that do not in themselves take the form of either conscious feelings or representations. The amygdala is, then, literally one of the "concealed gardens and plantings" of which Nietzsche speaks, implicated in a set of relays with other more open gardens. LeDoux suggests that it is for the most part a good thing the amygdala is wired to the cortex, for it imparts energy and intensity to that center needed for the latter's formation of representations and practical decisions. And, I suggest, those gaps and dissonances between the amygdala and the cortex, and between it and the hippocampus (the site of complex memories), may create some of the frictions from which creativity in thinking and judgment arises. How, though, can the amygdala be educated? It is under variable degrees of control by the cortex, depending on the context. But, also, since its specific organization is shaped to an uncertain degree by previous intensities of cultural experience and performance, either it or, more likely, the network of relays in which it is set may be susceptible to modest influence by rituals and intersubjective arts thematized by religions of the Book and Nietzscheans, respectively.

So, if the first quandary of secularism is bound up with uncertainties in the line of demarcation it pursues between private and public life, the second is that its forgetting or depreciation of an entire register of thought-imbued intensities in which we participate requires it to misrecognize itself and encourages it to advance dismissive interpretations of any culture or ethical practice that engages the visceral register of being actively. The secular understanding of symbol and ritual reviewed by Asad provides one index of this combination. A whole litany of dismissive misinterpretations of Nietzschean and Foucauldian arts of the self provides a second.[14]

The Secular Public Sphere

We now need to draw this preliminary engagement with secular accounts of thinking and discourse into coordination with a conception of public space that has become hegemonic within Euro-American secularism. For to engage its presentation of public life is to go some way toward explaining how the plurality of secular self-interpretations noted earlier becomes organized into a hierarchy. And it helps to set the table for another conception of public life that more actively appreciates the visceral register, that engages the role of micropolitics, and that embraces a more expansive and generous model of public discourses. Let's begin with Kant. Kant struggled to give "universal philosophy" primacy over ecclesiastical (Christian) theology in a way that has become authoritative for secularism. And his passage from an account of the proper organization of the university to the proper organization of public discourse is also exemplary.[15] Card-carrying secularists are very often university academics as well as citizens of a state. And they often pursue the same mantle of authority in each domain. Most pertinently, the way in which they imagine the contour of one institution regularly infiltrates into the mode of governance they project into the other.

In *The Conflict of the Faculties,* Kant's immediate objective is to curtail the authority of the faculty of ecclesiastical theology within both the German university and the larger political culture.[16] His concern is that since (Christian) ecclesiastical theology is governed by texts and practices sunk in the medium of history and sensibility, the claim by each ecclesiastical "sect" to moral supremacy is likely to meet with an equal and opposite claim by others. His object is to cleanse the university and public life of the adverse effects of sectarianism. This is to be accomplished by elevating universal philosophy, also known as "rational religion," to the authoritative position previously reserved for Christian theology. Kant asserts that

> a division into sects can never occur in matters of pure religious belief. Wherever sectarianism is to be found, it arises from a mistake on the part of ecclesiastical faith: the mistake of regarding its statutes (even if they are divine revelations) for essential parts of religion. . . . But since, in contingent doctrines, there can be all sort of conflicting articles or interpretations. . . . , we can readily see that mere dogma will be a prolific source of innumerable sects in matters of faith unless it is rectified by pure religious faith.[17]

Kantian philosophy is then wheeled out to fill the place of ecclesiastical authority just vacated. But, as *we* now know from repeated experience after Kant, the claim of an upstart to occupy the authoritative place of a teetering authority succeeds best if the upstart plays up the arbitrariness and divisiveness of the resources its predecessor drew upon while sanctifying and purifying the source from which it draws. Kant imagines himself to be up to the task. He elevates a generic Christianity called "rational religion" above sectarian faith, anchoring the former in a metaphysic of the supersensible that, so the story goes, is presupposed by any agent of morality. In the process, he degrades ritual and arts of the self without eliminating them altogether, for these arts work on the "sensibility" rather than drawing moral obligation from the supersensible realm as practical reason does. The point is to deploy them just enough to render crude sensibilities better equipped to accept the moral law drawn from practical reason. Secularists later carry this Kantian project of diminishment a step or two further.

To secure the authority of philosophy over theology, Kant then reduces moral judgment to practical reason alone. The program of anointing one discipline by degrading the other is pursued in the following formulation:

> For unless the supersensible (the thought of which is essential to any-
> thing called religion) is anchored to determinate concepts of reason,
> such as those of morality, fantasy inevitably gets lost in the transcen-
> dent, where religious matters are concerned, and leads to an illumin-
> ism in which everyone has his own private, inner revelations, and there
> is no longer any public touchstone of truth.[18]

Kant anchors rational religion in the law of morality rather than anchoring morality in ecclesiastical faith. That is, he *retains* the command model of morality from Augustinian Christianity, but he *shifts* the proximate point of command from the Christian God to the moral subject itself. This, with significant variations, becomes a key move in later secular models of public life. But it also engenders a legacy of uncertainty and instability that still haunts the secular problematic. For authoritative moral philosophy and rational religion are now only as secure as the source of morality upon which they draw. And morality as law now itself becomes anchored only in the "apodictic" recognition by ordinary human beings of its binding authority. To tie *this* knot of recognition tightly Kant must continue his attack on the relative difficulties ecclesiastical theology faces in anchoring morality directly in the commands of God:

> Now a code of God's *statutory* (and so revealed) will, not derived from
> human reason but harmonizing perfectly with morally practical reason
> toward the final end—in other words the Bible—would be the most
> effective organ for guiding men and citizens to their temporary and
> eternal well being, if only it could be accredited as the word of God
> and its authenticity could be proved by documents. But there are many
> difficulties in the way of validating it.... For if God would really speak
> to man, man could still never *know* it was God speaking.... But in some
> cases man can be sure that the voice he hears is *not* God's; for if the
> voice commands him to do something contrary to the moral law, then
> no matter how majestic the apparition may be...., he must consider it
> an illusion.... And ... we must regard the credentials of the Bible as
> drawn from the pure spring of universal rational religion dwelling in

every ordinary man; and it is this very simplicity that accounts for the Bible's extremely widespread and powerful influence on the hearts of the people.[19]

It is a significant move to give morality priority over ecclesiology, but Kant's rational religion still shares much structurally with the "dogmatic" ecclesiology it seeks to displace. First, it places singular conceptions of reason and command morality above question. Second, it sets up (Kantian) philosophy as the highest potential authority in adjudicating questions in these two domains and in guiding the people toward eventual enlightenment. Third, it defines the greatest danger to public morality as sectarianism within Christianity. Fourth, in the process of defrocking ecclesiastical theology and crowning philosophy as judge in the last instance, it also delegitimates a place for several non-Kantian, nontheistic perspectives in public life. Thus, as Kantian philosophy is elevated to public preeminence, the pre-Kantian philosophies of Epicureanism, Spinozism, and Humeanism are devalued because of the priority they give to sensible life and an ethic of cultivation, respectively, over the supersensible and a morality of command. Moreover, a series of post-Kantian philosophies such as Nietzscheanism, Bergsonism, Foucauldianism, and Deleuzianism are depreciated in advance on similar grounds. For denigration of these latter perspectives sets a crucial condition of possibility for the authoritative regulation of religious sects in public life by universal philosophy.

Later, neo-Kantian simulations of secularism, then, consist of a series of attempts to secure these four effects without open recourse to the Kantian metaphysic of the supersensible. Secularism, in its dominant Western forms, *is* this Kantian fourfold without metaphysical portfolio. The slogans "political not metaphysical," "postmetaphysical," "beyond metaphysics," and even "pragmatic" often provide signals of this attempt, although they occasionally set the stage for attempts to refigure secularism. My sense is, as I will argue later in this chapter and further in the last, that recent attempts to be postmetaphysical often complement secularism by depreciating the visceral register of intersubjectivity and investing too much purity into politics. At any rate, the third quandary of contemporary secularism is that its advocates often disavow dependence upon a metaphysic of the supersensible to fend off sectarian religious struggles in the public realm while they then invoke authoritative conceptions of thinking, reason, and morality that draw them perilously close to the Kantian metaphysic of the supersensible as they ward off contemporary defenders of an ethic of cultivation. Secularism functions most effectively politically when its criticisms of a public role for Christian theology are insulated from its corollary disparagements of nontheistic, non-Kantian philosophies.

The Kantian achievement, however, is cast from fragile crystal. For what if one contends, as Gilles Deleuze does, that the "apodictic" *recognition* by ordinary people upon which Kantian morality is grounded in the first instance is actually a secondary formation reflecting the predominant Christian culture in which it is set? Now the same objections Kant brought against the arbitrary authority of ecclesiology can be brought against him. And this difficulty returns to haunt other attempts to secure secular authority in the public realm after Kant, even by secularists who eschew reference to the Kantian supersensible. The return of Kantian charges against the philosophy that issued them leads one to wonder whether every attempt to *occupy* such a place of unquestioned authority reenacts the plot of Greek tragedy in which all parties promising to resolve an obdurate conflict in the same old way soon find themselves succumbing to it.

Kant introduces defining elements into the logic of secularism, but he himself does not construct a complete philosophy of secularism. His obsequious deference to the prince, his explicit dependence on the supersensible, his hope that a natural teleology of public life will promote rationality in the public sphere by automatic means, and his hesitancy to include most subjects within the realm of public discourse render him a forerunner rather than a partisan of secularism.[20] Nonetheless, most contemporary secularists attempt to secure the Kantian effect by Kantian and/or non-Kantian means. This implicates them, though to varying degrees, in a cluster of protectionist strategies against (a) the intrusion of ecclesiastical theology into public life; (b) the academic and public legitimacy of nontheistic, non-Kantian philosophies; (c) the exploration of the visceral register of thinking and intersubjectivity; (d) the admiration of creativity in thinking; (e) the related appreciation of the politics of becoming by which the new comes into being from below the operative register of justice and representational discourse; and (f) productive involvement with experimental practices of micropolitics and self-artistry. These intercoded interventions are pursued in the name of protecting the authority of deliberative argument in the secular public sphere, that is, of securing the Kantian effect.

Let's look at how one effort to secure the Kantian effect by non-Kantian means unfolds in the early work of Jürgen Habermas, when he traces the emergence and decline of "the public sphere" in modern Western societies. In *The Structural Transformation of the Public Sphere*, Habermas draws sustenance from Kant without endorsing a metaphysic of the supersensible.

According to the Habermas story, a small, vibrant public sphere shone brilliantly for a brief time in postmedieval Europe. Salons, coffeehouses, and weekly periodicals coalesced to foster a public that received ideas disinterestedly and debated them in a way that allowed "the authority of the better argument" to prevail. Early theorists who cataloged this sphere, including Kant, eternalized the historically contingent conditions that rendered it possible. But this historical practice of publicity, critical reason, and pursuit of a free public consensus set a model for public life transcending its immediate place of approximation. Unlike most secularists, the early Habermas (this changes later) finds this moment of evanescence to be short-lived. One element in his account of its fall from grace, however, may express a more pervasive proclivity in secular conceptions of public discourse.

By the middle of the twentieth century, under pressure from an expanding welfare state, the sophisticated capacities of corporate and political manipulation, and so on, the authentic public sphere had given way to a false copy. Consider some summary formulations from Habermas to capture the character of this decline:

> Put bluntly, you had to pay for books, theater, concert, and museum, but not for the conversation about what you had read, heard, and seen and what you might completely absorb only through this conversation. Today the conversation itself is administered. Professional dialogues from the podium, panel discussions and round table shows—the rational debate of private people becomes one of the production numbers of stars...; it assumes commodity form even at "conferences" where anyone can "participate."[21]

> The sounding board of an educated stratum tutored in the public use of reason has been shattered; the public is split apart into minorities of specialists who put their reason to use nonpublicly and the great mass of consumers whose receptiveness is public but uncritical. Consequently it completely lacks the form of communication specific to a public.[22]

> The consensus developed in rational political public debate has yielded to compromise fought out or simply imposed nonpublicly.[23]

> A process of public communication evolving in the medium of the parties...obviously stands in an inverse relation to the staged and manipulative effectiveness of a publicity aimed at rendering the broad population...infectiously ready for acclamation.[24]

> The collapse of ideology...seems to be only one side of the process.... The other side is that ideology...fulfills, on a deeper level of consciousness, its old function.... This false consciousness no longer consists of an internally harmonized nexus of ideas..., but of a nexus of modes of behavior.[25]

I do not object, of course, to exploration of how the contours of public discourse shift with changes in their technological and economic context, nor to how structural binds created by the expansion of capitalism squeeze the space in which public discourse appears. But the early Habermas—for his position, as we shall see, changes later—inflects the account of this history in a particular direction. Interpreted through the perspective advanced here, the early Habermasian formulations first extract a desiccated model of discourse from early-modern salon conversations and then re-present the elements purged from those representations as potent modes of destructive effectivity concentrated in the present. On the line of elevated extractions you find rational argument, true publicity, public opinion, collective consensus, and political action; on the remaindered line of correspondences you find management, manipulative effectiveness, staging, interest compromise, unstable settlement, behavior, and infectious acclamation. Indeed, the early Habermasian projection of a past and future model of public life from which the visceral element is purged depends upon playing up the negative potency of that very element in the present. For if the visceral dimension were treated as both inappropriate and ineffective, the most powerful contemporary impediments to actualization of the model of rational public consensus would disappear too. It would become more difficult to explain why the present is so degraded. The postulated potency of this dimension, then, might lead you to think that a reworked version of it should be folded into the ideal of discourse itself. But if the degraded element were reworked and incorporated into the model, the Habermasian imagination of sufficient and authoritative argument would be jeopardized. The early Habermasian contempt for existing public opinion is determined in part, then, by Habermas's infectious insistence upon an authoritative model of argumentation from which the visceral element is subtracted. The sufficiency of the secular model itself fades once the visceral element it can neither eliminate nor manage is folded back into it.

How might emendation of the secular be pursued? Such an attempt seems to require a series of revisions in secular simulations of public argumentation. In place of the Habermasian ideal of a consensus between rational agents who rise above their interests and sensibilities, you might substitute that of *ethically sensitive, negotiated settlements* between chastened partisans who proceed from contending and overlapping presumptions while *jointly* coming to appreciate the unlikelihood of reaching rational agreement on several basic issues; in place of a *reduction* of public discourse to pure argument, you might appreciate *positive possibilities in the visceral register of thinking and discourse too,* exploring how this dimension of subjectivity and intersubjectivity is indispensable to creativity in thinking, to the introduction of new identities onto the cultural register of legitimacy, and to the possibility of contingent settlements in public life; in response to the quest for rational purity in moral motivation, judgment, and authority, you might explore an *ethic of cultivation* in which a variety of constituencies work on themselves to attenuate that amygdalic panic that often arises when you encounter gender, sensual, or religious identities that call the naturalness, rationality, or sanctity of your own identities into question, and in which each constituency works to cultivate generosity and critical responsiveness in its negotiations with alter-identities that help it to be what is; and in response to the secular demand to leave controversial religious and metaphysical judgments at home so as to hone a single public practice of reason or justice, you might pursue a generous *ethos of engagement* between a plurality of constituencies inhabiting the same territory and honoring different moral sources. And so on.[26]

I sense that amygdalic pressures working on secularists may push some to ignore the next point, but nothing in the above carries the implication of eliminating argument, rationality, language, or conscious thought from public discourse. It merely insists that these media are always accompanied and informed to variable degrees by visceral intensities of thinking, prejudgment, and sensibility not eliminable *as such* from private or public life. To participate in a multitrack model of subjectivity and intersubjective relations, then, is to work on each of these fronts in relation to the others, seeking to infuse an ethos of care for the plurovocity of being into partisan modes of thinking, discourse, and judgment. It is not even, as I will address shortly, that everyone would have to endorse *this* practice of care (for care can come from multiple sources) to participate in the pluralized public life endorsed here. It *is,* however, that most would come to appreciate the profound element of *contestability* in the practice they do endorse. And they would incorporate that recognition positively into the way they engage other visions of public discourse in actual public life. That cardinal virtue is yet to be folded into most models of secular discourse with which I am familiar. Indeed, the Kantian inspiration of much of modern secularism, in its ambition to enable (Kantian) philosophy to wrest public moral authority from ecclesiastical theology, militates against it. Neither Kantian philosophy nor the secularism that follows it is alone responsible for this effect. It also involves pressure from ecclesiastical forces upon secular practices. But once it is understood that secularism is a political settlement rather than an uncontestable dictate of public discourse itself, the possibility of reworking that settlement under new conditions of being takes on new significance.

Pluralizing the Secular

By the mid-1980s, the Habermasian version of secularism had become chastened and moved closer to the Rawlsian model. While Rawls now seeks to ground secular justice at least partly in an overlapping cultural consensus without invoking "controversial" religious and metaphysical conceptions, Habermas has moved more actively to a postmetaphysical stance. One can understand the pressures pushing each in that direction. While each had expected the fervor of religious controversies to abate as the years rolled by, it has in fact intensified. So by eschewing reference to controversial metaphysical assumptions in their own forays into public life, secularists hope to discourage a variety of enthusiastic Christians from doing so in turn. Sometimes, indeed, such an agnostic stance folds the admirable virtue of forbearance into public debate. But the cost of elevating this disposition to restraint into the cardinal virtue of metaphysical denial is also high. First, such a stance makes it difficult for its partisans to engage a variety of issues of the day, such as the legitimate variety of sexual orientations, the organization of gender, the question of doctor-assisted death, the practice of abortion, and the extent to which a uniform set of public virtues is needed. It is difficult because most participants in these discussions explicitly draw metaphysical and religious perspectives into them, and because the claim to take a position on these issues without invoking controversial metaphysical ideas is soon seen to be a facade by others. Academic secularists are almost the only partisans today who consistently *purport* to leave their religious and metaphysical baggage at home. So the claim to being postmetaphysical opens you to charges of hypocrisy or false consciousness: "You secularists quietly bring a lot of your own metaphysical baggage into public discourse even as you tell the rest of us to leave ours in the closet." Finally, metaphysical abstinence increases the pressure on secularists to pretend that actually operative reason, in one form or another, is sufficient to the issues at hand, even in the face of their own insights into how cultural specificities, contingent elements, and artificial closures help to set operative conditions for actual practices of discourse and judgment. Habermas, for instance, after eschewing the transcendental status of the Kantian supersensible, first underlines uncertainties and contingencies that rejection implies for his perspective and then tries to recapture the Archimedean point he has just let go:

> Transcendental thinking once concerned itself with a stable stock of
> forms for which there were no recognizable alternatives. Today, in con-
> trast, the experience of contingency is a whirlpool into which every-
> thing is pulled: everything could also be otherwise, the categories of
> the understanding, the principles of socialization and morals, the con-

stitution of subjectivity, the foundation of rationality itself. There are good reasons for this. Communicative reason, too, treats almost everything as contingent, even the conditions for the emergence of its own linguistic medium. But for everything that claims validity *within* linguistically structured forms of life, the structures of possible mutual understanding in language constitute something that cannot be gotten around.[27]

Habermas now acknowledges more actively the role of sensibility in reflection and the role of contingency in the formation of sensibility. But he still tries to preserve the Kantian effect by non-Kantian means, substituting the presumption of rational decidability built into the logic of linguistic performance for the necessary presupposition of the supersensible. But it is now fair enough to ask, Why is that condition of discourse the *only* one treated as if it "cannot be gotten around"? What about visceral and contingent elements within thinking and discourse? Can they be gotten around? Or that problematic relation between the unthought (which only a contestable metaphysical assumption could assure you is already preshaped like thought) and its *translation* into thought? If you were to say that all three of these characteristics form constitutive conditions of thinking and discourse, and if you then acknowledged, as Habermas now does, the ideal of rational agreement to be a counterfactual never actually realized in practice, you would already have the makings of a more robust, ambiguous, multivalent model of discourse. Its ambiguity would reside in the need to push on one dimension of discourse (say, hidden contingencies folded into an operative presumption of universality) just after you had played out another (say, the presumption of possible accord). Now a new Habermas could say: It is impossible to participate in discourse without projecting the counterfactual possibility of consensus; but, hey, since each attempt to interpret the actual import of that counterfactuality in any concrete setting is also problematical and contestable, this stricture does not rule out in advance religious or nontheistic metaphysical perspectives that exceed the terms of the postmetaphysical alternative my younger self endorsed as necessary.

What, then, is the thought behind the thought that drives the actually existing Habermas to give singular primacy to one dimension of discourse over all others? Perhaps, at a visceral level, it is a reiteration of the Christian and Kantian demands to occupy the authoritative place of public discourse. The imperative to occupy that place of authority may be bolstered by another preliminary drive, that is, *the political* sense that a non-Kantian, religiously pluralized world would fall into either disorder or religious tyranny if its participants did not endorse a single standard of rational authority, regardless of the extent to which such a standard can in fact be secured transcendentally.

In an age of globalization and the accentuation of speed in so many domains of life, a cultural pluralism appropriate to the times is unlikely to be housed in an austere postmetaphysical partisanship that purports to place itself above the fray. The need today, rather, is to rewrite secularism to pursue an ethos of engagement in public life among a plurality of controversial *metaphysical* perspectives, including, for starters, Christian and other monotheistic perspectives, secular thought, and asecular, nontheistic perspectives. A new modus vivendi is needed to replace the Kantian achievement in which a few fundamental differences *within Christianity* were relegated to the private realm in the name of a generic rational religion or a generic reason. Here pluralism would not be grounded in one austere moral source adopted by everyone (say, a universal conception of rational religion, or discourse, or persons, or justice). It would be grounded in an ethos of engagement between multiple constituencies honoring a variety of moral sources and metaphysical orientations. Such an ethos *between* interdependent partisans provides an existential basis for democratic politics if and when many partisans affirm without deep resentment the contestable character of the fundamental faith they honor most. Such reciprocal affirmations across considerable variety in faith and belief enable mutual forbearance in public debate and the periodic assembly of majority assemblages. Such reciprocal affirmations enable a generous ethos of public engagement, then, even more than they follow from it. Significant currents already operative in contemporary life point toward the possible consolidation of such an ethos, even as intense constituencies mobilize against that very possibility.[28]

Let us simulate modifications in the secular model of public discourse by pursuing points of connection among several academic perspectives that have tended to be insulated from one another heretofore. We draw Kantian philosophy, Habermasian thought, post-Nietzschean thought, and one form of Christian theology into engagement during a time in which Habermas circumscribes such engagements and Rawls doubts their desirability. We proceed, of course, in a partisan way, while simultaneously seeking to open up the terms of conversation with others.

In a recent essay titled *Postmetaphysical Thinking,* Habermas identifies metaphysics with the attempt to "secure the precedence of identity over difference and that of ideas over matter."[29] Such a definition places Plato under the rubric of metaphysics, as it does Christian philosophers such as Augustine, Aquinas, Kant, and Hegel. But what does it say about diverse non-

Platonic and non-Christian perspectives in the history of the West represented by such names as Epicurus, Lucretius, Spinoza, Hume, Nietzsche, Bergson, Freud, Levinas, Butler, and Deleuze? Are they metaphysical or postmetaphysical? Each conveys a set of fundamentals that differ from the set christened as metaphysical by Habermas, yet none, in the most obvious sense of these phrases, gives precedence to "identity over difference and...ideas over matter." Once you encounter these perspectives, and also keep in mind how each fundamental reading of the world is bound up with particular orientations to ethics, identity, and politics, the Habermasian constitution of metaphysics begins to feel provincial. And the pretense to be postmetaphysical now gives off a hollow sound.

Consider a Deleuzian metaphysic. It invokes a non-Kantian transcendental field of (as I call it) the infrasensible. The infrasensible, like the supersensible it tracks and challenges, does not *exist* in the world of appearance. As a virtual field made up of elements too small to be perceptible and/or too fast to be actual, it insists below and within culturally organized registers of sensibility, appearance, discourse, justice, and identity. The amygdala, for instance, subsists on this register, projecting effects into the world of conscious thinking, feeling, and judgment without itself being *in* that world. Thinking itself for Deleuze (and Epicurus, Spinoza, Bergson, Freud, and Nietzsche too) operates on more than one level; it moves on the level of the virtual (which is real in its effectivity but not actual in its availability) and that of the actual (which is available to representation, but not self-sufficient). Infrasensible intensities of proto-thinking, for instance, provide a reservoir from which *surprise* sometimes unsettles fixed explanations, new *pressures* periodically swell up to disrupt existing practices of rationality, and new *drives to identity* occasionally surge up to modify the register of justice and legitimacy upon which established identities are placed. Again, this is so because the swarm of intensities emanating from the infrasensible are too multiple, finely meshed, and fast to be captured entirely in the coarse nets of explicit identity, conscious representation, and public appearance.

How does Habermas relate to such a perspective? Unlike most Rawlsians, he does take note of its type. But he then delegitimates it through his typification of it. He subsumes it under the labels "irrationalism" and "negative metaphysics." Here Habermas recapitulates Kant beautifully, binding his attempt to defang Christian ecclesiastical metaphysics to an effort to push nontheistic/a-Kantian metaphysical orientations below the field of intellectual eligibility.

How does Habermas make this move? First, he equates such an orientation with a loss of bearings essential to political and ethical life. It is received as inherently pessimistic and despairing, even though its partisans seldom present it in that light.[30] Second, he projects onto it a claim to secure the certainty of its own stance that *is* operative in other metaphysical doctrines and in the Habermasian perspective. Thus: "Every comprehensive, closed, and final system of statements must be formulated in a language that requires no commentary and allows of no interpretations, improvements, or innovations that might be placed at a distance."[31]

Habermas, then, is postmetaphysical in that he places none of his basic assumptions — except one — above the possibility of modification or reconfiguration. But Deleuze and Nietzsche, whom I call non-Christian metaphysicians, take this perspective a step further. As I read them, they first treat their basic presumptions to be contestable suppositions and then strive to interpret and act through them. For, first, these fundamentals are antisystematic. They carry within them the expectation that no theoretical system will ever be complete; that every explanation will periodically meet with surprise; that each identity is to a considerable extent an entrenched, contingent formation situated at the tense nexus between the self-identification of its participants and modes of recognition institutionally bestowed upon it; that a formation typically contains internal resistances or remainders; and that it might become otherwise if some of these balances shift. Second, the Deleuzian metaphysic reconfigures the standing and shape of the Kantian transcendental field without eliminating it altogether. It is transcendental in residing above or below appearance, but not in being unquestionable or in authorizing a morality of command. This, then, is metaphysics without the claim to apodictic authority or epistemic certainty, a combination that eludes the Habermasian division between metaphysical and postmetaphysical thought.

Put this way, a couple of potential points of contact now emerge between these two different perspectives. Habermas plays up elements of contingency and uncertainty in a doctrine that transcendentalizes the linguistic presupposition of a possible consensus. And Deleuze acknowledges the need for rules and norms for discourse to proceed while thinking that surprising changes might unfold in rules now presumed by Habermas to be fixed. Yet this line of potential communication across significant difference — a line enlarging the field of discourse rather than curtailing it — cannot be pursued until the definitive barrier Habermas poses to it has been addressed. For, at precisely this point of possible connection between two opposing perspectives, Habermas pulls out the hangman's noose of critical philosophy and lowers it around the neck of the Deleuzian: "All such attempts to detranscendentalize reason continue to get entangled in the prior conceptual decisions

of transcendental philosophy, decisions in which they remain trapped."[32]
"Negative metaphysics" has now been rendered null and void.

But is the noose tied that tightly? Most of those on the block already acknowledge how often they become entangled in the coils of paradox. Deleuze, for instance, insists upon it. But he also reads the anxious imperative to avoid paradox at all costs as a sign that the philosopher in question still treats Kantian models of recognition, common sense, and the upright character of thought as if they were apodictic. For only if they were apodictic would the encounter with self-referential contradictions and paradoxes necessarily show thinking to have gone awry. Does the Habermasian noose, then, muffle those who call into question the upright character of thought? For Deleuze, the encounter with paradox is sometimes a *sign* of the limit of thought and an *indication* of a reservoir of fugitive elements below and within thinking that might inspire creativity in thinking itself. This is the Deleuzian "field of immanence" upon which part of thinking is located. Deleuze, like Nietzsche, seeks to alter the mood or sensibility within which the encounter with paradox occurs. He welcomes the encounter in a way that both recalls one side of Kant and confounds the Habermasian attempt to secure the Kantian effect.

> Philosophy is revealed not by good sense but by paradox. Paradox is the pathos or the passion of philosophy. There are several kinds..., all of which are opposed to...good sense and common sense. Subjectively, paradox breaks up the common exercise of the faculties and places each before its own limit....At the same time, however, paradox communicates to the broken faculties..., aligning them along a volcanic line which allows one to ignite the other, leaping from one limit to the next. Objectively, paradox displays the element that cannot be totalized within a common element, along with the difference that cannot be equalized or cancelled at the direction of good sense. It is correct to say that the only refutation of paradoxes lies in good sense and common sense themselves, but on condition that they are already allowed everything: the role of judge as well as that of party to the case.[33]

Once these different responses to the occasion of paradox become clear, Habermas can criticize and resist a Deleuzian metaphysic, but he may not be able to produce a postmetaphysical rationale to rule it definitively out of public discourse. If that is so, it now seems imperative, on Habermasian terms, to enter into dialogue with it, to pursue a critical dialogue in which neither party insists upon being the final judge above the fray as well as party to the case. Because Deleuze requires rules of discourse to proceed and Habermas increasingly acknowledges contingent elements in the conditions of discourse, a new avenue of communication opens up across difference. Each party, certainly, may press the other to clarify itself and, perhaps, to revise itself. The Habermasian charge of performative contradiction, for instance, presses Deleuzians to clarify their orientation to paradox.[34] By proceeding along a path of agonistic respect and selective indebtedness, these academic parties can now simulate an expansive practice of public discourse, one in which the number of parties grows, the issues expand, and the encounter with paradox has been decriminalized.

We can, then, simulate discourse in one direction beyond the parameters of Habermasian permissibility. But what about public engagements between those who bring religious faith with them into public debates and those who eschew reference to a personal god or rational religion. Rawls would rule that discussion out of public life; the postmetaphysical matrix Habermas invokes points more hesitantly in the same direction. "Communicative reason," Habermas says, is treated by "negative metaphysics" as "the colorless negative of a religion that provides consolation." But Habermasian reason neither shrieks out heroic slogans against a universe without consolation nor offers religious solace. It

> neither announces the absence of consolation in a world forsaken by God nor does it take it upon itself to provide any consolation. . . . As long as no better words for what religion can say are found in the medium of rational discourse, it will even coexist abstemiously with the former, neither supporting it nor combatting it.[35]

This seems to announce that while communicative reason would purge public discourse of post-Nietzschean perspectives (in the name of coherence) it would practice respectful coexistence with powerful institutions of religious consolation. That is a fairly good reproduction of the Kantian effect. But surely there is a less self-effacing way to engage theistic perspectives in public life. Only a colorless demand to be postmetaphysical would stop you from exploring them.

In *Difference and Repetition* Deleuze finds a way to engage Kantian and Kierkegaardian orientations to religious faith. There is a dramatic moment, he says, when Kant is poised between a critique of ecclesiastical theology and a defense of rational theology. In that fissure other nontheological alternatives flash by for a second, only to be forgotten through insistent Kantian presentations of recognition and common sense. To pursue one of those nontheistic paths would be to open a public dialogue with Kantian religion as well as with the ecclesiological doctrines Kant sought to contain. But Rawlsian and Habermasian versions of secularism refuse to walk through that door.

Let us address the Deleuzian engagement with Kierkegaard. Kierkegaard represents a phase in high Christianity after the necessity of Kantian rational religion has been called into question. In Kierkegaard, faith relinquishes its mooring in a Kantian postulate of reason. It then seeks to make up that deficit through an increase in intensity. "Kierkegaard and Peguy are the culmination of Kant, they realize Kant by entrusting to faith the task of overcoming the speculative death of God and healing the wound in the self." Faith unavoidably changes its character in their hands. The experience of faith now becomes ambiguous: it is "no more than a condition by default, one lost in sin which must be recovered in Christ."[36]

This means, I take it, that the divine object of devotion is treated *as if* it were once there to faith in its fullness so that the faithful can hold themselves responsible for its loss and pursue an imagined future of its recovery. Faith now becomes ironized so that it can also be intensified. Such a movement backward and forward, the faithful disclose, makes a profound difference in your general bearing, your ethical conduct, and the rich horizon of being toward which you are opened. This is repetition with spiral effects, rather than bare repetition.[37] Kierkegaardian faith, however, repeatedly bumps into gaps or feelings of estrangement between repetitions, when traces of faithlessness intervene inadvertently and unintentionally. Perhaps such an effect is bound up with the very ground of Kierkegaardian faith, giving it its impetus to intense practices of faithfulness. Deleuze, the a-theist, pounces upon this trace of faithlessness between repetitions. I would do so too, not to purge faith from the faithful or disenfranchise expressions of faith from public life, but to open a window within theistic *representations* for appreciation of recurrent moments of difference in faith from itself. Now, alongside the difference between two practices of representation another more volatile difference is forming, a difference that also *has the potential to connect the contending parties*. Each practice of faith (theistic and nontheistic) may contain an element of difference within itself from itself that tends to be blurred or obscured by the representations it makes of itself to others.

This difference between faith and its representation explains why two devout believers "cannot observe each other without laughing." Such laughter testifies to breaches that unavoidably occur within the house of faith.[38] For

> there is an adventure of faith according to which one is always the clown of one's own faith, the comedian of one's own ideal.... Eventually faith reflects upon itself and discovers by experiment that its condition can only be given to it as "recovered" and that it is not only separated from that condition but doubled in it.[39]

Deleuze deploys this ambiguity to give more room to the nonbeliever. "We have too often been invited to judge the atheist from the viewpoint of the belief or faith that we suppose still drives him . . . not to be tempted by the inverse operation — to judge the believer by the violent atheist by which he is inhabited, the Antichrist eternally given 'once and for all' within grace."[40] But, we can add, now a space also emerges to inform the dialogue between some *representatives* of theistic faith and some *representatives* of nontheistic gratitude for life. For if the true believer is a simulacrum of himself, in what relation does the nonbeliever stand to herself? Does the *nonbeliever* who, say, affirms a Deleuzian nontheistic transcendental often inadvertently project life forward *as if* it might perpetuate itself eternally? Epicurus, at least, thought so. This pre-Christian spiritualist, who treated the gods as if they were unconcerned with human life, counseled his followers to resist that recurrent moment when life projects its continuation after death so that they might overcome existential resentment against the contingency of life. Epicurus thus testifies to a visceral tendency to project life after death even before the advent of the Christian heaven. Do such projectionist tendencies reveal we who represent ourselves as nontheistic to be comedians of ourselves too, harboring truant moments of forgetful faith that belie the steadfastness we present to Christians and other monotheists whenever they press hard upon us? We too may exist in a condition that can "only be given . . . as 'recovered' and is not only separated from the condition but doubled over in it." Is it possible, then, for believers and nonbelievers from a variety of faiths to double over in laughter together on occasion across the space of difference? On principle? Doing so partly *because* each party harbors in itself an ineliminable element of difference from itself?[41] And partly because the dominant self-representation of each party contains within it an element of faith that is likely to remain contestable?

Yes, those differences within that support connections between tempt many to close off agonistic respect in this domain. But, still, the other possibility returns, to counter such a temptation — even if to pursue it we have to fashion reciprocal modifications in the very sensibilities in which theistic faiths and nontheistic faiths are set,[42] and even if the boundaries of secularism must be stretched to incorporate such relations into public life.

The step to which each party gives priority does have a distinctive effect on the type of character developed, the character of the ethic supported, the sources it draws sustenance from, and the political priorities supported, though none of these can be read from bare knowledge of the official stance. Repetition, in its spiral pattern, makes an important difference to the registers of belief, identity, and self-representation even while it does not erase all difference within these appearances. The earlier discussion of the multiple registers of intersubjectivity has already suggested this.

By placing a Deleuzian metaphysic and the temper in which it is set into conversations with Habermas, Kant, and Kierkegaard, we augment academic models of secular discourse. We also join Kant, Rawls, and Habermas in acknowledging the connection between models of academic discourse and conceptions of public life. We simply pursue that connection differently, stretching the parameters of secular discourse in a couple of directions without claiming the right to be final judge of each dispute as well as fervent party to the case.

2

Suffering, Justice, and the Politics of Becoming

Suffering and Ethics

People suffer. We suffer from illness, disease, unemployment, dead-end jobs, bad marriages, the loss of loved ones, social relocation, tyranny, police brutality, street violence, existential anxiety, guilt, envy, resentment, depression, stigmatization, rapid social change, sexual harassment, child abuse, poverty, medical malpractice, alienation, political defeat, toothaches, the loss of self-esteem, identity-panic, torture, and fuzzy categories. We organize suffering into categories to help cope with it, but often these categories themselves conceal some aspects of suffering, even contribute to them. This latter experience leads to the suspicion that suffering is not entirely reducible to any determinate set of categories. To suffer is to bear, endure, or undergo; to submit to something injurious; to become dis*organ*ized. Suffering resides on the underside of agency, mastery, wholeness, joy, and comfort. It is, therefore, ubiquitous. Severe suffering exceeds every interpretation of it while persistently demanding interpretation. Without suffering, it is unlikely we would have much depth in our philosophies and religions. But with it, life is tough—and often miserable for many.

Does the polycultural character of suffering reveal something fundamental about the human condition? And how contestable and culturally specific are the medical, psychological, religious, ethical, therapeutic, sociostructural, economic, and political categories through which suffering is acknowledged and administered today? Is "suffering" a porous universal, whose persistence as a cultural term reveals how conceptually discrete injuries, wounds, and

47

agonies are experientially fungible, crossing and confounding the fragile boundaries we construct between them? Or is it a barren generality, seducing theorists into metaphysical explorations removed from specific injuries in need of medical or moral or religious or political or therapeutic or military attention? Any response to these questions draws upon one or more of the theoretical paradigms already noted. A political theorist might focus on power struggles between disparate professionals over the legitimate definition and treatment of suffering. An evangelist might minister instances that flow from a crisis of faith. And a physician might medicate theorists and spiritualists burned out by the projects these faiths commend. Is the bottom line, then, that today people go to the doctor when they really need help? Perhaps. But they might pray after getting the treatment. Or file a malpractice suit. Or join a political movement to redesign the health care system. Sufferers are full of surprises.

Secularism recognizes the importance of suffering and the ethical necessity to respond to it. Indeed, one of its major justifications is the promise to stop the suffering caused by religious wars. But secular thinkers often think that suffering is always easy to recognize and categorize. To speak more responsively to suffering is to contest that assumption. And to do that we will eventually engage the problematic relations among Rawlsian secular justice, suffering, and "the politics of becoming."

John Caputo, in a fascinating study titled *Against Ethics,* seeks to cut through the abstractions of contemporary ethical theory. He places suffering at the center of moral attention. Drop judging and punitive gods. Forget Rawls. Bypass Nietzsche's coldness toward sufferers. Avoid entanglement in the coils of Derrida. Pour salt on Foucault's critique of normalization. Be wary of the spiritualism of Immanuel Levinas. Step outside the conflictual world of political partisanship. Concentrate instead on suffering of the flesh, and on the obligation of those in the vicinity of suffering to respond to it. Let's make obligation, Caputo says, palpable, specific, situational, and guttural. Let's rescue it from secularism, theology, and philosophy. Let's respond to suffering without mediation by a god, a Greek ideal of beauty, a teleological principle, a veil of ignorance, an overlapping consensus, or a (non)metaphysics of *differance* to govern the response.

Obligation is not commanded on high, nor is it grounded in reason, nor does it filter into life through mystical experience. Caputo, a theologian and philosopher, has gone practical. He still loves the old texts. But obligation, he says, simply happens: "Obligation means the obligation to the other, to one who has been laid low, to victims and outcasts. Obligation means the obligation to reduce and alleviate suffering."[1]

Moral codes grounded in a law of laws, such as the commands of a god or the dictates of a categorical imperative, are too blunt, crude, and closed to respond to suffering equitably. Those grounded in a fictional contract are not much better. Besides, both types purport to ground morality in certitudes that are highly debatable. People spend so much time debating the certitudes they never get around to suffering. Even moralities built around appreciation of humans as essentially embodied beings tend to slide over suffering — though they come closer. The thing to do is to move through gods, transcendental commands, principles, contracts, and bodies to the experience of human flesh. "Flesh is soft and vulnerable. It tears, bleeds, swells, bends, burns, starves, grows old, exhausted, numb, ulcerous. . . . Flesh smells."[2] Flesh is the soft, perishable medium in which suffering occurs. "What is suffering if not this very vulnerability of the flesh, this unremitting unbecoming. This liability to suffer every breakdown, reversal and consumption?"[3] If you bind suffering to flesh and flesh to obligation, you both cut through systems that try to ground obligation in some solid finality and you render obligation more sensitive to the palpable hunger, sickness, desperation, and helplessness humans often face. Flesh moves you from us to them, without complex argumentation. We are all made of it.

Caputo knows things are not quite that simple. He knows that to reach the flesh it has been necessary to write an entire book entangled in a host of controversial arguments. But, still, he hopes he has built a cantilever upon which a certain amount of moral weight can be placed. He hopes to pull us away from metaphysics and systematic doctrines toward the suffering and obligation that both inspires the constructions of metaphysics and engenders its obfuscations. "Flesh fills metaphysics with anxiety."[4] Flesh, first, challenges the systematicity that governs metaphysics. For flesh is vulnerable. It absorbs burdens, blows, injuries, and shocks. It compromises agency. Flesh suffers. But the very vulnerabilities of flesh, second, often prod humans to construct metaphysical systems to elevate them above its softness, smell, and bloodiness. (Caputo does not evince old worries about temptations of the flesh.) Or it prods them to embrace systems that show why limits of the flesh are deserved. But you never escape the flesh, and Caputo counsels you to stay close to it as you let obligation happen.

Can such a recipe be followed? Caputo concedes formally that he relocates himself in the world of metaphysics even as he struggles to write himself out of it. For he uses an inherited language.[5] Caputo has read his Derrida. Indeed, he has written books on language. Nonetheless, we can stay close to the experience of suffering, Caputo thinks, if we strive for "metaphysical minimalism."

> Minimalism is a metaphysics without a meta-event, a kind of decapi-
> tated metaphysics. . . . Minimalism lets events happen, lets them be, lets
> them go, without imposing grand and overarching schemata upon them,
> without simplifying them. It has decided to come to terms with intract-
> able plurivocity.[6]

Caputo, I should tell you, loves many of the prophets he criticizes. He loves Abraham, Kierkegaard, Nietzsche, Deleuze, and Levinas, for starters. Well, I love Caputo. I love his critical engagement with monotheistic and secular moralities alike. I respect his quest to bring suffering back to the center. I appreciate his sense of the fragility of obligation and his wariness of the quest to secure solid foundations for it. I love much in his sensibility. But, still, Caputo, in order to make obligation simple, has submerged some of the complexities of suffering. A few blemishes still remain on Caputo's skin.

His "metaphysical minimalism" contains some admirable ingredients, but it does not succeed in its objective. Rather, Caputo replaces a familiar set of metaphysical doctrines with an alternative that is just as fundamental. It is also profoundly contestable. Moreover, Caputo does not identify anything within his perspective (within the perspective I share up to a point) that might *inspire* the spirit of obligation he pursues. You are either moved or unmoved by the stories Caputo tells. Obligation either "happens" or it does not. And Caputo's "minimalism" may compel him to reduce his injunctions to the "I" too often: "I feel"; "I avoid;" "I love;" "I must." Minimalism reduces Caputo to a Christ figure without transcendental portfolio. Either *he* moves you to read suffering as he does, or nothing happens.

Most significantly, Caputo's metaphysical minimalism impels him to treat devastated groups and helpless individuals as *paradigm* objects of obligation. Sick, homeless, helpless individuals. Peoples laid low by floods, conquest, famine, holocaust. Caputo issues a model of obligation in which virtuous helpers are moved by the helplessness of the needy: "The power of obligation varies directly with the powerlessness of the one who calls for help, which is the power of powerlessness."[7]

Such situations often occur, and their importance is undeniable. But they may not pose the most difficult cases in politics and ethics. The perspective that arises from Caputo's examples are poorly equipped to deal with the very forms of suffering secularism also tends to ignore or deflate. For some of the most difficult cases arise when people suffer from injuries imposed by institutionalized identities, principles, and cultural understandings; when those who suffer are not entirely helpless but are defined as threatening, contagious, or dangerous to the self-assurance of hegemonic constituencies; and when the sufferers honor *sources* of ethics inconsonant or disturbing to these constituencies. And this suffering, too, invades the flesh. It engenders fatigue; it makes people perish; it drives them over the edge. To simplify obligation in a political era of pessimism, Caputo has quietly emptied ethics of its political dimension.

The most difficult cases require a public *ethos of critical engagement* between interdependent, contending constituencies entangled in asymmetrical structures of power. Indeed, sometimes acting upon obligations to the deserving poor and victims of natural disaster, while important, also provides a moral cover for the obstinate refusal to negotiate a generous ethos of engagement with constituencies in more ambiguous, disturbing, *competitive* positions. The most complex ethical issues arise in those contexts where suffering is intense and its visitation upon some is bound up with securing the self-confidence, wholeness, transcendence, or cultural merit of others. That is, the most intense, intractable cases of suffering are political in character. They often revolve around what I will call the politics of becoming.

The politics of becoming occurs when a culturally marked constituency, suffering under its negative constitution in an established institutional matrix, strives to reconfigure itself by moving the cultural constellation of identity\ difference then in place. In such situations either the suffering of the subjugated constituency or the response required to open up a new line of flight for it is not acknowledged by some of the parties involved. Under these circumstances it takes a militant, experimental and persistent political movement to open up a new line of flight from culturally induced suffering. The movement strives to modify the identity institutionally imposed upon it by redefining those institutionally entrenched definitions. Success is never guaranteed. Such a movement, to succeed, must extend *from* those who initiate cultural experiments *to* others who respond sensitively to those experiments, even when the experiments disturb their own sense of identity.

I bestow honor, then, upon the politics of *becoming,* not the politics of realization of an essence or universal condition already known in its basic structure by all reasonable persons. Indians, slaves, feminists, Jews, laborers, homosexuals, and secularists, among others, have participated in the politics of becoming in the past few centuries in Euro-American societies. But many citizens who now acknowledge the fruits of these movements, who repudiate the negative marks institutionally inscribed upon others in the past who participated in them, also forget how the politics of becoming proceeds when it is actually in motion. They treat retrospective interpretations of the politics of becoming as if the interpretations and institutional standing it helped to bring into being were "implicitly" available to participants when things were in motion. They act as if the initiating constituency either exposed *hypocrisy* in the profession of universal rights by the dominant group or prompted a cultural *dialectic* that fills out the logic already implicit in a just society. They reduce the politics of becoming to a social logic. And that attitude ill prepares them to respond to the *next* surprise in the politics of becoming in a reflective and sensitive way.

Caputo is wary of both the model of hypocrisy and the model of dialectical progress. I am with him here. But his minimalist appreciation of culture and metaphysics flattens out the modes of suffering he can recognize. Caputo's perspective may appear "minimal" by comparison to the models of a commanding (Christian) god and/or a teleological principle. Measured by these two perspectives, it *lacks* a final authority or a fundamental purpose of being. Lacking these supports, Caputo seems compelled to give (apparently) simple examples of suffering and to make obligation just "happen."

For the two interdependent traditions Caputo resists appear to exhaust metaphysics only if *meta* is (mis)translated as "beyond."[8] But if you construe metaphysics to be any reading of the fundamental character of things, it becomes clear that every positive cultural interpretation is inhabited by a metaphysical dimension. The call to metaphysical minimalism now becomes either a command to forget the perspective that moves you or a doomed attempt to live, act, judge, and respond without engaging in positive interpretation.[9]

Caputo takes a step in the direction I endorse when he speaks of an "intractable plurivocity" coursing through things. But his drive to minimalism stops him from pursuing this thought. Does he lament the *loss* of a god who could communicate clear commands or draw us closer to the fundamental design of things? His critical reading of Nietzsche suggests this possibility, anyway; for Caputo reduces the thinker who pursued the theme of fundamental plurivocity more than anyone preceding him in the West to the visionary of a cold, cruel, world indifferent to suffering. Often Caputo bypasses the element of joyfulness, abundance, and possibility Nietzsche locates in the multiplicity of being; and the Nietzschean generosity he does acknowledge is never pure enough to fit the disinterested model of obligation he demands.

My Nietzsche offers a positive metaphysic that breaks with some familiar options presented under the titles teleology, theological voluntarism, and secularism. But he does not embrace metaphysical minimalism either. He resists the "passive nihilism" that so readily accompanies such a liquid diet. Nietzsche affirms that concerted action is impossible without interpretation, that every particular interpretation invokes a fundamental conception of the world, and that every interpretive perspective remains questionable and contestable. He affirms, that is, life, in its ambiguous conditions of possibility. So Nietzsche interprets actively from within a distinctive, contestable reading of the fundaments of things. Here is one formulation of those fundaments, offered by Zarathustra, while preaching about "Old and New Tablets":

> When the water is spanned by planks, when bridges and railings leap over the river, verily those are believed who say, "Everything is in flux...." But when the winter comes..., then verily, not only the blockheads say, "Does not everything stand still?"
>
> "At bottom everything stands still"—that is truly a winter doctrine....O my brothers is everything not in flux now? Have not all railings and bridges fallen into the water? Who could still cling to "good" and "evil"?...The thawing wind blows—thus preach in every street, my brothers.[10]

Several thoughts mingle in Zarathustra's saying. Things are mobile at bottom, rather than still or fixed. This experience of the mobility of things has profound, corrosive effects upon winter conceptions of nature, divinity, identity, truth, and ethics that have prevailed in the West.

However, winter thoughts keep reinstating themselves in ways that treat the cultural ice as if it were frozen all the way down. This drive to find a solid bottom becomes powerful when suffering is intense; it can also be powerful when the identity of others unsettles your own claims to self-certainty. Moreover, the very character of language and limitations in our abilities to retain very many complex ideas at one time further reinforce the return of winter doctrines. You cannot dispense with them altogether or finally. But sometimes people struggle against these multiple pressures, doing so to open up a line of flight from intolerable suffering and/or to come to terms self-critically with cruelties against difference that often accompany the singular hegemony of winter doctrines.

Zarathustra's perspective is both paradoxical and contestable. He can point to multiple disturbances and surprises that disrupt each new winter doctrine; he can provide *pointers* to a fundamental mobility of things that exceeds the reach of definitive demonstration. But he cannot set this contestable experience of mobility within things in the cement of truth. Truth cannot be a relation of correspondence for Nietzsche. For truth changes its *place* as well as its meaning in his thought. "Truth," in one of its valences, is those indispensable cultural productions that freeze things (representations of nature, identities, moral codes, and so on) temporarily and incompletely. Truth, as the cultural sedimentation of a perspective, occurs in a "regime of truth," as Foucault would say. On another register—for Nietzsche plays with "truth"—the Nietzschean true *is* the flux and potential for mutation circulating through the solid formations of social life and nature (for nature itself is unfinished), the surplus and noise that circulate through every solid formation, disturbing well-laid plans and creating possibilities for new becomings. Thus preach in every street my friends. Truth, when it is layered in its complexity, casts off the dimension of final *solidity* so crucial to the correspondence model while retaining the dimension of *fundamentality* invoked by that model. The true becomes unsusceptible to final or complete correspondence because of its very character. By disaggregating elements the correspondence model binds together Nietzsche, uncovers an alternative orientation to truth. Along *this* dimension, Nietzsche is closer to a-theologies of god(s) as absence, excess, or "nothing" than to secular conceptions of truth as correspondence, coherence, rational consensus, or pragmatic success.

Nietzsche and Zarathustra tap into this fugitive experience, cultivating *gratitude* for the rich abundance of life. They cultivate gratitude for the surplus and porosity that endows life with mobility. Such a gratitude is "religious" without necessarily being monotheistic. It may find more intense expression in some times than others.

> What is astonishing about the religiosity of the ancient Greeks is the lavish abundance of gratitude that radiates from it. Only a very distinguished type of human being stands in *that* relation to nature and to life. Later, when the rabble came to rule in Greece, *fear* choked out religion and prepared the way for Christianity.[11]

Gratitude for the abundance of life, then, carries a contestable conception of being into ethics and politics.[12] But such a temperament is not located above the play of identities, institutions, and principles. It is inserted into these media, rendering them more responsive to that which exceeds them, more generous and refined in their engagements with difference. Without the infusion of such gratitude, high-sounding principles will be applied in stingy, punitive ways. A theistic or nontheistic perspective that exudes gratitude for being can promote an ethic of generosity while trimming some of the cognitive fat from its theological or secular diet.

This contestable faith in the abundance of being, this impious, nontheistic reverence for life, can render a postsecular ethic both more alert to the fragility of ethics and more open to the play of difference in cultural life. These two dispositions support one another. Those inspired by an ethos of generosity can participate in the politics of becoming without having to ground their ethic in something solid, fixed, or frozen. Because we can act ethically without being commanded by a god or transcendental imperative, we can also deploy genealogy, deconstruction, and political disturbance to cultivate responsiveness to movements of difference. For we do not need external or certain foundations to act ethically. The dissolution of foundations does not automatically dissolve ethics: it does so only for those who cannot be ethical without being ordered to do so. We do not pretend that obligation just happens either. Acceptance of obligation grows out of a protean care for the world that precedes it.

A nontheistic, postsecular ethic thus situates itself within the experience of the constitutive *indispensability and fragility of ethics*. It renounces the assurance of solid grounds for morality out of ethical concern, out of the concern to move those unnecessary and injurious limits that the defenders of solid foundations too often impose to protect their foundations. Those who participate in such an ethic cultivate critical generosity to those differences upon which the specification of their own identities depend, in part by responding to those differences outside that are regulated in themselves to enable them to be what they are, and in part by recalling that they inhabit a world where the admirable possibilities of being outstrip the time and corporeal capacity of any particular individual or culture to embody them all.

Perhaps most important of all, the themes reviewed so far do not render Nietzsche indifferent to suffering, as Caputo sometimes suggests. Rather, they drive him to make a critical division *within* suffering. He resists pity for those who demand a winter doctrine to redeem the suffering that comes with life or to prove why human beings deserve to be punished. For such doctrines, he thinks, express persistent resentment against the flesh, the limited capacity to know, the vulnerability to disorganization, and the susceptibility to death that mark the human condition itself. They express resentment against the very conditions of possibility for life. Existential resentment, in Nietzsche's view, helps to engender stingy moral ideals, tight conceptions of truth, closed practices of identity, restrictive judgments of normality, and cruel systems of punishment. Every individual and culture struggles with ressentiment, according to Nietzsche. And every generous disposition also issues in resentment, anger, or fear on occasion. Indeed, such responses are sometimes appropriate to specific circumstances. But moral dispositions governed by ressentiment too often wage cultural war against the diversity of life in a quest to transcendentalize what they already are or purport to be. Or so Nietzsche thinks.

Above all, Nietzsche refuses to shy away from that suffering that the self must impose upon itself to become something distinctive and admirable.

The refinement and maintenance of an admirable mode of individuality, for example, requires considerable work by the self on the self. Since "to do is to forgo" the very achievement of a particular form of individuality carries losses and sacrifices with it. "How is freedom measured, in individuals as in nations? By the resistance which has to be overcome, by the effort it costs to stay *aloft*."[13] Any way of being involves considerable work to stay aloft. Too many individuals and groups both resent this condition of life and take revenge on others because of it. The key is to overcome the drive to convert that suffering needed to keep you aloft from fueling resentment against those internal and external differences that help to define what you are through contrast to them.

My Nietzsche, then, is not against compassion per se, despite what Caputo and several other commentators suggest. He resists compassion for selective modes of suffering to express it actively for others. As he puts the point: it is "compassion, in other words, against compassion," one type of compassion against another.[14] Nietzsche pits compassion for that suffocated by the normalizing politics of "good and evil" against compassion for existential suffering. The latter must be redirected, and the demand to which it responds must be overcome, if an ethic of generosity in relations of identity\ difference is to be cultivated. Nietzsche, again, might better have striven to find positive possibilities within the mode of suffering he finds most offensive and dangerous. But he, like everyone else in *this* respect, is still *compelled* to be selective with respect to suffering. His open selectivity challenges concealed principles of selection in other moral perspectives.

There are plenty of ways I dissent from Nietzsche: his cultural aristocraticism, which prizes becoming and plurality among a "noble" (though not necessarily moneyed) few while condemning "the herd" to a cultural dogmatism it is said to be predisposed toward; his (sometimes appealing) fantasy of residing on the margin of society beyond the reach of organized politics; his tendency (following from the first two themes) to neglect the *politics* of becoming in favor of cultivating individual distinctiveness; his profound ambivalence toward the basis and effects of gender duality; his periodic delight in petty cruelty against carriers of ressentiment; his occasional expressions of regret that people are no longer prepared to be "stones" in a cultural edifice; and so on. I do not, then, endorse every theme people of various stripes connect to the name "Nietzsche." But Nietzsche does prompt me to suggest that you can cultivate an admirable ethical disposition without anchoring it in the commands of a god or reason and that you are in an excellent position to address affirmatively the politics of becoming when such a disposition is attached to Zarathustra's conviction that there is an ineliminable element of mobility in things at bottom capable of upsetting the best-laid plans at unexpected junctures.[15]

The Politics of Becoming

By *the politics of becoming* I mean that paradoxical politics by which new cultural identities are formed out of unexpected energies and institutionally congealed injuries. The politics of becoming emerges out of the energies, suffering, and lines of flight available to culturally defined differences in a particular institutional constellation. To the extent it succeeds in placing a new identity on the cultural field, the politics of becoming changes the shape and contour of already entrenched identities as well. The politics of becoming can thus sow disturbance and distress in the souls of those disrupted by its movement. In a (modern?) world where people are marked and known through their identities, difference and becoming are ubiquitous. If each positive identity is organized through the differences it demarcates, if difference circulates through it as well as around it, if movement by some of these differences compromises its quest to present itself as natural, transcendent, or self-sufficient whole, then the politics of becoming often imperils the comforts through which dominant constituencies are reassured.[16] The question of ethics with respect to the politics of becoming is this: Which sort of suffering is most worthy of responsiveness at a particular historical moment, that which the politics of becoming imposes on the stability of being or that which established identities impose upon the movement of differences in order to protect their stability? In contemporary U.S. culture the operational answer often precedes the question. Here, entrenched codes of morality and normality weigh in heavily on the side of being, stasis, and stability without even acknowledging that the scales are tipped that way. And this is probably true more generally as well. To attend to the politics of becoming is to modify the cultural balance between being and becoming without attempting the impossible, self-defeating task of dissolving solid formations altogether.

The politics of becoming is paradoxical. A new cultural identity emerges out of old injuries and differences. But because there is no eternal model it copies as it moves toward new definition, and because it meets resistance from identities depending upon its neediness or marginality to secure themselves, the end result of this politics is seldom clear at its inception. Indeed, becoming often proceeds from inchoate suffering and hopes that are not crisply defined until a new identity has been forged through which to measure those injuries *retrospectively*.

If and as a heretofore stigmatized identity attains a more positive standing, it still may be an exaggeration to say that it has arrived at what it truly is at bottom or in essence. No positive identity can be judged final in a world where identities are organized through the differences they regulate and a certain capacity for mobility persists in things. Of course, it is often hard *not* to pretend such a final state has been approximated. The presumptions of (at least) European languages press in this direction. So do persistent human interests in regularity of expectation and the stability of justice. But a successful movement of becoming stirs up this cultural field of identities, standards, and procedures; *it thereby alters to some degree the measure by which its previous suffering and the responsibility of others to it is culturally defined.* Moreover, the new movement, if it is not squashed, engenders new intrasubjective and intersubjective differences as it proceeds. And as it enables new possibilities it might also engender new modes of suffering not yet crystallized as officially recognized injuries.

The politics of becoming is purposive without being teleological. It engages actors who, as they pursue a particular line of flight rendered available to them, do not remain fixed enough across time to be defined as consistent and masterful agents. Those who initiate the politics of becoming often make a significant difference without knowing quite what they are doing. In this respect they amplify underappreciated dimensions within human freedom in general.

The politics of becoming requires specific conditions to flourish. It flourishes in a culture that is inclusive economically, that is already *pluralistic* to a considerable degree, and that has cultivated an ethos of critical responsiveness to new drives to *pluralization*. Here many constituencies appreciate a little more actively the uncertain element of historical contingency in their own constitution, and this discernment informs their responses to movements by alter-identities to reconstitute the terms of their institutional identification and regulation. The responding constituencies recognize, in turn, that to create space for the politics of becoming they must render *themselves* available to modification in one way or another. They convert the cultural disturbance of what they are into energy to respond reflectively to new lines of flight. If they are pluralists, they appraise each new drive to identity first according to the likelihood it will support a culture of pluralism in the future.

An ethos of responsiveness to becoming is never entirely reducible, then, to obedience to a preexisting moral code. Some elements in the existing code itself must be modified if space is to be opened for something new to emerge. In a pluralizing culture two interdependent dimensions of ethics are poised in tension: the *obligation* to abide by the existing practice of justice and morality and *cultivation* of an ethos of critical responsiveness to the movement of difference. Without a moral code, the regularity of judgment expected by existing constituencies would be lost. But a congealed code also poses dumb, arbitrary barriers to the politics of becoming. This closure and clumsiness is what Nietzsche means by the "immorality of morality." While a moral code is indispensable to social regulation, judgment, and coordination, it is also too crude, blunt, and blind an authority to carry out these functions sensitively and automatically, particularly when new and surprising modes of suffering are encountered. An ethos of critical responsiveness, when active, navigates between these constitutive, interdependent, and discordant dimensions of ethical life.

In U.S. history positive examples of the politics of becoming can be found in antislavery movements, feminism, gay/lesbian rights movements, the introduction of secularism, the effort to place "Judeo" in front of the "Christian tradition," the right to die, and so on. Few participants in such movements interpret themselves entirely through the politics of becoming. Many claim to pursue an essence that has been culturally occluded, or to fill out a universal set of rights that contains hypocritical exclusions. Yet some difficulties speak against the sufficiency of these self-interpretations. The collision of two claims to universality is likely to create an implacable conflict over which one gains the title of *the* natural, true, or intrinsic identity. And when the winners of one round are convinced what they are touches the ultimate truth of being, they are ill prepared to come to terms with the work upon themselves needed when a new round in the politics of becoming begins.

And there is always another round in the politics of becoming. For, in a world where things are mobile at bottom, the final essence of things never arrives. Let us, then, set these general formulations in the context of a couple of contemporary examples, examples poised in that uncertain space between obscure suffering and the possible consolidation of something new.

Jan Clausen is a beneficiary of and participant in gay and lesbian movements in America. Because of them it became more feasible for her to establish affectionate, sensual relations with women without self-hate and without encountering quite as much social stigmatization as heretofore. She knows these collective achievements are partial and precarious. But through them she has developed a critique of "essentialist thinking" and come to terms more actively with the constructed, conflicted, and sometimes mobile character of sexual identity. While "socially powerful groups have a stake in promoting the illusion of unconflicted identity because maintenance of their power depends on keeping in place a constellation of apparently fixed, 'natural,' immutable social relationships," Clausen joins others in engaging the "resistance to identity which lies at the very heart of psychic life."[17] The community she belonged to until recently believes, for example, that both "heterosexuality" and "homosexuality" are complex organizations of sensual energy rather than cultural fixtures to be graded according to a natural scale of normality and abnormality.

Clausen, though, recently found that this collective knowledge did her little good when her affections shifted from a woman to a man. She faced charges of betrayal and responses of rejection strangely reminiscent of those she had encountered in disturbing the code of heterosexual normality. These responses were understandable, given the beleaguered condition of gay and lesbian communities. Still, they may point to powerful tendencies in most cultural groupings to naturalize what they are; they may suggest how the naturalization of identity functions simultaneously to protect collective bonds, to provide security for its members, and to create hardships for those whose contingent condensation of life and desire does not fit into defined cultural slots.

Clausen's "interesting condition" shows how the politics of becoming at one historical junction regularly solidifies into a mode of being at another. For Clausen, alert to a fluidity of desire that may settle for a time and then start moving again, needs a new social movement to modify one she still identifies with to a considerable degree. Clausen's interesting condition enables her to amplify a common, though rather subterranean, experience of ambiguity and resistance within identity. It encourages her, therefore, to become more responsive to other unconventional sensualities struggling to form themselves within the social matrix. Out of such a series of intersections between old and new participants in the politics of becoming, she can hope for a new cultural coalition to bestow greater ethical attention upon becoming itself. As she puts it, experience "in a particular community of women convinces me that all human connections are risky, fragmentary, and non-ideal"; but participation in coalitions between disparate social constituencies connected by multiple knots of affinity and sympathy also convinces Clausen of the possibility of people combining together "from incredibly different places" from time to time to support the politics of becoming.[18]

Mrs. Lin, a daughter of Chinese intellectuals who died while being abused during the Cultural Revolution in China, is in a more abject situation. Her "symptoms" include headaches, difficulty sleeping, poor appetite, low energy, anxiety, and fantasies of death. They lead to the diagnosis of neurasthenia by Chinese psychiatrists, while they might issue in the diagnosis of depression in the United States.

> For a North American psychiatrist, Mrs. Lin meets the...criteria for a major depressive disorder. The Chinese psychiatrists...did not deny she was depressed, but they regarded the depression as a manifestation of neurasthenia....Neurasthenia—a syndrome of exhaustion, weakness, and diffuse bodily complaints, believed to be caused by inadequate physical energy in the central nervous system—is an official diagnosis in China; but it is not a diagnosis in the American Psychiatric Association's latest nosology.[19]

Arthur Kleinman, a medical anthropologist with degrees in medicine and psychiatry as well, doubts that either diagnosis fits the case perfectly.[20] While the first focuses on bodily symptoms and the second on psychological states, neither pays much attention to the complex intersections between social stress, corporeal experience, and professional diagnoses of the symptoms that issue from this combination. And Kleinman's extensive interviews with Mrs. Lin convince him that her situation cannot be "diagnosed" until the stresses, punishments, and dislocations imposed upon her as a cultural dissident are drawn into the diagnosis. If they are incorporated, the prescribed responses to Mrs. Lin's condition will include changes in the system of social stress and surveillance in which her suffering occurs. Psychiatry will become more explicitly engaged in the political context in which it is always already set.

In the United States, too, there is considerable resistance to a cultural broadening of psychiatric perspective. It would require psychiatrists to explore complex relations between social stress and bodily experience; to study how corporealization of cultural experience occurs; to explore general limits to the human body's tolerance of stress, disruption, fixed routine, and so on, and to reflect upon the connections between contemporary practices of medical diagnosis and the professional identities psychiatrists themselves seek to maintain. It would implicate psychiatrists in wider political debates from which the narrow *medicalization* of suffering and illness now protects them. Mrs. Lin, and her equivalents in the United States, need a political movement to reconfigure the psychiatric approach to mental disorder. Such a politics of becoming would profit from recent movements in the States that sharpened awareness of complex interconnections between social stress, human suffering, medical diagnosis, and medical treatment in the domains of race, gender, and sexuality.

Any such movement would be filled with uncertainty and risk, of course. Even Arthur Kleinman shies away from it. His last chapter is not titled "Social Movements and the Psychiatric Sensibility," but "What Relationship

Should Psychiatry Have to Social Science?" The latter is doubtless an important topic. But it stretches the experience of psychiatry while remaining within the bounds of academic interdisciplinarity. Kleinman, I suspect, would be responsive to a new political movement to connect psychiatry, social stress, and corporeal experience, a movement that opened up new investigations in psychiatry by altering the cultural pressures in which it occurs. His subject position, however, makes it difficult to *initiate* such a politics of becoming.

Justice and Becoming

The element of paradox in the politics of becoming is that before success a new movement is typically judged by the terms through which it is currently depreciated, and after success a new identity emerges that exceeds the energies and identifications that called it into being. We are morally primed to expect a new identity to precede our recognition of it; but, given the paradox of becoming, the way in which this moral expectation closes off lines of flight from suffering often turns out retrospectively to have been immoral. An ethos of critical responsiveness negotiates these discordant imperatives: it ushers new identities through the barriers normality and morality pose to becoming. Participants in such an ethos appreciate how something admirable might become out of obscurity or difference.

Critical responsiveness bears a family resemblance to liberal tolerance. Tolerance is typically aimed at minorities whose identity is already stabilized, and it typically flows from those at the cultural center to those on the margins. Tolerance is an admirable virtue, even though a limited one. Critical responsiveness is aimed at constituencies in the process of renegotiating the identities through which they have been culturally recognized and institutionally regulated. Critical responsiveness is bestowed as a new identity is forming through the politics of becoming. Most important, critical responsiveness often involves comparative shifts in the self-identification of the constituencies who offer it. Thus where tolerance implies benevolence toward others amid stability of ourselves, critical responsiveness involves active work on our current identities in order to modify the terms of relation between us and them. Critical respondents themselves enter into practices of self-modification in the very process of changing their recognition and treatment of the others already in motion. For example, as heterosexuals respond to the politics of becoming by which a previous history of medicalization and demoralization of homosexuality is reconfigured they are also pressed to acknowledge for the first time that heterosexuality is not firmly grounded in the universality of nature, the commands of a god, or the automatic outcome of normal sensual development. This latter modification is not simply a matter of a change in verbal self-definition, though that is important too. Since the organization of a sensuality occurs on several registers of being, the cultivation of critical responsiveness often requires diligent work by the responding constituencies upon their own visceral registers of being. Similarly, for "whites" to participate in challenges by "blacks" to established assumptions of racial difference is to come to terms palpably with how whiteness has been culturally constructed by aligning diverse skin shades and tones with a paradigm set of social privileges, a gender-graded code of parenthood, and middle-class expectations.[21] Critical responsiveness to the claims of difference often calls forth a partial and comparative denaturalization of the respondents themselves; it thereby opens up other possible lines of mobility in what the respondents are. These effects are possible because every effective movement of difference modifies the institutional constellation of identities through which it has been differentiated. And if these changes are to be consolidated, a corollary set of changes will be required in such institutions as family life, marriage law, military rules, church membership, tax practices, medical benefits, and curriculum organization. It is thus not too surprising that the time in which the politics of becoming seems to move at a faster pace than heretofore is also the time in which counter drives to the fundamentalization of disturbed identities become tempting.

Consider, then, the ambiguous relation the institution of justice bears to the politics of becoming. The politics of becoming, when it achieves a modicum of success, repositions selected modes of suffering so that they move from an obscure subsistence or marked identity *below* the register of justice to a visible, unmarked place *on it*. In a modern world of justice as fairness between *persons*, this means that modes of being consciously or unconsciously shuffled below normal personhood become modified and *translated into the dense operational rubric of personhood itself through the politics of becoming*. A mode of suffering is thereby moved from below the reach of justice to a place within its purview; and now the language of injury, discrimination, injustice, and oppression can apply more cleanly to it. It is *after* a movement crosses this critical threshold that a mode of suffering fits into the practice of justice.

Thus the coarse practice of justice regularly poses barriers to the politics of becoming before providing support for it. Failure by many secular theorists to acknowledge this fundamental ambiguity at the center of justice disables them from registering the importance of an ethos of responsiveness to justice itself. This does not mean that the politics of being (justice, common standards, shared understandings, and so on) is irrelevant to ethico-political action. It is indispensable to it. It means that critical responsiveness is essential to a practice of justice that would be crude and incomplete without it.

Take John Rawls. I will concentrate here on two ways in which the Rawlsian rendering of "persons" engaged in "fair cooperation" poses ill-considered barriers to the politics of becoming in the process of trying to develop a (nearly) self-sufficient theory of justice.

Rawls now concurs that justice as fairness cannot be derived from the calculations of rational agents. The outcomes of rational calculations depend upon the premises adopted. Self-interest, for instance, does not serve as a sufficient basis for justice. "What rational agents lack is the particular form of moral *sensibility* that underlies the desire to engage in fair cooperation as such."[22] What else is needed, then? Well, agents of justice are "reasonable" people. They are willing to accept reciprocal limits. Rawls's use of the word "reasonable" may suggest that this sensibility is a necessary companion of rationality, while it seems to me to be better understood as a kissing cousin of traditional theories of virtue.[23] For by what procedure or mode of argument is reasonableness attained? On what logic is it grounded? Rawls says the disposition comes from a fortunate cultural tradition that already embodies it. Though for reasons yet to be discussed Rawls does not like to emphasize this point, it is nested within cultural practices never entirely reducible to a logic or rationality.

Note that Rawlsians are now unable to find the sufficient rational ground for justice they habitually accuse post-Nietzscheans of lacking. Reasonableness finds its grounds in itself if and when it is already widely shared in a cultural tradition. But what does a Rawlsian moralist appeal to when such a tradition is deeply conflictual, or weak, or active in some domains and absent in others? What do Rawlsians appeal to, that is, when the appeal is most needed? Rawls has nothing compelling to say in such cases. This is because, in a way reminiscent of John Caputo, Richard Rorty, and Jürgen Habermas, he rules "comprehensive doctrines" out of public discourse in order to protect the impartiality of justice. But the Rawlsian imperative to silence at such junctures has become a politically dangerous eccentricity. Since every other contemporary constituency articulates some of its most fundamental presumptions as it presses its claims in public life, the secular liberalism of John Rawls functions to marginalize secularists on some of the most hotly contested issues of the day.

Sure, Rawls and Rawlsians still claim that unreasonable people explicitly refuse to recognize what their conduct in other domains "implicitly" presumes. But, given the slack, uncertainty, and slipperiness within the operational terms of public discourse, there is always more room to slip out of such a putative logic of social implication when people are motivated to do so than Rawls wants to acknowledge. Better put, one side of the Rawlsian doctrine points in the direction of this acknowledgment while that acknowledgment is resisted when the specific practice of justice is up for discussion.[24] The moral power of the logic of cultural implication itself grows to a considerable degree out of the sensibility it purports to sustain rather than the other way around. No cultural logic is sufficient to the practice of morality or justice. The reasonableness Rawlsian justice seeks thus rests upon fungible cultural dispositions and conventions.

Post-Nietzschean gratitude for life and its ambiguous conditions of possibility, while not widely thematized today and insufficient to *guarantee* the production of such a sensibility, does speak at the precise juncture where Rawlsians lapse into silence. Moreover, it joins some theological perspectives such as those provided by Levinas, Ricoeur, and Jaspers in challenging all the way down the theistic and secular fundamentalisms Rawls himself resists.[25] For this fundamental perspective anticipates noise, surplus, and inchoate energy coursing over and through every culture and every winter doctrine. It draws an ethic of generosity partly from those energies and attachments that exceed established conventions rather than resting it on a fictive juridical ground, or binding it entirely to the existing shape of existing cultural conventions, or drawing it entirely from a logic of cultural implication too loose to carry out the job by itself. It therefore has resources to draw upon in fighting cultural forces disposed to the moral negation, punishment, or marginalization of differences that disrupt their sense of naturalness or self-assurance. Nor is it pressed to hide ugly forces within contemporary life behind a veil of ignorance to protect the fiction that existing conventions ("the overlapping consensus") sufficiently sustain the cultural background (the "reasonableness") justice requires. And, of course, this very appreciation of irreducible surplus alerts democratic post-Nietzscheans to the insufficiency of justice to itself and, therefore, to the need to cultivate critical responsiveness to the politics of becoming.

The second, most direct, way in which Rawls stymies the politics of becoming follows from his conception of the person. The loss of traditional grounds for "the good" means, Rawls says, that justice must be insulated as much as possible from irresolveable debates over the good. So Rawls seeks a fixed conception of persons appropriate to justice as an internal practice, dependent only on the (supposedly modest) externality of cultural reasonableness. Sure, Rawlsians say a thin conception of the person allows concrete persons to develop rich, individual selves. But the very formality of this permission obscures how dense cultural differentiations and hierarchical rankings of *types* of self (identities) always precede and shape the practice of justice. It deflects ethical attention from thick cultural determinations of what is already inside, marginal to, and excluded from personhood *before* justice as fairness appears on the scene. A veil of ignorance thus screens from justice as fairness the ethical importance of becoming.

This way of putting the point exaggerates slightly. Rawls, as we saw in chapter 1, now acknowledges how the fortunate becoming of secularism out of a historically specific "modus vivendi" forms the indispensable political background to justice as fairness. This thought about the ethicization of a modus vivendi contains valuable possibilities, and I am indebted to Rawls on this point. *But secularism is the last historical moment in the politics of becoming Rawlsian categories authorize us to acknowledge.* Rawls wants to freeze the liberal conception of the person and the secular conception of public space today while everything else in and around the culture undergoes change. The result is to surround justice with a stingier sensibility than Rawls intends. Persons just are, for Rawls, at least after the modus vivendi of secularism. "No constructivist view, including Scanlon's, says that the facts that are relevant in practical reasoning and judgment are constructed, any more than they say that the conceptions of person and society are constructed."[26] Then he states the effects of this theme for slavery:

> In claiming that slavery is unjust the relevant fact about it is not when it arose historically, or even whether it is economically efficient, but that it allows some persons to own others as their property. *That is a fact about slavery, already there, so to speak,* and independent of the principles of justice. The idea of constructing facts seems incoherent.[27]

Rawls levels persons to make social facts simple. And he carries out these two assignments to secure an unequivocal conception of justice. But the most relevant fact about slavery, to many slaveholders and defenders, was that "slaves" did not count as full "persons." Defenders of slavery could accept the Rawlsian formula of fairness to persons while contesting its application to those who do not measure up to the relevant standards. Rawls would say that they were simply wrong in this respect: his judgment fits the facts about persons while slaveholders misrepresented them. This formulation has a point, as long as it is treated as shorthand for a more complex claim. That is, defenders of slavery abstained from steeping themselves in the unfamiliar civilization of those who were violently wrested from it and then enslaved; they failed to explore whether their own civilization was more closed than it had to be in its interpretations of the enslaved; and they refused to run disturbing social experiments that might challenge their judgment about the natural incapacities among those enslaved while pressing them to alter key dimensions in their own economies of cultural identity and production. But in treating his retrospective judgment of the injustice of slavery as if it were derived from a timeless and sufficient concept of persons, Rawls again buries two crucial dimensions in the politics of becoming: (a) the importance of dense, institutionally embedded discriminations between traits, dispositions, and sensibilities that cross the threshold into personhood and numerous culturally defined afflictions, incapacities, inferiorities, liabilities, disorders, and defects that are placed, to one degree or another, *below* that threshold; and (b) the importance of periodic, disruptive political performances in breaking up, moving, and challenging elements in those dense historically specific codes of cultural presumption that invade and surround us at any specific time and enter into the operational coding of personhood and justice. Thus in the United States at various times over the past two centuries, slaves were said to be inhabited by natural incapacities that pushed them below the threshold of full persons; John Brown, the abolitionist, was widely declared to be a monomaniac, a type, I believe, no longer recognized in the official nosology of psychiatry; women were said to be equipped for the immediate ethics of family life but not for the abstract deliberation essential to public life; atheists were (and still often are) said (e.g., by Tocqueville and the America he registered) to be too materialistic, narcissistic, and selfish to hold public office, though each was person enough to participate in employment, commerce, and military liability; "homosexuals" were (and often are) said to deserve justice as persons *and* to be marked by an objective disorder and/or sin shuffling their sensualities below the reach of justice; "postmodernists" — occupying today the subject position previously reserved for atheists — are said to be cool, amoral, and nihilistic, lacking the prerequisites to be taken seriously as moral agents; doctors who assist terminally ill patients in dying were (and often are) defined as murderers because of the generic Christian injunction against taking one's own life; and Rawls himself now treats the mentally retarded as something less than full persons because they cannot participate fully in the practice of "fair cooperation" upon which his scheme of justice rests. In these cases either significant changes in interpretation of the extent to which the parties measure up to the existing code of personhood or changes in the implicit composition of personhood itself have been initiated. In most cases both were required. And in no case is either argument or the establishment of simple facts, previously overlooked, sufficient to the change. In each case a shift in sensibility informs the changes in interpretation and composition.

Rawls is superb at acknowledging the justice of newly acknowledged claims and constituencies once the politics of becoming has carried their voices within range of his hearing. Within a period of thirty years or so, Rawlsians have acknowledged the claims of Indians, women, and gays *after* a series of social movements began to reshape the complex institutional determinations in which they had been set. But Rawls pretends (and his categories presume) that he is *now* in the same position with respect to a large variety of unpoliticized injuries today that he is with respect to constituencies whose cultural identification and institutional standing have already been modified through the politics of becoming. Most crucially, he also acts as if his own identity (as "a person") can remain untouched and unchanged as he responds to new and surprising movements of difference. But a political struggle that moves "homosexuality" from a place below the register of justice to a place on that register also challenges the visceral experience of exclusive sensual naturalness upon which heterosexual identity had been based. In doing so, it elevates, as it were, a new dimension of being into the rubric of personhood itself. That elevation involves changes in the self-identifications of heterosexuals, and it opens the door to further pluralizations of sexuality. Once these two initiatives have made headway—supported by a critical responsiveness irreducible to justice—the question of justice now becomes pertinent in the domains of military practice, marriage law, child rearing and adoption, employment discrimination, curricular organization, and so on. And the resolution of these new issues of justice now helps to shape cultural practices in those domains. Exploration of these connections, therefore, discloses the relation of dissonant interdependence between critical responsiveness, personhood, and justice.

The point is not to criticize previous "oversights" of Rawlsians, as if *we* have a god's-eye view above the fray that they lack. *Such a model of moral criticism would merely reiterate secular, Rawlsian insensitivities to the politics of becoming.* The point, rather, is to press Rawlsians (and others they stand in for) to *cultivate a bivalent ethical sensibility responsive to both the indispensability of justice and the radical insufficiency of justice to itself.* For it is extremely probable that all of us today are unattuned to some modes of suffering and exclusion that will have become ethically important tomorrow as a political movement carries them across the threshold of cultural attentiveness and institutional redefinition. This is so because each effective movement of difference toward a new, legitimate cultural identity breaks a constituent in its previous composition that located it below the operational reach of personhood and justice by rendering it immoral, inferior, hysterical, sinful, incapacitated, unnatural, abnormal, irresponsible, mono-maniacal, narcissistic, nihilistic, or sick.

Often enough, of course, such a movement does not succeed; and some-times it should not. In some cases many critical respondents eventually con-clude that they have good reason to refuse some of its claims, even after the movement has opened up previously obscure issues. But, and this is the pertinent point, some of those reasons themselves come sharply into view through the politics of becoming rather than preexisting as a pile of criteria and arguments before its appearance. The constitutive uncertainty at the center of becoming does not defeat the central point [28] It, rather, re-minds us how ethical uncertainty haunts the politics of becoming and how important it is to those who care for the plurivocity of being—or who come to a similar sentiment from different directions—to cultivate an ethos of crit-ical responsiveness irreducible to a fixed moral code or abstract conception of the person. For often enough, obscure pains, objective disorders, low lev-els of energy, perverse sexualities, basic inferiorities, uncivilized habits, hys-terical symptoms, inherent abnormalities, and unreliable work dispositions become reconfigured through a politics of becoming and critical respon-siveness that first exceeds the official reach of justice and then places new dimensions of life on its register. These effects show justice to be an essen-tially ambiguous practice, insufficient to itself. No general concept of the person can resolve that constitutive ambiguity into a sufficient code or set of criteria: it will be either (like the Rawlsian model) too formal to reach deeply enough into the density of culturally constituted identities or (like the communitarian model) too specific to respond to diverse possibilities of being that may turn out to be acceptable or admirable after the politics of becoming presses them into being. It is better to respond to this constitutive ambiguity by cultivating critical responsiveness to the politics of becoming, acknowledging that the practice of justice is indebted to an ethical reserve it is incapable of subjecting to definitive regulation.

Rawls is pulled by the demand that things be still at bottom. He wants—after the historical becoming of secularism—persons and the generic facts about them to remain stationary so that liberal justice can be (nearly) suffi-cient unto itself. One should offer a moment of tribute to those who cling to such a winter doctrine during difficult times. They do honor one impor-tant dimension of ethical life in the face of forces that press relentlessly against it. But it is even more important to remember that things don't stay still. Even the dense, unconscious coding of personhood shifts over time. Those doctrines of secularism that appreciate the politics of becoming with respect to, say, the advent of secularism itself tend to freeze this result into a theory of justice, persons, and rationality insufficiently attuned to the persistence of becoming. This drive to stillness is the crucial, secular, Rawlsian sensibility to contest by those who think the politics of becoming is not finished. The idea of an ethos of engagement explored in chapter 6 is indebted to the Rawlsian theme of an overlapping consensus. But, in contrast to the latter idea, it both appreciates the role that cultivation of a sensibility along several registers of being plays in ethics and negotiates a generous public ethos between a variety of constituencies who bring aspects of their fundamental religious and metaphysical orientations into public life.[29]

Dialectical Progress and Becoming

But isn't it time for those who seek to refashion secularism to become reasonable? Doesn't the trajectory of change in the shape of Western universals reveal a historical dialectic that fills the universal out progressively? Doesn't it show, retrospectively, how historically tolerable suffering imposed upon slaves, women, Indians, atheists, and homosexuals was actually unjust, and hence how the enlargement of justice draws us ever closer to the universal as such? If we can't be strict Rawlsians, can we not at least become neo-Hegelians?

We *can,* indeed. It is perhaps impossible not to from time to time—whenever we honor the politics of becoming retrospectively. Rawls, for instance, is a neo-Hegelian with respect to the historical becoming of secularism. And there *is* ethical value in treating the latest filling out of persons as approaching more closely to the highest standard of personhood. It is just that this valuable ethical imperative soon bumps into a discordant ethical concern: to pursue practices of genealogy, deconstruction, political disturbance, and the politics of becoming through which contemporary self-satisfied unities are rendered more problematic and more responsive to new movements of difference. Attunement to the politics of becoming, then, engenders a bivalent ethical sensibility in which critical tension is maintained between two interdependent and dissonant ethical imperatives.

I resist, then, the winter satisfaction of dialectical progress without being able either to forgo its comforts at some moments or to disprove it definitively.[30] Perhaps, even under conditions of goodwill, the entry of new identities into a cultural constellation, if and as they relieve palpable modes of suffering, often enough eventually engender in their turn a series of new surprises, including unexpected and poorly articulated modes of suffering. The publication of these obscure and unexpected injuries will, if we are lucky, become entangled in a new round in the politics of becoming. What if (a) the energy and suffering of embodied human beings provides a starting point from which becoming and critical responsiveness proceed *and* (b) no intrinsic pattern of identity\difference on the other side of suffering consolidates being as such? Would it not then be wise to maintain *ethical* tension between being and becoming, even to sanctify becoming so as to counter powerful tendencies normally in place to tilt ethico-political energies in the other direction?[31]

When a dialectical rendering of the politics of becoming suggests that the most recent identities are also the most true, natural, or advanced, it discourages proponents from cultivating that partial, comparative sense of contingency in their own identities from which responsiveness to new claims of difference might proceed. A dialectician is always poised in front of a final act always about to commence *or a dialectical reading of things cannot be vindicated.* For how could a dialectical reading of things be sustained unless the standard that redeems it is now discernible in vague outline just over the horizon? Contemporary dialecticians, therefore, proceed as if they were on the cutting edge of the last historical moment. Most have learned just enough from the record of Hegel, Marx, and Fukuyama to refrain from shouting this presumption out.

If a politician of the dialectic thinks that things have been developing up to *this* penultimate moment on the edge of stasis, the politician of becoming thinks it is critical at this same moment to initiate the politics of becoming in some domain and/or to cultivate critical responsiveness to some forces pressing for the modification of existing stabilizations. Moreover, the politician of becoming thinks a generous ethos emerges when a number of constituencies engage actively and more generously those differences in themselves and others the regulation of which enables them to be what they are. This end, then, forms a regulative *ideal* for the politician of becoming, a complex, final act never entirely susceptible to completion because some of its components cannot be synchronized perfectly with the others at any particular time. It places two politicians of difference fairly close to one another for a moment. If these two types were to converge upon an ambidextrous characterization of the regulative ideal, other differences between them would diminish, though they would still debate which *vocabulary* best expresses that connection and what *balance* between being and becoming must be sought at any particular moment. Such debates remain crucial to the ethics of engagement, as long as the tension between being and becoming persists, enough people care about the constitutive tension between suffering and the play of cultural possibility, and public discourse remains relatively open.

3

Liberalism, Secularism, and the Nation

Forgetting the Nation into Being

Nationalism, we are often told, is dangerous and elsewhere. It is in Sri Lanka, Ireland, Iraq, Russia, Bosnia, Israel, Palestine, Quebec, and so on. But, we are also told, the nation-state is a Euro-American invention; and it exists here and now in secular, democratic countries. What if the image of the nation reflects a chimera more than a possible achievement?[1] What if a world organized around the presumption of states as nations engenders cruel and dangerous modes of exclusionary politics, and secular ideals of individualism, minority rights, and democracy function simultaneously as important obstacles to these tendencies and problematic sources of them? Then secular liberalism would be entangled in the nationalism its most valiant devotees also resist. It would be divided against itself, helping to inspire the imagination of the nation *and* to offer leads through which to value it. To revalue the nation-state would be to rework secular liberalism; and to rework the latter would be to release admirable elements from the image of the nation in which they too often remain encased.

But what was the nation? The *Elementary Latin Dictionary* says that *natio* means "a birth, origin," also "a breed, stock, kind, species, race, tribe," and "race of people." The *OED* seconds this, saying that in early European uses, race or stock was primary to the image of a nation, while in later uses the idea of a people formed through a common history takes on more salience. This etymology helps. For in either case—either where race is taken to form the essential *basis* of a people or where the unity of a people is said to be *irreducible* to race per se—the image of the nation remains closely

73

bound up with the image of race. Sometimes race provides a nation with a putative basis of unity; sometimes it provides the paradigm *form* of unity a nation is to approximate by other means, say, in its language, religion, or memories. For a populace united by race was thought to be single rather than multiple, centered and given in its unity rather than pluralized and improvised, bound together fundamentally rather than superficially, and readily recognizable by others through visible signs. The putative basis of this or that nation may reside in a single race, religion, language, set of memories, constitution, or some combination thereof, but its *form* of unity seems to be inspired by the traditional imagination of race. This resonance between two uncertain images of "unity" may help to explain why race is so often reinvoked by nationalists when the aspiration to be a nation faces severe threats.

But this resonance exposes a problem in the image of the nation: race provides the paradigm from which the image of nationhood is formed, while the idea of a unified race itself has become highly dubious. Every time somebody tries to coordinate the elements and boundaries of a particular race the historical record confounds the attempt. Today race is widely understood to be a fable through which a people might consolidate its unity rather than the paradigm of what collective unity as such looks like. Is the very imagination of the nation, then, extrapolated from a dubious model of human unity? Put another way, once race forfeits its place as either basis of or model for nationhood, *what material exemplars of unity now sustain the image of the nation?* What could it now mean to *be* unified as a nation? A nation can't simply refer, say, to a peaceful state in which most people most of the time honor the laws. For that begs the question: maybe somewhere an effective state is made up of multiple constituencies, *marked* by numerous indeterminacies and hybridities; *divided* along lines of ethnicity, language, religion, irreligion, ethical sources, and sensuality; and *connected* by corollary ties too multiple in type and varied in intensity to be summarized by a simple image or picture. To call such an effective state a nation would stretch the image of the nation to the breaking point. It would not help you to figure out what is added to a state when it becomes a nation, or, more pertinently, what it *exceeds* when it is not one. Appeals to nationhood would not resolve, say, what sort of cultural ethos a democratic state needs to function effectively.

Ernst Renan, the nineteenth-century French nationalist, was perplexed by these issues. He took the nation to be essential to citizenship in a modern state. Without the bond formed by nationhood, citizens would be unwilling to risk death to defend the state or to fight for its glory. And without this will to sacrifice, the state could not sustain itself. But Renan could not delineate quite what a nation was. That is, for Renan a nation is a form of unity, but the unity need not always come from race, religion, or language. Indeed, he finds race to be a dubious basis of nationhood because its purity so readily dissolves under the scrutiny of the critical historian. "The truth is that no race is pure, and that to base politics on ethnographic analysis is tantamount to basing it on chimera."[2] A common religion often forms the basis of a nation, but not always. Even a common language is not entirely necessary, as, according to Renan, the experience of Switzerland shows and the relaxed attitude in (nineteenth-century) France toward the evolution of the French language attests.[3] The unity of a particular nation might be formed out of any combination of these elements, as long as they are supported by two other ingredients:

> A nation is a soul, a spiritual principle. Two things, which are really only one, go to make up this soul or spiritual principle. One of these things lies in the past, the other in the present. The one is the possession in common of a rich heritage of memories; and the other is actual agreement, the desire to live together, and the will to continue to make the most of the joint inheritance. Man, gentlemen, cannot be improvised. The nation, like the individual, is the fruit of a long past spent in toil, sacrifice and devotion. Ancestor worship is of all forms the most justifiable, since our ancestors have made us what we are.... To share the glories of the past, and a common will in the present; to have done great deeds together, and to desire to do more—these are the essential conditions of a people's being.[4]

Above all, then, nationhood is founded on shared memories of sacrifice and a common will in the present. It is refined by its memory of the enemies it faced in the past. Its victories fill it with glory. Its defeats fill it with the determination to reverse that result in the future. What's more, a nation is formed out of "a long past spent in toil, sacrifice and devotion." Time must move slowly for a nation to be. A common fund of memories forged over long, slow time, and a current will to express that inheritance in the future: these form the crucial constituents in the soul at the center of a nation.

Renan notes two other factors. The first is that not only race but any memory upon which a nation is founded could be pluralized, eroded, or rendered uncertain by critical history. So every nation, whatever the elements upon which it is grounded, requires a selective national memory to be.

> To forget—and I will venture to say—to get one's history wrong, are essential factors in the making of a nation: and thus the advance of his-

torical studies is often a danger to nationality. Historical research, in fact, casts fresh light upon those deeds of violence which have marked the origin of all political formations, even of those which have been followed by the most beneficial results. Unity is always realized by brute force.[5]

Forgetting the violence through which unity has been forged out of variety is critical to the imagination of a nation. But this means that any element previously rendered unnecessary by Renan might now return as a possible source of unity. A nation might be based on the unity of race, a unity grounded in forgetfulness about the multiplicity from which it was formed. Renan himself says that something like that occurred in nineteenth-century France. It might be grounded in glorious religious wars of the past. But above all, a nation is grounded in forgetfulness of arbitrary violences and exclusions from which it was forged: its unity is actually founded on "brute force," but its image varnishes that brutality with a veneer of necessity, beneficence, and innocence.

While Renan emphasizes how critical history can undermine the unity of a nation, his account suggests inadvertently how another force might generate the same effect. When the *tempo* of history quickens, the fog of forgetfulness needed to form a single soul out of multiplicity might not form so readily. Does the easy self-confidence of a nation, then, depend upon the experience of history as long, slow time?

What is the *shape* of this unity grounded in forgetfulness? Is it a smooth unity or one crossed and cracked by the effects of violences in its past? What about, say, Amerindians and former Mexicans who still inhabit the territorial state created through their conquest? What about remnants of paganism circulating through a predominantly Christian culture? Or the sons and daughters of communists in a capitalist state? Or the descendants of those previously enslaved by the state? Or those whose ancestors lost a bitter civil war? Or those once constituted as a "nation of Jews"? And what about forgetfulness of the present in the present? How difficult is it today to forget the corrosive effects nomadic capitalism has on the experience of the nation? Particularly when this nomadism of investment, advertising, production, and consumption both compromises the spatiotemporal conditions of nationhood and forms part of the self-definition of the nation. Does forgetfulness form the basis of the nation *and* create a standing reserve of threats to it? Perhaps the incomplete inability to forget provides the source of those experiences of anxiety, threat, and loss that perpetually haunt the quest for nationhood. Perhaps the nation is based upon its explicit enemies and haunted by the effects of its forgotten past. Maybe the indefinite sense of insecurity always discernible at the center of a nation helps to explain why those internal constituencies defined by nationalists to be enemies of the people are so often figured as volatile and nomadic (Jews, Gypsies, Indians, homosexuals, welfare recipients, atheists, promiscuous women, unpatriotic men). Is the speed of late-modern time simultaneously the most elemental adversary the modern nation encounters and struggles to locate outside itself?

Renan, perhaps reasonably enough, given the time in which he writes, is silent about such issues. He insists that a nation is essential to unity, that national unity is essential to a healthy state, and that sluggish time fosters unity. But he does not address the shape and tightness of unity itself or the effect of speed on the composition of a nation-state. He is so absorbed in how the commonalities of his time have been formed through long, slow time and to how the commonalities that form a nation (race, religion, language, memories, and so on) vary from nation to nation that he forgets to probe further into the spatiotemporal conditions of nationhood itself.

A Liberal Image of the Nation

Renan is neither a liberal nor a secularist. He imagines the nation in the language of honor, blood, sweat, sacrifice, devotion, and suffering. And he wants time to move slowly so that it is possible to absorb cultural diversities into the territorial unity of a nation. Secular liberals are allergic to these words and moods: to the liberal, Renan's vocabulary signals a desire to sacrifice the happiness, rights, and vitality of some to the comfort, superiority, and honor of others. Moreover, Renan's appeals devalue the quest of liberals to rectify violences and injustices still sedimented into established practices. Still, secular liberal resistance to conservative nationalism may be weakened by its own presumptions about the nation as a necessary condition of democratic governance. Take John Stuart Mill.

Mill honors individuality, tolerance, agitation of public opinion by creative minorities, and active participation by people in their own governance. But Mill also propagates models of civilization, secularism, progress, and nationality that mark and delimit this first set of dispositions. To rethink Millian secularism and liberalism is to explore the subterranean channels by which these two lines of thought define and delimit one another.

Civilization, for Mill, is an advanced mode of living and governance. Generally growing out of a Christian culture, it equips people with the discipline, character, disposition to regular obedience, and appreciation for rule of law necessary to representative government. Not all "peoples" are susceptible to the civilizing process:

> Nothing but foreign force would induce a tribe of North American Indians to submit to the restraints of a regular and civilized government. The same might be said, though somewhat less absolutely, of the barbarians who overran the Roman Empire. It required centuries of time, and an entire change of circumstances, to discipline them into regular obedience even to their own leaders, when not actually serving under their own banner.[6]

Mill does not follow Tocqueville in treating the violent displacement of Amerindians to be essential to the installation of a new democratic civilization. Still, such an implication may hover over the first sentence. Civilization is something given to "peoples," one people at a time, over "centuries of time." It involves a long, slow, progressive process of discipline that renders a people capable of regular obedience, restraint, respect for rule of law, and a streak of independence. While Mill himself is a secularist, that secularism reflects its implication in the Christendom from which it emerged. Thus peoples such as the Chinese and Egyptians, who chanced upon some of the prerequisites of civilizational progress, were unable to press it very far forward on their own. "Such cases are frequent and are among the most melancholy cases in history. The Egyptian hierarchy, the paternal despotism in China, were very fit instruments for carrying those nations up to the point of civilization they attained. But having reached that point, they were brought to a halt through want of mental liberty and individuality."[7]

What, first in Judaism and then in Christianity, prepares a people to become a civilized, democratic nation? While the Jews had "an absolute monarch and hierarch," that was not the most distinctive thing about their culture:

> These did for them what was done for other oriental races... subdued them to industry and order and gave them a national life. But neither their kings nor their priests ever obtained... the exclusive molding of their character. Their religion, which persons of genius and a high religious tone regarded... as inspired from heaven, gave existence to an inestimably precious unorganized institution—the Order (if it may be so termed) of Prophets.[8]

Restrained dissidence between the priests and the Prophets installed an "antagonism of influences which is the only real security for continued progress."[9] Christianity, particularly after the devolution of Christendom into a European world of states, continues this creative antagonism of forces within the nation. It is therefore through Jewish and Christian culture above all that a territorial people acquires the civilizational conditions of possibility for representative government.

Civilizational development is crucial to a possible world of democratic nation-states. Creative minorities within each monotheistic people provide the critical sparks that propel the nation toward "further improvement." So only a particular kind of nation enables individuality. That means that the parameters of Millian individuality and rights are fixed in advance by the civilizational shape of the nation in which they are set. This latent theme carried forward into contemporary doctrines of liberalism and secularism makes it more difficult than it might otherwise be for many defenders of individualism and rights to negotiate with constituencies not already enclosed in the matrix of monotheism, mastery over the land, and morality endemic to Europe. The operational boundaries of individuality, rights, and justice are quietly set in advance by the parameters of the liberal nation. But these boundaries themselves are being challenged by the extended pluralism and the acceleration of pace that mark secular states of the West today. It is pertinent to note, then, that a "minority" for Mill is very often a creative constituency *above* the general run of people culturally, morally, and educationally; but they are *part of the people* in its major linguistic, religious, and moral heritage.[10] Mill defines secular intellectuals as crucial counterpoints to the weight of public opinion, religious authority, and bureaucracy in the modern nation-states of Europe. The prophets and intellectuals he invokes, though, typically belong to the "people" or the "nation" they agitate.

Civilizational progress, though often shaky and never inevitable, forms the principal vector of Millian history. This precarious line of historical development points toward a world of "peoples" ranked according to their levels of civilizational attainment. An intercoded vocabulary of civilization, progress, peoples, nations, and races is very prominent in *Considerations on Representative Government*. Mill, who views the world through the eyes of a recent administrative officer for Indian affairs (1856–58) and a potential tourist, *supposes the world of his time to consist already and for the most part of territorially separate peoples*. His quest for representative government, already stressed by pessimism and anxiety, would collapse into despair if the initial presumption of a world of territorial peoples were shaken profoundly.

A world of territorial peoples. Mill speaks, variously, of "*a race* who have been trained in energy and courage," of how foreign rulers can sometimes be "of the greatest advantage to *a people*," of "uncivilized *races* ... averse to continuous labor of an exacting kind," of "*a rude people*," of "the form of government which is most effectual for carrying *a people* through the next stage of progress," and of "a hundred other infirmities or shortcomings in *a people* ... which might disqualify them from making the best use of representative government."[11] *The Millian world already comes out-*

fitted with territorial peoples, and only because it is so equipped can representative government hope to consolidate itself on a few spots on the earth. The idea of biological inheritance seems to move in and out of Mill's account of national unity, but a world of peoples, nations, races, and tribes, each shaped by stable interaction over a long stretch of time on the same territorial space, is always prominent. In those cases where "a people" occupies the same territorial space, it deserves to have its own state. "Where the sentiment of nationality exists in any force there is a *prima facie* case for uniting all of the members of the nationality under the same government."[12] This sentiment is admirable as a protest against empire; it does not speak, however, to those numerous cases in which a variety of constituencies divided along numerous dimensions occupy the same territorial space.

Peoples, territories, time. Mill may sense that the conceptions of territorial space and historical time governing his analysis are less than fully appropriate to the time in which he himself lives. Mill *is* aware that the contemporary tempo of life is accelerating. But he mentions this historical shift in tempo only in the context of a hope to convince "the people of England" of the value of proportional representation when their traditions of local representation incline them against it. "But unfamiliarity is a disadvantage which, when there is any real value in an idea, it only requires time to remove. And in these days of discussion, and generally awakened interest in improvement, *what formerly was the work of centuries often requires only years.*"[13] But what would it mean if this world of territorial peoples forged through slow centuries of experience and improvement, to the extent it existed when Mill was writing, has become increasingly dispersed and pluralized in the century or two after Mill? Would Mill's aspiration to representative government collapse? Or would he argue that the acceleration of speed is matched by the ability of governments to organize a populace into a people faster than heretofore? If he were to argue the latter, what burdens and sacrifices would be imposed on those who have the furthest to go to participate in the nation?

We might pursue these questions by asking, again, what *is* the Millian image of a people? And why is that image so crucial to democratic governance? "A portion of mankind," Mill says, "may be said to constitute a nationality if they are *united* among themselves by *common* sympathies which do not exist between themselves and others." It is this unity and commonality that makes them "desire to be under the same government."[14] Notice how critical the indeterminate ideas of unity and commonality are to the image of a nation. The centrality of these uncertain ideas to Mill becomes more conspicuous when you notice how often they are invoked without elaboration. Consider them again, even as Mill explains, now in accord with Renan, how variable the *sources* of unity might be:

> Sometimes it is the effect of *identity* of race and descent. *Community* of language and *community* of religion greatly contribute to it. Geographical limits are one of its causes. But the strongest of all is *identity* of political antecedents: the possession of a *national* history and consequent *community* of recollections; *collective* pride and humiliation, pleasure and regret, connected with the *same* incidents in the past.[15]

Several points are pertinent. First, Mill invokes the language of commonality, identity, community, same, and collective to imagine nationality, but he does not explain how tight, centered, or close identity must be to *be* identity. It is this constant combination of indispensability and uncertainty within the image of the nation that sets it up to be a condition to be remembered but never known, pursued but never present, absent but never eliminable as an end. Any regulative ideal, surely, is impossible to realize fully. But the image of the nation seems to be marked by a sense that *the density at its very center* is both always indispensable to it and always insufficiently available. This distinctive combination in the regulative ideal of the nation makes the state particularly vulnerable to takeover attempts by constituencies who claim to embody in themselves the unity that is necessary to the nation but so far absent from it.

Second, Mill employs the nation, as we saw earlier, to explain political rule by a state, but he also refers to a long period of political rule on the same territory to explain the formation of a nation. This appears most dramatically when he uses the phrase "national history" to help explain how a nation comes into being. His ambiguous rendering of the temporal dimension of nationhood does not discriminate enough (for me) between (a) a series of interactions over a long period between diverse constituencies of multiple types forming an ethos of engagement across those multiple lines of difference and (b) a series issuing in a centered nation governed by the intercoded commonalities listed by Mill. The failure to address this distinction helps to explain why Mill's territorial maps are two-dimensional and national rather than three-dimensional and rhizomatic. For when you fold intraterritorial struggles of the past into a three-dimensional map—made up of longitude, latitude, and time—the violences upon which the current image of the nation is grounded become more visible. If you scrap the temporal dimension and reduce it two spatial dimensions, that violence is more readily forgotten. The credibility of Mill's story of progress toward the advanced nation is enhanced by such cartographies of forgetfulness.[16] In the film *The Man Who Fell to Earth,* David Bowie—playing the one who drops in—feels the painful traces of past violence as he walks across the ground of Texas. Such temporal sensitivity can become debilitating if it is allowed to overwhelm, but Millian liberalism needs to incorporate a larger dose of it into its maps of contemporary life. If it did so it might not set its insistence upon the unity of a people into such a benign picture of territorial integrity.

Third, Mill generally says that commonality of race, religion, and language may or may not be crucial to a particular nation, but the actual examples he gives of nationalities that should be recognized as states, nationalities ill prepared to become democratic states, and diverse peoples dispersed across the same territory who lack nationhood and therefore are in a poor position to achieve statehood are often delineated by some mixture of these three elements. His emphasis upon terms such as *identity* and *unity* discourages him from exploring more actively indeterminacies and hybridities circulating through the unity citizens represent themselves to have or probing critically the unexamined idea of unity itself. Mill, of course, possesses impressive resources through which to pursue these questions, as anyone can see who examines his thinking about freedom, individuality, participation, and tolerance. But he does not apply these categories to the idea of the nation because he (generally) presumes the nation to be an essential condition for their existence. The Millian image of the advanced nation as a condition of representative government ushers forth a liberalism divided against itself.

Perhaps every theory and every regime is divided against itself in certain respects. And certainly, as Mill himself suggests, such divisions often enable freedom if they are approached in the right spirit. But it seems to me that the regulative ideal of the nation, in particular, leads to an experience of politics in which a black hole subsists and persists at the center of political culture. This constitutive lack at the center of the nation provides a standing temptation for some bellicose constituency to occupy it, doing so by claiming that it *embodies* in its ethnicity, faith, loyalty to the past, and/or commitment to the true source of public morality the missing essence of the nation. The regulative ideal I endorse, more rhizomatic in the mulitiple lines of difference and connection it supports, also encounters discrepancies between itself and actuality. Pursuit of this ideal, however, requires negotiations between diverse constituencies in which each assumes more modesty with respect to what it is and more generosity toward constituencies that deviate from it. The discrepancies between this ideal and actuality are multiple. But because they do not assume the form of a lack at the very center of culture, they do not lend credibility to the emergence of a single, heroic constituency claiming to embody in itself the traits and virtues needed by the nation as a whole. Such a layered, plural ideal is thus more resistant to contending drives to occupy a fictive center than is the image of the nation. The decentering of the nation is pertinent to the refashioning of secularism.

The Second Image

The dominant tendency in Mill's orientation to the nation can be condensed into a sentence: "For the preceding reasons, it is in general a necessary condition of free institutions that the boundaries of governments should coincide in the main with those of nationalities."[17] But there is another strain in Mill's thinking, already intimated by clauses such as "in general" and "in the main." It emerges when Mill bumps into "parts even of Europe" — the place where civilization has reached its highest pitch — where the territorial conditions of nationhood are absent.

> The population of Hungary is composed of Magyars, Slovaks, Croats, Serbs, Romanians, and in some districts Germans, so mixed up as to be incapable of local separation; and there is no course open to them but to make a virtue of necessity and reconcile themselves to living together under equal rights and laws.[18]

Mill thinks that "Hungary" is an exceptional case rather than a dramatic version of the typical case. His dominant vision of liberal representative government requires it to be so. But, it might be objected, Mill thinks Hungary is exceptional because of the peculiar *virulence* displayed by diverse nationalities occupying the same territory. This extremism, perhaps, makes the territory unsusceptible to representative government. Mill is definitely concerned about the virulence of the nation, but he does not quite explore the tragedy of Hungary in a way that opens up critical reflection into the very image of the nation. He does not, for instance, warn other territorial states against the very project of nationalization, calling upon them to cultivate intersections, hybridities, and alliances among ethnic, religious, sensual, and linguistic diversities to *avoid* collapsing into the quagmire of the future former Yugoslavia. In the case of "Hungary," he suggests that "there is no course open to them but to make a virtue out of necessity and reconcile themselves to living together under equal rights and laws."

Then Mill notices that many "nations" have a predominant population punctuated by significant minorities on the same territory — the Basque in Spain and France, "the Welshman or the Scottish Highlander," and so forth. What can a liberal do in such cases? He says:

> Whatever really tends to the admixture of nationalities and the blending together of their attributes and peculiarities in a common union is a

> benefit to the human race. Not by extinguishing types, of which, in these cases, sufficient examples are sure to remain, *but by softening their extreme form and filling up the intervals between them.*[19]

This language can be taken either to follow a model of national assimilation or to move toward a more multifarious pluralism, depending on how you inflect "common union" in relation to "extreme form" and "filling up the intervals." The commendation would definitely incline in the second direction if Mill represented the intraterritorial diversity of "Hungary" to disclose the typical case and if he treated the general need to be the cultivation of intraterritorial pluralism in which a variety of constituencies divided along several dimensions negotiated an ethos of mutual engagement and collaboration. Such a shift would stimulate thinking about how destructive the pursuit of the nation is to democracy itself. For the current former "Yugoslavia" reveals how contending demands to occupy the ethnic center of a territory marked by numerous ethnicities and faiths fosters violent discord and war. In our time—and to a significant extent in his, too—the image of the nation reflects a chimera: the same image that fills many with hope for national unity engenders cultural and civil wars between parties contending over the right to occupy the constitutive lack at its center.

Mill himself, though, hesitates to pursue the course he opens up. He thinks "that to render this admixture possible, there must be peculiar conditions."[20] The peculiar conditions obtain when the dominant nationality is also the one that has attained the highest level of civilization. Tragic results are in store if the smaller group is also the more civilized or if "the nationalities which have been bound together are nearly equal in numbers and the other elements of power."[21]

Mill might be entirely right. A strong historical case could be made in support of his thesis. But if so, and if the condition this nineteenth-century secular liberal treated as the exceptional instance today approaches more closely to the norm, then the future prospects for both democracy and liberalism are bleak. Perhaps, then, we should explore the premise that Mill is half right and half wrong. Perhaps he is right that as long as the image of the nation retains hegemony it will be difficult to secure democratic states under circumstances of intraterritorial diversity but wrong in thinking that only in very rare circumstances is it possible to craft a more multidimensional, pluralist democracy. Of course, recent history in several parts of the world supports Mill's presumption, even if there are discernible countertrends. But we are uncertain to what degree this history itself embodies the self-propelling belief on the part of its major participants that nationhood is necessary to a democratic state. History is best viewed as a source of caution here and not an absolute guide. Up to the seventeenth century, it encouraged people in Europe to say that Christianity itself requires a single Church to be its authoritative representative on earth; up to the eighteenth, that constitutional democracy is an unlikely prospect to replace monarchy; up to the nineteenth, that secularism is an unlikely organization of public space; and up to the late twentieth, that gay rights and gender equality are incompatible with a civilization inspired by predominantly Christian principles. The emergence of new possibilities through the politics of becoming, for both better and worse, periodically breaks the mold of history. If, then, you pursue the possibility of democracy without a nation, and if you draw attention to such possibilities already inscribed to some degree in the actual practices of several states, the subordinate strain discernible in Mill may be susceptible to further amplification and development.

The Instability of Nationhood

If you fast-forward to the onset of the twenty-first century, the old image of the nation retains its hegemony while attempts to actualize it engender a series of cultural wars. Civil war replaces wars between states as the most common form of war, and cultural war without military portfolio extends the range of strategies available to warriors of the nation. The most distinctive feature of this time is the acceleration of *tempo* in the domains of capital investments, military practice, cultural communication, identity formation, population migrations, tourism, and disease transmission. The acceleration of tempo can stimulate the experience of historically contingent elements in those ethnic, religious, gender, sexual, linguistic, and moral identities that inhabit you. And it can open up the contestability of selective assumptions about being that you prize. But as long as the nation appears indispensable to the democratic state even as its actual attainment keeps retreating into the future, these very experiences of contingency and contestability are likely to foster reactive pressures to resanctify the traditions of nationhood just disturbed. For speed can be deployed on behalf of returning to the putative experience of nationhood said to be jeopardized as well as on behalf of cultural pluralization. In contrast to the national imaginary, then, we might make the following observations about the contemporary conditions of nationhood.

1. A nation is something that has been or will be but never is at any actually existing moment. Its most fervent advocates today imagine it to be something that has been lost, must be (re)instated, or both. Its promise as future unity is thus defined less by positive exemplification than by marking a set of constituencies who deviate from it in need of assimilation, correction, punishment, or elimination. The pursuit of national unity is founded

on decisions of exclusion and punishment, whereas its achievement is predicated on the end of arbitrary violence. The forgetfulness of the nation, then, exists along at least two dimensions: forgetfulness of the past violence on which it is grounded and concealment of the constitutive lack always subsisting at its center by holding a set of devalued constituencies responsible for that lack.

When nationalists in the United States, for instance, demand laws to punish flag burners, they inadvertently expose the black hole at the center of the nation. Why not just pull out five new flags each time one is burned? The rage engendered by flag burning expresses anxiety that the flag covers up the hole at the center of the nation. And it functions to fill that hole with a symbolic substance. The rage, in effect, was already there before a flag was burned. To burn it is to uncover for a moment the emptiness at the center of the nation; to punish burners is to allow a set of angry, white, Christian, male patriots the right to *occupy* that vacant center and to *embody* in their being its otherwise uncertain directives. Flag burning and the punishment of flag burners coalesce to reveal the lack in the nation and to mobilize constituency energies to cover it through occupation.[22]

2. The nineteenth-century image of the nation gained its place as a source of authority, allegiance, and communication in the democratic state in part because the nation was presented as a *universalizable* mode of being. That is, it was presented as a form potentially available to every people on every territory organized as a state. In such a world the legitimacy and stability of each nation is supported by the recognition it receives from other nations. But at least by the last third of the twentieth century, and probably before, it has become clear that the state as nation is *not* a universalizable form. As former colonized populations scattered within territorial states that deny them standing, refugees, boat people, civil war, and cultural war all reveal in their diverse ways today the quest to achieve equivalence between nation and territorial state fosters drives to exclude, silence, liquidate, or assimilate large sections of the population already there. One index of the contemporary nonuniversalizability of the ideal of the nation resides in the increase in the number of civil wars by comparison to interstate wars; two of its signs are the numbers of refugees and boat people. Boat people wander the seas after being pushed out by forces of nationalization in their home states and before they are defined to fit into the national profile of another. The conjunction of the globalization of economic life and retention of the image of the nation lies behind these events and signs. Given population dispersion within and between politically organized territories, and given

the finite space on the face of the globe, there is not enough contiguous space of the right type for every putative people to occupy as a nation-state.

The high reputation of the nation itself rested upon the hope, articulated by Tocqueville, Kant, Hegel, Renan, and Mill to varying degrees, of a future in which each "territory" would be occupied by a politically organized "people." Today, however, the nation has become a form that can be promised to some only because it is denied violently to others. The cry of (re)nationalizers, "Go back where you came from," reveals how much the nation retains its aura of necessity amid the loss of its early promise of universalizability. The very indefiniteness of "where you came from" signals that while there is no room here there is probably none there either.

3. The image of the nation and the idea of democracy are bound together in an uncertain relation of interdependence and strife. The assumption built into various conceptions of democracy inspired by Rousseau, Kant, Tocqueville, and Mill is that a democracy must be a nation *if* it is to be. But, on the other hand, numerous devotees of democracy valiantly point out how this or that attempt to build or restore a nation imposes exclusions and violences incompatible with minimal values of democratic dignity and participation. The imperative image of the nation sustains democratic hopes, but it also pushes democratic diversity and rights toward restrictions and exclusions that jeopardize the democratic project.

4. The contemporary magnification of obstructions to the nation does not dampen popular pressures to (re)nationalize. On the contrary, as the rocky trail to the nation encounters multiple forces that impede its achievement, drives to renationalization often become more intense and ruthless. Globalization, for instance, does not mean the end of the nation as an aspiration. Rather, it foments drives by constituencies injured by global market pressures to reinstate the image of the nation to compensate for those losses. The problem is that these compensations typically involve blaming vulnerable constituencies outside the imagined parameters of nationhood for the loss of jobs and so on, when these very effects are generated by global capital forces that must be met by state, regional, and global counterorganizations of labor, consumer groups, environmental organizations, and the like. The demand to renationalize intensifies as the possibility for its achievement weakens.

Secularism and the Nation

If the image of the nation is impossible to actualize, if attempts to do so foster otherwise unnecessary exclusions and violences, to what degree, then, is it possible to denationalize the democratic state? I want to explore this question without appealing to a deep, comprehensive explanation of why the nation retains so much power over the modern imagination. The idea is to remain content with a thin account, one that points toward modes of intervention that pluralize the state without itself purporting to provide a more sufficient account of why the nation persists as an ideal. A deep, comprehensive explanation might combine generalities about political organization in the late-modern time (including factors I have alluded to, such as the division of the world into states, the aspiration for self-rule within each state, the insecurities fostered by globalization in a world of states, and the acceleration of tempo) with some fundamental condition of humankind that propels the quest for a fundamental law or unity of being. The potential value of such an account is that it might explain why the modern image of the nation is so persistent and so difficult to dislodge. Its most salient risk is that it explains the phenomenon on the basis of factors assumed to be so deep that the *quest* for nationhood would now appear *immovable* even in its falsity. The nation would now acquire the stature of a necessary fiction, and attempts to rework the national imaginary would be resisted on the grounds that the attempt to do so would unleash virulent drives to reinstate the law of the master somewhere else. Deep, comprehensive explanations risk congealing experimental intervention in precisely those domains where historical experiments of thought and action are most needed. In this domain, I prefer the practice of Michel Foucault and Gilles Deleuze to, say, that of Friedrich Hegel and Slavoj Zizek. They offer explanations, but don't try to render them complete, deep, or uncontestable. They give priority to experimental intervention over deep explanation, expressing through the superficiality of the former a certain appreciation for the elements of opacity, uncertainty, mobility, and surprise circulating through existing practices. Experimental intervention, you might say, is superficial in its explanations out of appreciation for the fugitive mobilities, contingencies, and dissonances coursing through institutions, structures, and identities, not because its proponents "forget" or "fail" to offer accounts deep enough to cover the phenomena.[23] This is one of the things Nietzsche meant, in the statement quoted in chapter 2, about how the Greeks were "superficial out of profundity." We post-Nietzscheans doubt that the protean energies flowing through the institutional organization of things are in themselves susceptible to complete, deep, categorical explanation, and we suspect that deep, profound explanations freeze historically specific factors that might otherwise be moved or nudged in productive ways. Our superficiality is, then, considered.

Let us, then, return to Mill, whose secular political philosophy some-times resonates with this call to studied superficiality. For Mill, in his domi-nant formulations, democracy requires a people as one of its prime condi-tions of possibility. And a populace requires long, slow time on the same territorial space to become a people. Unfortunate peoples who do not en-gender antagonistic elements within themselves sufficient to spark a progres-sive march through history are unlikely to attain representative government without considerable outside help. Finally, a world consisting mainly of ter-ritorial *peoples* provides the best hope for democracy anywhere. Stated in such stark terms, without qualification, the Millian vision is disturbing. Its image of the world is challenged by shifts in the pace of history, changes in the scope of population migration, and the absence of many territories that fit its descriptions and prescriptions. Under such conditions the future of secular liberalism itself depends upon reworking the problematic of the na-tion. Such a reworking will recover and intensify valuable ideas of minority, dissent, dissidence, and "sympathy" within Millian thought by pulling them out of the image of the nation in which they are encased. It will be indebted to Mill in its deviations from him. One way to start might be to disaggregate the (dominant) Millian image of the nation. There are three basic elements in Mill's version.

1. There is the element of *unity* through a significant set of identities or commonalities. *Which* list of elements is unified (say, race, religion, lan-guage, justice, memories, or constitution) varies to some degree from na-tion to nation. But some such list must be brought into correspondence for a nation to be. A *liberal* nation, then, would be one in which the national majority extends tolerance to an assortment of minorities clustered around the vital center. Such an image *is* compatible, then, with variety and diver-sity and difference. It is how diversity and difference are imagined in relation to a constitutive cultural center that is definitive. Similarly, a *progressive* na-tion is one that locates an element of dissidence at its center, allowing it to move forward toward representative government. The Millian image of the nation is thus typically arboreal in form; it takes the shape of a tree, with limbs of variety and diversity branching out from the trunk. It resists eleva-tion into a rhizomatic pluralism, in which a plurality of constituencies divided along several dimensions enter into a complex network of differences and connections informed by a general ethos unmarked by a single cultural con-stituency at the center.

2. There is the element of *identification* with the center, in which af-fection or allegiance flows from the members to the symbolization of what

they all share. A modern nation, after the pluralization of Christendom, is thus said to allow citizens to be attached to something larger than the family and more palpable than an abstract universal. This explains how a hint of the divine and the universal so readily attaches itself to the particularity of a nation. The nation, as the soul of the state, renders the state more than an instrument for private interests or an apparatus through which laws backed by coercion are concocted. The nation makes sacrifice, rights, justice, tradition, visceral identification, obligation, and representation possible in the modern world. Moreover, the soul of the nation provides a point of potential belonging and allegiance for minorities who seek to become assimilated to it.

3. There is the nation as indispensable conduit of cultural *communication*. This element is prominent in the Rousseauian image. Rousseau wants a people to share rough equality of economic circumstance so that the events of history will be experienced in similar ways by all citizens. When the troubles of some become transparent to all, no constituency is so easily tempted to deceive others or to pretend that their troubles are false. Rousseau consolidates political communication through a common center in Poland by calling for a national style of dress, religion, family authority, language, memories of victory and defeat, and foreign peoples to "despise" without hating.[24] Economic equality also plays a role for Mill in the logic of national communication, but a common language, memories, and victories and defeats play the largest role.[25]

These three threads of unity, allegiance, and communication are woven into the image of the nation, then. If one is pulled out, the other two are likely to come unstrung as well. The anxiety of nationhood, then, is the feeling that its fabric is always becoming too loose, too weak, too threadbare to carry out its central functions. The nation is *always* on the verge of loss. If you live in a time where the organization of time, space, and people splinters the lived experience of nationhood, while the nation monopolizes the political imagination of identity, allegiance, and communication, you live in a time when intransigent constituencies press each state to renationalize itself by attacking its enemies within and without held responsible for the experience of a lack where the center is supposed to be.

The contemporary secular response to the will to nationhood under adverse historical conditions of actualization is to cling to the three centered functions while thinning out the medium that promotes them. Secularists, as we saw in the first two chapters, often convert the idea of a national center into that of a public sphere. They then respond to the various moments in the politics of becoming that seek to purge the center of evils such as racism, aboriginal displacement, compulsory heterosexuality, the subordination of women, and religious conformity *by pulling more and more elements out of the center.* The center now becomes reduced to allegiance to a common constitution, or a set of generally stated rights, or the practice of justice, or an authoritative mode of public argument.

The Rawlsian and Habermasian strategies to secularize the nation do not seem entirely wrong to me, but they do encounter limits and risks that call their sufficiency into question. To cling to the old logic of the nation while shucking off much of its historical filling is to present yourself to staunch nationalists as a weak, uncertain, unreliable defender of the cultural logic you endorse. When people now experience uncertainty at the center, and when they also encounter the insufficiency of proceduralism to the democratic state, they are likely to blame the hegemony of secularism and liberalism for these failings. And some are then likely to present themselves forcefully as ethnic, religious, linguistic *embodiments* of the national tradition that has been allowed to lapse. The thinned-out center becomes an invitation to occupation by bellicose constituencies who claim to embody in themselves the national vitality in need of restoration.

The logic of secular nationality is vulnerable to attack from one side as "abstract" and "empty"; it is susceptible to criticism from another as "hypocritical." Abstract because the pale, secular image of the nation is drained of dense, palpable, living examples that give it vitality; hypocritical because it secretly draws cultural sustenance from the "private faith" of constituencies who embody the European traditions from which Christian secularism emerged. Late-modern constituencies who simultaneously embody the traditional ethnic, religious, and linguistic accoutrements of the nation and feel themselves to be dislocated by immigration and/or the global economy are now drawn into attacks against secular hypocrisy and recruited into drives to renationalize the state. Liberal secularism is placed on the defensive, partly because its very idea of a center around which everything else revolves invites other constituencies to fill that center more densely and belligerently.

Not only does the secular model of the nation place its supporters on the defensive, it may also disable creative and experimental thinking by secularists themselves about the distinctive time in which we live. For today the challenge is to explore distinctive pluralities of political identity, allegiance and communication irreducible to liberal, secular, communitarian, or chauvinistic images of the nation.

Multidimensional Pluralism

It may be timely, then, to experiment with another image of political attachment and communication within and around the state. It bears debts to the secular perspectives just reviewed without recapitulating the experience of public culture they promote. It shares Mill's sense that a dense culture is crucial to the procedural success of democratic politics without endorsing his image of the nation. It draws inspiration from the secondary strain in Mill to support a more diversified, nonnational pluralism.

This image reworks the idea of a cultural center surrounded by diverse, satellite minorities. It also honors proceduralism and the practice of justice while finding them to be insufficient to the density of public culture. Nor is public culture reduced to an abstract mode of deliberation in which people always leave (or pretend to do so) their diverse private faiths and visceral modes of judgment at home when they enter public life. Rather, the cultural center is pluralized along multiple dimensions and the procedures of governance are set in this dense plurality. Public culture inside and outside the state is now constituted by multiple minor*ities,* divided along more numerous lines of religion, linguistic habit, economic interest, irreligion, ethnicity, sensuality, gender performances, and moral sources of inspiration than Mill felt compelled to acknowledge. These constituencies share overlapping commitments to each other and to a set of procedures, but this sharing now takes the form of a general ethos negotiated between constituencies honoring a variety of moral sources. This is the overlapping consensus of John Rawls reworked. For here, partisans bring selective dimensions of their religious, ethnic, sensual, gender, and moral sensibilities into public engagements whenever the issue makes it pertinent to do so. The public ethos in which struggle, debate, and settlement are set does not have one anchor; it is refined under new spatiotemporal conditions as several constituencies come to terms more actively with historical elements of hybridity and interdependence in what they are, affirm the profoundly contestable character of those religious or moral sources that inspire them the most, and register the violent and destructive consequences in the past engendered by futile pursuit of the nation.

Cultural density now becomes rhizomatic rather than national. Its density is made up of intersecting and interdependent *minorities* of numerous types and sorts who occupy the same territorial space and who negotiate an ethos of engagement between themselves. How far can such an image be actualized? It is uncertain, since it depends so crucially on other factors, such as the strength of the economy and the character of the ethos negotiated between them. But when such a regulative ideal enters into active contestation with the national image of public life, it now becomes possible to identify numerous lines of connection, communication, and allegiance within and between minorities. The image of a tolerant or intolerant *public center* inclines toward that of complex *networks* of interdependence and intercommunication unfiltered through a definitive racial, ethnic, religious, linguistic, sensual, or transcendental center. Now the claim by any cultural constituency to *occupy* the lack at the center of the putative nation will be met by suspicion from numerous sources. Perhaps that constituency seeks to transcendentalize its own habits and conventions to ward off the anxiety cultural pluralism engenders in it. When no single constituency is given the right to occupy the definitive center, each becomes more free to explore multiplicities already circulating through it and each becomes obliged to try to convince others to listen to it without already receiving acknowledgment as the embodiment of cultural normality against which the others are to be measured.

In such a regulative ideal, already competing to some degree with the image of the nation in several countries, it is false to say that no one now has anything to go on or that the possibility of collective action in concert through the state has been lost. Rather, several constituencies have a lot to go on in pursuing lines of affinity, communication, and negotiation with numerous others; several overlap in ways too various to be summarized in advance by an overarching image of the nation or reference to a few simple "interests." When contending claims to occupy the authoritative cultural center are called into question, a cultural network of multiple lines of allegiance and communication already in place becomes more visible. Several constituencies now find themselves well placed to probe and develop connections they have with numerous others. Mill's idea of "sympathies" is highly relevant here, but it is now released from the image of the nation in which it was trapped.

Even if such a multifarious state were democratic, there could be no ironclad guarantee that things would not break down into violent discord. But once the logic of the nation has become pluralized along several dimensions, the most dangerous source of violent fragmentation has been attenuated. For when the pressure to fill the vacuum at the center of the nation is relieved, it becomes more difficult for any constituency to claim that its own way of being embodies the lost, necessary essence of the nation. A virulent source of cultural war, cultural gridlock, and tyranny created by contending claims to occupy the authoritative center has therefore been surmounted. Many will now know from experience that it is not necessary to democratic life itself that one authoritative constituency occupy the cultural center; many who are sympathetic to one degree or another with one claimant or other to that authoritative role will find themselves better able to resist the premise upon which its claim to cultural sanctification is based.

As critical work upon the image of the nation registers previously obscure lines of connection, it enlivens the possibility of further elaboration of the network. The political culture emerging is reducible neither to a republican model of the nation nor to a procedural model of the state. Rather, it draws selective elements from both while reworking each. It is invested with presumptive respect for electoral procedures, the rule of law, and the practice of rights while it remains open to the probability that the existing practice of rights, justice, and legitimacy will later appear to have foreclosed ways of being that need to be honored. Critical responsiveness is a cardinal virtue of multidimensional pluralism.

But isn't this just too good to be true? Doesn't an unnational, democratic state require much more? Might not the debate over which procedures are essential become too divisive, encouraging some constituencies to try to override them? Aren't class and racialized inequalities, for instance, currently too intense in many places to render such a rhizomatic image credible? Yes, yes, yes. But by giving preliminary voice to a positive counterimage, it becomes possible to explore its limits and needs for augmentation without falling right back into the lack of the nation. For such objections to multidimensional pluralism reinvoke the idea of the nation when it is the drive to nationhood that has helped to protect the inequalities of class and race.

Consider the question of possibility. It once seemed impossible to most intellectuals in the West, for instance, to be moral without anchoring morality in common commitment to a single God. Once this apparent imperative was challenged through lived experience with a variety of monotheists, atheists, agnostics, and secularists, it became possible for some (it is still uncertain how many) to admire a larger variety of sources of moral inspiration and responsibility. In the case before us, the long-term aspiration is to come to terms with limits and debts of a rhizomatic state without reinstating the image of the nation.[26]

A democratic state animated by multiple lines of intercommunication and allegiance needs rights, electoral politics, and diverse memories to sustain itself.[27] But these elements are now no longer described aptly through the secular metaphoric of a thin center. Rather, the supporting culture is dense without being as highly centered as chauvinistic nationalists demand. A *pluralized network* is now supported by a modus vivendi between multiple constituencies in which most give up the claim to *embody* in themselves the living essence of the nation. "Our" memories become more pluralized in type and number when we experience "us" to be pluralized along several dimensions. In the United States, for instance, the memory of Martin Luther King awakens the idealism of Christian religion in some, the struggle against the legacy of slavery in others, the role of the FBI in neutralizing putative enemies of the nation in others, the importance of social movements in reconfiguring the existing shape of diversity in others, the forgotten plight of the white underclass in others, the dangers of political activism in others, and several of these in some constituencies. *The key is to break the link between the importance of memories as crucial reference points in cultural communication and the existence of an unmarked constituency endowed with final authority to represent them.* Once this dangerous link is broken, exactly which memories are critical and which things in each memory are timely become objects of political engagement as much as points of departure for it. Now sharing is filtered through a pluralized complex and situated within a general ethos drawn from multiple sources. Sharing is not thinned out; it is thickened and pluralized through the networks of intercommunication in which it is set.

A democratic state now becomes a state with multiple, overlapping lines of identity, allegiance, and communication. Participants in these lines of communication practice forbearance in political initiative and cultivate an ethos of engagement that is generous in its presumptions about others. And the members of a state have multiple loyalties, including those to constituencies and issues that transcend the boundaries of the state itself.[28] The democratic adventure now becomes enlivened while the character of its risks shift. The old risks were, first, that "we" (for advocates of the nation typically imagine *themselves* to occupy its center, just as believers in a universal God do) might not be able to get "them" to do or be what we say, and, second, that contending claimants to the center will tear each other apart in cultural or civil war. The new risk is that a culture of multidimensional diversity will not be able to organize complex political assemblages to maintain its own general conditions of existence. Both the arboreal image of the democratic nation and the network image of the democratic state encounter risks, then. My wager is this: significant shifts in the late-modern experience of time, space, and identity mean that the former risks are now more severe than the latter.

To sustain a network image of politics situated in an ethos of engagement is to affirm the importance of democratic participation through intrastate social movements, majority state assemblages, and cross-national, nonstatist movements. It is also to foster an ethos of *engagement* between multiple constituencies on the same territory honoring different moral sources.[29] Here several constituencies concede that while each may project universality into the moral source that inspires it, none is in a position to consolidate that faith with a definitive argument. Now the classical competition between moralities honoring different sources becomes attenuated. And new possibilities open up for an ethos of diversity forged out of restrained competition and selective collaboration. To the extent a pluralized we participates in a general ethos inspired by several moral sources, democratic politics comes to terms ethically with the new world. Contemporary shifts in tempo, population migration, economic globalization, and ethical engagement, then, provide some degree of support to one another in setting preliminary conditions of possibility for this modus vivendi.

Now, of course, were such a pluralized ethos to become dominant, it *could* be said to occupy the old center. And it *would* produce a set of limits and exclusions. Hence the predictable charge: "You presuppose, Connolly, what you protest against," etc., etc., etc. The point is not to deny this formal(istic) rejoinder. It is, rather, to explore how the distinctive ethos fostered by a *pluralized* we differs in its density and shape from more singular perspectives—to see how it speaks to new conditions of existence unlikely to disappear and enables more constituencies to interact with dignity on the same territory than otherwise possible. The crucial thing is not, as reductionists would insist, that both images set limits. It is that under contemporary conditions of political being, the limits set by rhizomatic pluralism speak more profoundly to the political need for peaceful coexistence within a dense cultural life than do the models of the regular individual, proceduralism, and the nation.

Such changes in the grain and fiber of politics are no less imaginable today than the modus vivendi of secular liberalism was in several Christian nations a few centuries ago. That earlier modus vivendi even provides an inspiration of sorts. Its terms were only vaguely imagined prior to its consolidation; and for a time it curtailed destructive civil wars while opening up cultural space to *improvise* a public ethos between a variety of sects within Christianity. We need new improvisations today, those that rework rather than eliminate secular, liberal practices of majority rule, minorities, progress, dissent, rights, sympathy, tolerance, and creative dissidence. The shape of such a complex can be glimpsed only in uncertain images and hypothetical outlines. A measure of luck would be needed first to secure such a modus vivendi and then to refine it by ethicizing it. The desired effect might emerge, for instance, out of a conjunction among the moral exhaustion of some nationalizing constituencies, the sense of shame of others, and the positive mobilization of yet others who have seen through the pretexts of nationhood. To encourage that possibility, the historic imagination of secularism and liberalism must be refashioned.

4

Freelancing the Nation

If you are a politician, journalist, or academic over fifty in contemporary America, there is a definite expectation that you confess before discussing drugs and drug policy. This demand reflects the sense that we know where the drug problem in America started, what dangers drugs pose, how to respond to those dangers, and who ought to preside over the responses. More pointedly, it conveys the judgment that the generation of Americans now called upon to wage war on drugs is the same one that initiated a decade of drug fantasies in the mid-1960s. Those over fifty are guilty. Confession might cleanse our souls, clear our minds, even give us a chance to become born again. It would signify our obedience to the very culture of America jeopardized by the drug culture. It would return a measure of moral authority to us by displaying our *obedience* to the culture that makes morality possible. And that would be its point.

Perhaps you once found cocaine to be an aphrodisiac. Or that LSD discloses profound truths otherwise unavailable to rationalists and technocrats. Or that marijuana enhances your sensitivity, enabling you to experiment with new thoughts and ways of life in a corrupt culture.

The typical confessional goes like this: "I was a liberal secularist (New Leftist, recreational drug user, countercultural radical) in the sixties. But now..." Here is my version: I am an amateur when it comes to drugs. I smoked and inhaled a little pot in the good old days. I sometimes take aspirin for pain relief. I drink white wine, whenever the social occasion allows it. I still love the runner's high. And I claim to have risen to "the zone" in basketball a few times, though most of my former playing partners doubt it. I have yet to become addicted to the drugs I understand to be most dangerous, such as cocaine, religious fervor, tobacco, nationalism, or heroin. Even academic drugs of choice such as alcohol, rationalism, Prozac empiricism, and deconstruction remain under pretty decent control—though some may argue with me about this. There is a danger of denial in this domain.

As one amateur sees it, there are a few modest things that might be done to reduce the self-destruction and social violence accompanying the most addictive drugs. First, since poverty, homelessness, and powerful street drugs are often found in the same neighborhoods, we might conclude that the last of these often involves protective responses to material deprivation, demoralization, and hopelessness. So intensive federal, state, and local action to provide jobs, housing, education, and safety to the poorest communities is the most crucial thing.

Second, several now illegal drugs might be decriminalized and either sold by the state or sold privately and taxed. Drug policy in the Netherlands might provide a model to emulate and adapt to the American setting. State proceeds from legalized drugs would go entirely to drug information, prevention, and treatment programs. That would reduce the tendency of the state to become dependent on this source of revenue. Every attempt would be made to gear the sites and levels of expenditures for prevention and treatment to the level of drug income received from specific communities. Advertisement and places of use for these drugs would be restricted about as much as they now are for tobacco. Indeed, I would increase the regulation of tobacco advertisement currently aimed at children and teenagers. One side effect of decriminalization would be to reduce pressures toward corruption within local police departments, for no illegal drug trade (or prostitution or gambling) flourishes anywhere unless a section of the police are involved. And police corruption is one of the great dangers facing a democratic culture.

Third, drugs that are the most highly addictive, mind destroying, and contributive to violence would become illegal. But I am not sure which these are. Suppose we treat alcohol as a benchmark. If it remains legal—and my wine habit makes me hope it does—then other drugs with similar pleasures and dangers attached to them will be legal too. Both legal and illegal drugs would be accompanied by educational programs about addictive risks attached to them, with attempts to acknowledge any element of uncertainty that attaches to these judgments as well. Once the stark line of differentiation between legal and illegal drugs/medications is breached, a series of questions will now be more susceptible to thoughtful exploration. Is Prozac always preferable to cannibus as a treatment for depression? How does the latter compare to now legal medications with respect to reducing pain and nausea in cancer patients? Does nicotine have positive medical uses above and beyond the effects smoking it has on pleasure and health?

Should users of drugs (to be) deemed illegal receive criminal penalties? I don't think so. Perhaps we/they should be fined. And voluntary treatment programs should be expanded. Should there be drug testing in workplaces? Again, I don't think so. Every attempt should be made to reduce state and corporate practices of surveillance in this domain, for they constitute serious threats to the ethos of a democratic society. But *performance* tests in high-risk jobs do seem reasonable.

That's about as far as my amateurish thinking has proceeded to date. There are notable dangers in my approach. If the last two parts were adopted while the first part was ignored, the whole thing would surely fail. The approach would suffer the fate that has already befallen much of the welfare state: conservatives would charge that it had failed after a real try, conveniently forgetting that its essential connection to jobs and good education had never been enacted. Moreover, treatment programs and performance tests could become corrupted or misused. There is also a risk that the state could become dependent on the funding provided by drug revenues, even though the proposal tries to guard against that effect. Finally, judgments about which drugs are the most dangerous can easily be influenced by political considerations about which drugs are most widely used in what communities. Certainly that is the case today. Each of these issues needs extensive debate; no response is free of risk.

But by far the most devastating objection to such a proposal is that it is culturally unrealistic and politically utopian in the current context of American politics. The proposal, in short, is the abstract scheme of an amoral academic, one out of touch with the standards of individual responsibility, religious belief, criminal punishment, national identity, and antistate sentiment of the political culture in which it is set.

But such a punitive context is more intense in the United States than in most other countries. For example, in Australia in 1997 the government proposed an experiment to provide heroin at below street price to those who wanted to reduce gradually the dosage upon which they had become dependent. The experiment, later dropped, carried dangers as well as possibilities; but the pertinent point is that public discussion of its pros and cons was situated in a context quite different from that found in the United States. An editorial in the *Canberra Times* conveys some of the difference. It is headlined "Sanity at Last on Drug Trial":

> Heroin is a nasty, addictive drug..., but there has been so much propaganda about heroin that a large majority of the population greatly over-estimate its effect on the human body. [Nonetheless]...a large number of people...are beginning to realize that the effect of heroin prohibition on the body politic is far more pernicious than its effect on the human body of those unfortunate to be addicted....
>
> With prohibition and penalties in place, providers of the drug have to take higher risks or have to pay other people more to take those risks for them. It means the price of the drug on the street goes up.... A significant proportion of users (by no means all) become addicted and willing to pay a very high price for their drug....Invariably they spend their own assets with destructive effects on family and friends.... Prohibition over the years has created large numbers of small-time dealers who actively try to get others hooked. The higher the penalties, the greater the risk, the higher the price, and the greater profits for big dealers....There is enough money to bribe police and even judicial officers to protect the big and medium dealers.[1]

The gap between the formulations made in this editorial without creating a huge uproar of protest and the narrow range of permissible statements available to an American newspaper is revealing. How did the constriction occur? What are its political effects?

Drug/Culture Wars

Bill Bennett knows people like me. He may even be obsessed with us. At least he talks about us a lot. We are of the same generation. He and we have spent large parts of our adult lives in the university. Most of us, like him, drink spirits freely. And each of us, as a type, is energized, even intoxicated on occasion, by the appearance of the other type. The only thing is that Bennett is far more effective at identifying, marking, and demonizing my type than my type has been at replying to him. We don't seem to understand how he feeds off us, how he uses us to engender, enlarge, and energize the "cultural war" he wages. Maybe we can learn a thing or two from this former philosophy teacher, secretary of education, drug czar, Republican publicist, and contemporary intellectual of the American nation.

In *The De-Valuing of America: The Fight for Our Culture and Our Children,* Bennett defines the American condition as one of war between traditional working, religious, responsible Americans and a variety of elites in the media, the academy, and a few churches who have corrupted the culture:

> The battle for culture refers to the struggle over the principles, sentiments, ideas, and political attitudes that define the permissible and impermissible, the acceptable and the unacceptable, the preferred and the disdained, in speech, expression, attitude, conduct, and politics. This

battle is about music, art, poetry, literature, television programming, and movies; the modes of expression and conversation, official and unofficial, that express who and what we are, what we believe, and how we act.[2]

An "open declaration of war over the culture"[3] is necessary because over the past few decades "significant portions of American society have been culturally deconstructed" by liberal and radical elites, imposing "particularly devastating effects" on "our schools, colleges and universities, mainline churches, the legal profession, the Congress and others." Liberal artists, intellectuals, and journalists are indispensable foils in the war Bennett directs. Most things he opposes, for instance, are first put into the mouths of liberal intellectuals and then brought back to "the American people" as alien, amoral, abstract goods. Academic and media intellectuals inhabit a "preconceived reality," "walled off" from traditional values and realities. Bennett recognizes "typical academic myopia" because he participated in it before he was born again. "The old saw that a neoconservative is a liberal who has been mugged by reality applies to me." And "though I never used drugs, I had spent almost all of 1965 through 1975 on or around a college campus."[4]

Bennett forges two links between the academic and the drug user. First, the university of the late 1960s was the *place* where "America lost its moral bearings regarding drugs."[5] You might note that other candidates for this honor — such as the end of Prohibition, or the difficulty of getting through the day in desperate life situations, or the organization of commercial advertisement around consumption pleasures — are ignored or downplayed. They are too closely bound up with that side of the culture Bennett is out to defend. Second, the loss of character and demoralization associated with drug use in the inner city and elite art communities today corresponds to the "radical nihilism" and "cultural Deconstruction" that governs universities.

Once those two links are forged, Bennett can render suspect everything the academic says about drugs *because* of the suspicious source from which it emanates. He accents the difference between him and us by saying that academics interpret the world through abstract theories, while his postacademic conservatism emerges from "what I have seen with my own eyes, traveling up and down and back and forth across America and visiting hundreds of cities and schools over nine years."[6] Once the liberal media and academic elites have been rendered alien, those same elites can be deployed to devalue the ideas of anyone anywhere who sees things differently than Bennett does with his own two eyes. Even if they are on the front lines in that war. Listen to Bennett's denigration of cops who dissent from his war on drugs:

> During the tour of downtown [Detroit], one of the police officers accompanying me asked, "Why should a kid earn four bucks an hour at McDonald's when he can make two or three hundred dollars a night working drugs?"
>
> "For a lot of reasons," I said on that first tour, as I was to say a hundred times after. The police officer had picked up this line of reasoning from the media.[7]

Again:

> I expected that some of our biggest allies in our law-enforcement efforts would be the police and national leaders in law enforcement. And most street-level police and many police chiefs did support our strategy from the very beginning. But . . . increasingly I found that talking to some chiefs was like talking to some of the school superintendents I had encountered while Secretary of Education. . . . They spoke of deep social problems, alienation, and illiteracy. They sounded as they wished to sound, like contemporary social scientists. . . . They, too, had become theoreticians of society's woes.[8]

Media and academic elites provide the filter through which miscellaneous misfits formally within the constituency Bennett courts are marked and screened out. They now become defectors to the enemy in a culture at war. To erase the negative marks scrawled upon them, they must repudiate the preconceived, abstract, amoral worldview of journalists and social scientists. A confession would help.

So media and academic elites are crucial pawns in the cultural war Bennett wages. Bennett's political strategy is to draw members of the white working and middle classes, street cops, suburban dwellers, veterans, the military, sport heroes and team owners, conservative politicians, conservative religious believers, and working black urban dwellers plagued by street drugs and violence into a bellicose cultural coalition, a coalition mobilized and animated through hostilities to university intellectuals, liberal journalists and politicians, moderate school administrators, poor black residents of the inner city, illicit drug users, drug dealers, welfare recipients, philosophical police chiefs, and convicted felons. Each constituency on the latter list is marked by its rhetorical association with the others on that list; the most negatively marked constituencies on the list (e.g., prisoners and drug dealers) place stains of suspicion upon everything said and done by others associated with them. The lines of demarcation are clean: the "American people" value America; the amoral elements devalue it. Artistic, media, and academic elites of a liberal or secular cast provide the cultural insignia enabling anyone to judge who belongs where.

That is why Bennett himself must be so selective (so abstract) in his invocations of moral principle, the will of God, clean decisions, individual responsibility, and the American people. His principled invocations must support the lines of cultural division he contrives. Take alcohol. It is dissociated from other drugs—it is, in fact, not called a *drug*—so that the war against the paradigmatic drug populace does not become extended to constituencies at the epicenter of the cultural coalition Bennett constructs.

> One of the clear lessons of Prohibition is that when we had laws against alcohol, there *was* less consumption of alcohol, less alcohol-related disease, fewer drunken brawls, and a lot less public drunkenness. . . .
>
> I am not suggesting that we go back to Prohibition. Alcohol has a long, complicated history in this country, and unlike drugs, the American people accept alcohol. They have no interest in going back to Prohibition. But at least advocates of legalization should admit that legalized alcohol, which is responsible for some 100,000 deaths a year, is hardly a model for drug policy. . . . The question is, should we accept both legalized alcohol *and* legalized drugs? The answer is no.[9]

Some slick moves here. Alcohol is bracketed from "drugs," even though the former is implicated in issues of addiction, violence, and loss of self-reliance offered as paradigmatic reasons for a veritable war on drugs. Why? Well, this legal (un)drug is popular with working white males and unmarked minorities, while illegal drugs are associated with cultural elites, heterodox sexualities, and black ghetto dwellers. The moral/legal demarcation between drugs and alcohol enables the "American people" to be identified as that moral majority that would keep alcohol legal while using ghetto police sweeps, harsh prison sentences, new prison construction, and military interventions abroad to wage war on drugs and the target populations identified with them. It allows athletes to speak against drug use while posing in advertisements for alcohol. Assorted minorities who initially fit into neither formation—those who, say, would decriminalize drug penalties, or curtail commercial advertisement of alcohol, or build housing, public transportation, and public incentives to create jobs in the inner cities—are ushered out of the "American people" and into the disparate populace it targets for action. In Bennett's world no attention can be given to the case for treating alcohol, marijuana, and tobacco in the same way, perhaps legalizing all three, regulating their commercial advertisement, and using taxes from the sale of each for programs of drug education and voluntary treatment. These potential connections must be broken to maintain the master line of cultural division between valuers and devaluers, legitimate actors and illegitimate objects of action. Alcohol and crack are distinguished first and foremost by the battle lines governing the cultural war. So are tobacco and marijuana.

Bennett is a two-star general in this culture war. What distinguishes him from the other officers is his role as chief of war games. He tests possible tactics of engagement before they are adopted or rejected by those in charge of the war. Thus the most revealing moments in *The De-Valuing of America* occur when Bennett brags about "freelancing" in public. Bennett reviews an interview he participated in while still secretary of education and before the "war on drugs" had become refined. He first reiterated his usual litany of "heightened inspections of international cargo . . . , more prisons, higher fines, and, for parolees, longer probationary periods and regular drug tests."[10] Then Bennett, without prior authorization, called upon the American military to eradicate drugs in Latin American countries. "It is to be hoped we can do this in collaboration with foreign governments," he said, "but if need be we must consider doing this by ourselves. And we should consider broader use of military force against both the production and shipment of drugs." Here is Bennett on his own pronouncement:

> As I sometimes did, I was free-lancing. I hadn't received White House clearance for my remarks, and I heard through back channels that my remarks caused heartburn among some members of the Domestic Policy Council, and especially at the Pentagon. But I was not troubled. . . .
>
> This episode revealed a tactic I frequently used. I believed in what I said. But I would also try to throw out an idea with the intent of sparking a debate, to get the national conversation going in a new direction. . . . Sometimes this approach worked. This time it did.[11]

In what terms did it work? Well, reading between the lines, polls showed that the constituencies Reagan, Meese, and Bennett sought to mobilize were aroused by this approach. The introduction of the military into the equation allowed the drug war to take on real meaning. Equally pertinent, the proposal flushed out liberal journalists who had reservations about this conflation between the drug war and military intervention in other countries. The political effect was to place potent, masculine symbols of strength, will, and national power on one side of the culture war and traditional feminine signs of weakness, ineptness, and lack of will on the other. Bennett knows how to work on the visceral register. He simultaneously identifies the lack at the center of the nation, identifies the enemies who stop it from being filled, and disarms secularists who cannot offer an alternative to the image of the nation. His freelancing binds the war against vulnerable minorities at home to that against rebellious populations abroad by drawing the American military into both sides of the equation. It would fight abroad to stop the import of drugs into the ghettos at home. Reagan loved the political effect of this intervention, but took no direct action. George Bush, after winning the presidency and selecting Bennett to be drug czar, eventually enacted it.

On another occasion, during an interview with Larry King, Bill Bennett endorsed the sentiments of a caller who demanded that drug dealers be beheaded:

> I could see King's eyes light up. He asked for a clarification. "Behead?"
> "Yeah. Morally I don't have any problem with it," I said.
> "You would behead..." King began again.
> "Somebody selling drugs to a kid?" I said. "Morally I don't have any problem with that at all. I mean, ask most Americans if they saw somebody out on the streets selling drugs to their kid what they would feel morally justified in doing—tear them from limb to limb. . . .
> "What we need to do is find some constitutional and legally permissible way to do what this caller suggests, not literally to behead, but to make the punishment fit the crime. . . ." During the program I strongly rejected the calls for drug legalization and endorsed capital punishment for major drug sellers.[12]

Bill Bennett freelances again. The same dynamic is set in motion. Liberals are stunned and outraged. Public opinion—among the troops who count in the cultural war—is pulled toward Bennett and his moral toughness. Morality itself becomes bonded to Bennett's brand of vindictiveness. Soon, other conservatives join in. A new line is drawn in the mud. And every leader is now marked by where they stand on the death penalty for drug dealers.

The Reagan/Bennett/Gingrich political formula is first to block or cut "welfare state" approaches to the drug issue, then to blame liberals for laxity and moral weakness in this domain, next to use this failure as a pretext for further dismantling the welfare state, then to call for violent state policies as the only alternative to public inaction, and finally to brand those who protest the unconstitutionality, cruelty, or immorality of these proposals as paradigmatic agents of inaction and moral uncertainty.[13] The favorite targets of choice for Bennett are inner-city blacks and white intellectuals; but the former constituency does not need to be named explicitly because the cultural coding of terms like *drug dealers* and *drug war* is already available to the cultural troops. And secular intellectuals? We keep naming ourselves through our reactions to Bennett's freelancing.

Because the objective is to mobilize an angry cultural coalition out of a diverse, opaque section of the populace, Bennett operates as a war games simulator, experimenting loudly and brashly with words to see what it takes to shape and hold the appropriate friend/enemy constellation. You can be confident, for instance, that Bennett uses a different vocabulary when it comes to the question of what punishment Edward Meese deserves for breaking laws he was sworn to uphold. Nor is this moralist of the nation likely to demand a thorough investigation of charges that the CIA ignored or condoned drug trafficking by allies in the civil war in Nicaragua during the 1980s.

Prosecuting the War

The Bennett war on drugs is not very effectively addressed, then, if it is treated simply as a series of attempts to solve the problem of drug use. If that were the issue, it would suffice to show how expensive, ineffective, and intrusive the war has been. But if the real objective is elsewhere, failure on the policy front might even contribute for a time to success of the political agenda. If the objective is to identify an available population of urban drug users, drug dealers, media representatives, and liberal academics as targets of cultural war, then Bennett's tactics have succeeded. Bennett's direction of the drug war, thereby, resembles the relation of the maker of a blockbuster film to the audience mobilized by it more than that of a policy maker to a discrete problem. Take, for example, the killer shark in Spielberg's *Jaws*:

> A direct search for the shark's ideological meaning evokes nothing but misguided questions: does it symbolize the threat of the Third World to America epitomized by the archetypal small town? is it the symbol of the exploitative nature of capitalism itself (Fidel Castro's interpretation)? does it stand for the untamed nature which threatens to disrupt the routine of our daily lives? In order to avoid this lure, we have to shift perspective radically: the daily life of the common man is dominated by an inconsistent multitude of fears (he can become the victim of big business manipulations; Third World immigrants seem to intrude into his small orderly universe; unruly nature can destroy his home; etc.), and the accomplishment of *Jaws* consists in an act of purely formal conversion which provides a common "container" for all these free-floating, inconsistent fears by way of anchoring them, "reifying" them, in the figure of the shark.[14]

The war on drugs, in turn, concentrates and defines a series of vague, shifting resentments and anxieties in everyday life. What are they? They might involve, for some, the fear of black violence in the city. Or the loss of good working-class jobs, readily projected onto women and minorities who are said to have taken them. Or the shifting ethnic and linguistic composition of the country. Or the internationalization of corporations that disempowers American workers from acting upon the corporations that employ them. Or the reduced capacity of the state to control its fate in a globalized economy. Or the unsettling diversification of religious and irreligious creeds. Or the sense that the moral authority previously exercised by your constituency is now challenged on several fronts. Or the visible porosity of territorial boundaries. Or the sense that taxes are high while their positive effect on the quality of life is minimal. Or the vague sense that the tempo of cultural change is whirling out of control. Often, several of these combine together. Which anxieties and impulses to revenge are most salient for whom shifts and moves in unexpected ways; which symbo-operational programs are most pertinent changes with the cultural variations in the experience of threat and danger. Freelancing is necessary.

Bennett knows who his key constituencies are. He knows which agents of responsibility to avoid and which to target. But beyond those two boundary-setting conditions he must experiment to locate the most productive fears, mark the most vulnerable enemies, recruit the most available constituencies, identify the most potent tactics of mobilization and isolation.

What remains constant in the cultural war is the symbol of the nation, an abstract entity Bennett sees with his own two eyes. This abstraction speaks to the common sense of the core constituencies he courts. That is, it binds intense feelings of uncertainty, anxiety, and resentment to the memory of a nation lost. When liberals and deconstructionists misread the spirituality through which the Bennett partisans are mobilized, their protests are likely to invigorate it. If and to the extent they themselves implicitly participate in this spirituality, their calls for restraint and caution in its pursuit fuel charges of moral weakness and uncertainty against them. It may be important, therefore, to take the measure of this spirituality. Let us call it, provisionally, the common sense of a nation of regular individuals. Whenever Bennett invokes "the American people," "our culture," "our children," "the Judaeo-Christian tradition," "family values," "real people," and "common sense," he summons a spiritual image of the nation in which each regular individual is a microcosm of the nation. The nation is a macrocosm of the regular individual; the regular individual is a microcosm of the nation. The church, the nuclear family, the elementary school, the media, and the university are the institutions called upon to maintain each primal unit as a reflection of the other. If and when the nation begins to fall apart, some of these institutions are held responsible.

The endlessly reiterated phrase "the American people" captures this combination precisely: it speaks at once to a general yearning for identity between individual and nation and conveys the idea that a diverse host of individuals, perhaps even a majority, fall outside this essential unity. It sustains the image of an ethnic, religious, linguistic center under grave duress; it thereby marks as immoral, weak, or unrealistic pursuit of a pluralistic culture with multiple lines of connection among diverse constituencies honoring divergent sources of morality.

What drug users, drug dealers, inner-city residents, non-European immigrants, state bureaucrats, homosexuals, liberal church leaders, secularists, atheists, liberal arts academics, and liberal journalists share is that each constituency contains a large number of people who deviate in various ways *as individuals* from the spirituality of a nation of regular individuals. For while it may feel strange to some to be placed with these others on the same line of associations, what all participants share is the fact of deviation from the national norm of the regular individual. As a crucial corollary, any individual initially marked by one or more of these ascriptive liabilities can become a full-fledged member simply by asserting aggressively the conventional code of the nation: individual responsibility for your own fate, unfettered faith in the capitalist market, belief in a moral god, the readiness to obey those who embody the spirit of the nation, commitment to the opportunity society, opposition to the welfare state, support for family values, identification with the military as ultimate guarantor of the nation, commitment to normal sexuality, and the collection of all these dispositions under the general heading of common sense. Hence the honored individuality of Clarence Thomas, Robert Bork, George Will, Jeane Kirkpatrick, William Bennett, Midge Decter, Lynn Cheney, and Rush Limbaugh, participants in institutions otherwise taken to be part of the problem. The strategy is to be generically skeptical toward the state, fervently committed to the authority of a nation of regular individuals, and selectively disposed to state action when it patronizes the nation by waging cultural war on those who deviate from the code of regular individualism.

Most fundamentally, since the *empirical average* in America today splits and diversifies in response to a series of endemic pressures such as changing patterns of immigration, the acceleration of speed in cultural communications, the globalization of capitalist economic relations, and the effects of these forces in magnifying the experience of contingency in the racial, sexual, religious, and ethnic identities that inhabit us, the spirituality of a nation of regular individuals is maintained by political invocations of a putative past when this unity was present; by the repetitive exhibition of contemporary policies, ethical codes, and styles of living that deviate from the spiritual norm; and by the threat that the culture will die a horrible death unless it reinstates this fictive past. But there never has been a time when the nation was intact, and today the invocation of a nation of regular individuals eventually catalogs a majority of the populace into diverse deviants in need of correction. The drive to realize this ideal of the nation entails extensive programs of social engineering and punishment doomed to fail in producing their putative end. But, again, the failure of this cultural war to eliminate drugs or reinstate the nation is very compatible with the success of these campaigns in disabling the state from acting to support the economic and cultural conditions of multidimensional pluralism.

The common sense of "the American people," then, is held together by the political designation and cultural segregation of constituencies that negate it; the promise of return to a nation lost is kept alive by militant campaigns against those groups and dispositions said to be responsible for the loss. Some potential targets are politically unavailable, however, given the projected dissonance between the spirit of the nation and the clumsiness of the state. Agents of capital must not become central targets, for instance, even though they are probably more involved than any other constituency in those forces of change that scramble the common sense of the American nation. Capitalists remain a protected species because general faith in the market as the primordial mechanism of automatic regulation and individual freedom is the key that enables the *nation* to be turned against the social activism of the *state*. The agents susceptible to being held responsible, then, for the loss of the nation are liberals, secularists, drug users, state bureaucrats, drug dealers, deconstructionists, the irreligious, the media, and universities. The implication of drug dealers and the media in capital markets has to be laundered some to isolate them in the appropriate way.

If you resist the ugly drive to renationalization, it is important not to misidentify the adversary. When secularists, liberals, or deconstructionists, for instance, accuse those who purport to embody the spirit of the American nation of racism, they set themselves up for ferocious refutation. For the bellicose nationalist is not a racist, *if* by racism you mean (as the nationalist does) the view that some "races" are congenitally inferior to others. That definition does not fit, because individuals and families from any racial or ethnic group are deemed capable of assimilation to the American nation, if they work hard enough and assert the right identifications actively enough. The accusation of racism against renationalizers, then, opens the door to counteraccusations against the critics themselves. They reveal a typical academic incapacity to discriminate between the simple sin of racism and the virtue of nationalism. To make the charge of racism is to show that you simply don't get the simple idea of the nation. What *is* the relation between race and the spirit of national individualism, then? You are on more solid ground if you say that the impossible goal of assimilating everyone to the nation of regular individuals through private effort and formal opportunity produces negative race effects in contemporary America.

Similar traps are waiting in other domains, such as welfare policy and the public expression of religious faith. For example, "the American people" do not support one faith within Christianity, nor does this authoritative abstraction decertify separation of church and state as that principle has been interpreted within the Tocquevillian/American tradition. Rather, it sets faith in a less sectarian, monotheistic, moral God as *the* consummate sign of moral virtue and defining condition of legitimate participation in the politics of the nation. Do you pray? A yes or no answer will suffice. In this way the atheist, the agnostic, the secularist, the unitarian, the deconstructionist, and a few others are rendered morally suspect, without committing the American People to public enforcement of a particular version of Christianity or Judaism.

The war on drugs organized around military intervention, long prison terms, capital punishment, morality as crusade, and intellectuals as morally bankrupt provided an effective configuration of national symbols, antistatism, and punitive state action in support of the nation for a while. This potent signifier mobilizes floating anger and anxiety among white working- and middle-class males; identifies selective constituencies marked by urban location, race, and class for punitive action; relieves pressure on the state to support education, job training, and welfare; places a thin veil of deniability over the site and racial composition of primary targets; and opens dissenting media and academic elites to charges of moral ineptitude. The New Right's inversion of the New Left view of the drug experience contributes to the cultural potency of its war on drugs. While many on the cultural left in the sixties claimed that (some) drugs disclose deep truths hidden by the bureaucratic routines of mundane experience, the nationalist commanders of the drug war insist that these same drugs pull people away from verities of the nation that would otherwise shine through the experience of every regular individual. The deepest political connection between users of street drugs and academic secularists and deconstructionists, then, is that both types are too drugged to perceive or accept the unity of the nation. Forrest Gump is the counterexample here: his uncomplicated character opens him to the simple virtue of obedience to the nation, and his example implicitly recalls a (fictive) time when the issues of morality and politics were uncomplicated.

The war on drugs has played a critical role in the campaign to renationalize America. But freelancers such as Bennett have probably begun to sense that it is losing its cultural potency. Too many police chiefs may defect. Or the continuation of drug use may belie the effectiveness of the war. Or the very familiarity of this evil may fail to mobilize the appropriate cultural energies. Or exciting new signifiers of negations of the nation may displace it: prayer in the schools to resecure the religiosity of the nation, or the deportation of illegal aliens to restore the ethnic composition of the nation, or the definition of gay marriage as a generic threat to family values, or the call to reculturate the universities through state action to protect our children may well push the drug war into a modest, background position.

Freelancing, then, remains critical to signification of the nation. For powerful institutional forces—many fervently endorsed by the nationalizers themselves—operate to denationalize the contemporary democratic state. Even as the organizing symbols of negation shift, the primary targets of identification and the strategies of demonization pursued will remain fairly stable. The abstract spirit of the individualistic nation provides the vacant center around which cultural war is organized against liberals and deconstructionists.

Freelancing Pluralism

How can liberals, secularists, journalists, media critics, and deconstructionists respond over the long term to these strategies? The first temptation may be to lapse into silence, since so many avenues are full of traps. But a salient response may be to rework the roles of social scientist, political theorist, reporter, editorialist, philosopher, and policy analyst that many now accept. Neither deconstruction as the decoding of codes of violence within practices of rationality nor journalism as detached reporting of the events of the day to a secular public is sufficient to the times. Each of these role definitions has been neutralized, negated, or both by the internal difficulties besetting them and the cultural politics of the day. The need, first, is to cultivate ourselves as critical intellectuals who learn a trick or two from the political style of Bill Bennett. We seek to expose the impossible dream energizing Bennett's cultural war while also becoming more closely attuned to troubles, anxieties, and hopes that grip people in a variety of contexts. We experiment with themes that might tap into those concerns while moving people in more noble and generous directions. We become, thereby, freelancers of a different sort than Bennett, exposing the experiments of those who seek to divide the culture against itself, and articulating as best we can the assumptions, risks, and stakes governing our own cultural experiments.

As we proceed, it may be imperative to identify just how our adversaries seek to define us and what turns for others on the war games they play. Is it timely to participate actively in talk shows, then? To put ourselves on the line more often, without taking refuge behind the faded veneers of expertise, neutrality, or the sufficiency of critique? The initial objectives are to set up barriers against the political uses to which liberal and deconstructionist academics are put. For while we may see each other as adversaries along some dimensions, there is something to be learned from Bennett's systematic insistence on lumping secular liberals and deconstructionists together. We seek to learn from a variety of constituencies what troubles them even as we show more of them how the circumstances of their lives deteriorate as they buy into the cultural war fomented by Bennett and his buddies.

Many of us may conclude that it is timely to reconfigure the common sense of the nation of regular individuals. For Bennett is both right and wrong. He is right that a series of divisive cultural wars is inevitable as long as the sense of a nation lost remains common. He is wrong in his promise that a sustained cultural war could issue in attainment of this vision of the nation. For the very conditions that create nostalgia for a nineteenth-century image of the nation ensure that it can function today only as a clarion of cultural war, not as a positive achievement of democracy. It can mobilize anti-statism; it might even foster a punitive, corrupt police state. But it cannot nourish a positive state capable of acting in support of the institutional, ethical, and spiritual conditions of a pluralistic democracy. As long as this spirituality prevails, nationalists will enlist the state to promote the nation by attacking itself.

A central task of critical intellectuals today is to show how the assimilation of numerous constituencies to pursuit of a nation of regular individuals multiplies the internal and external enemies to be defeated while perpetuating many of the troubles that incite the drive. It might be timely to start by demonstrating how selective these appeals are. The obligation to national allegiance and sacrifice is simultaneously lifted from finance and industrial capital and applied all the more fervently to workers, parents, teachers, journalists, and consumers. Capital can invest anywhere; consumers should buy American. Corporations must expand internationally; workers must organize to keep foreign workers and products out. Consultants can advise any owner anywhere about anything; teachers and journalists must preach national virtues. Products and advertising are to be subjected to minimal regulation; media programming must embody the virtues of the nation. This asymmetry between the rights of capital and the obligations of other institutions must become a critical theme among those who seek to expose the illusions, injuries, and injustices accompanying the drive to renationalization.

Such critical forays are important, but they are insufficient unless joined to the demonstration of how a democratic culture flourishes best when it transcends the common sense of a nation lost. Today it is timely to place an alternative spirituality into active competition with this two-track model of renationalizing workers and disnationalizing capital. To turn back the charge that we are either amoral (liberal idealists of the neutral state) or agents of cultural fragmentation (deconstructionists and postmodernists), it is necessary to show how the effective performance of a pluralist, democratic state requires overturning the massive schemes of social engineering upon which renationalization is based, and how democratic action in concert through the state is a product of creative coalitions coming together from diverse places.

Again, as long as the nation is thought to be a necessary condition of public morality and democracy, demonstrations of its absence are likely to spur intensive constituency drives to occupy the vacant center of the nation. So critical forays against the idea of a nation must be matched by contributions to an alternative spirituality: to the ideal of a dense, multidimensional pluralism in which numerous constituencies differing along dimensions of ethnicity, gender, sexuality, religion, and metaphysical faith negotiate an ethos of engagement between them inspired in part by the general sense that no single constituency can hope to *embody* in its own being a center too diffuse and multifarious to be so represented.

As I said at the outset, I am an amateur in this territory. I feel the need to shed some of the innocence with which critical journalists and academics enter into political struggle with bellicose saviors of the nation. And to challenge the reductions, simplifications, and selective mobilizations of resentment through which self-proclaimed partisans of the nation appropriate the most potent symbols of morality, faith, virtue, and belonging. Multidimensional pluralism has the best chance to flourish when the constituencies constituting it overcome nostalgia for the innocence of a nation lost.

5

The Will, Capital Punishment, and Cultural War

A Brief History of Forgetfulness

The will, we are often told, forms a hinge of Western civilization because it is crucial to our practices of freedom, responsibility, and punishment. The will is one of those categories that has traveled the bumpy road into secularism from its inception in the sacred discourses of Judaism and Christianity. The priority of the will today points to metaphysical continuity between the old regime of Christendom and the secular modus vivendi fashioned out of that regime. Of course there are minority reports in and around these two traditions that seek to rework the will for ethical reasons. Epicurus, Lucretius, Spinoza, Nietzsche, Kafka, and Freud, for instance, all tell stories that challenge and modify the majority report.

Today murder is often said to deserve capital punishment because it is a *willful* act; and even many who oppose capital punishment are hesitant to do so by reconsidering the stability or priority of the will. But the hinge upon which these judgments of freedom, responsibility, and punishment turn has always been creaky. It may be that the case for capital punishment rests upon cultural *forgetfulness* of instability in the very idea of the will. Let us, then, examine forgetfulness in this domain, condensing long stretches of time into brief summaries so that the instability persistently stalking Western conceptions of the will stand out vividly.

1. "Father, forgive them, for they know not what they do" (Luke 23:34). It is uncertain, according to the scholars, whether Jesus said this on the cross or it was attributed to him later. Part of the case for the latter judgment is that the statement asserts a difference between Son and Father that Jesus

did not express so intensely elsewhere. Either way, the sentence prefigures an interminable struggle within Christianity. The father, on this reading, is a demanding figure with a soft spot in his heart, while the son is a gentle soul whose forgiveness expresses appreciation of the uncertainty and ambiguity in which violence is set. The son's sentiment, however, is not entirely independent of the father's passion: forgiveness becomes appropriate only after an injustice has been recognized. The language of will, in relation to responsibility, desert, and punishment, is not highly developed in the Gospels. The killers of Jesus, for instance, are deemed by the one who uttered that sentence to act as much out of ignorance as out of willfulness. For several centuries, before the will became crafted into a more powerful instrument of punishment, most Christians seem to have opposed the death penalty. The exemplary sacrifice of Jesus on the cross spoke against such a spirit of revenge.

2. "Why should it be? Mind commands body, and it obeys forthwith. Mind gives orders to itself, and it is resisted.... Mind commands mind to will..., but it does not do so. Whence comes this monstrous state? Why should it be?"[1] Augustinian (and Pauline) Christianity places the will front and center, setting the stage to translate the message of Jesus into a more punitive Christianity. Augustine deploys the will, first, to open conceptual space between his omnipotent, benevolent, creationist God and responsibility for evil in the world; second, to deepen human responsibility for vice on earth (virtue, in his thinking, is due to the grace of God and not to the will of the do-gooder); and third, to connect the image of humanity to the God who willed the world into being. The *divided will* appears in the world only after Adam, who was initially endowed with a pure, undivided will, disobeyed a divine command willfully. Henceforth, the "monstrous state" of human willfulness, whereby "mind gives orders to itself, and it is resisted" by itself. Volatility in the will is part of the punishment visited upon humanity for the first, free and original sin. Division, thereafter, is both constitutive of the Augustinian will and extremely problematic to it. For how can you be responsible for evil acts that flow from a will that is deeply divided against itself after the fall? Augustinian grace relocates the sense of injustice haunting the will, but it does not dissolve it.

The theme of division, needed by Augustinianism to protect divinity from responsibility for evil in the world, also threatens to throw the will back into the arms of those devils and heretics, the Manichaeans. The latter treat this division as a manifestation of the cosmic contest between the forces of good and evil. They deny the omnipotence of God to make sense of evil in the world. Augustine seeks to retain the theme of division while doing whatever is necessary to ward off the loss of divine omnipotence that threatens to accompany it. He responds punitively to the danger that his own acknowledgment of division in the will could be taken as a sign of a cosmic struggle between a limited God of benevolence and a God of evil:

> Let them perish from before your face, O God, even as vain talkers and seducers of men's minds perish who detect in the act of deliberation two wills at work, and then assert that in us there are two natures or two minds, one good, the other evil. They themselves are truly evil, when they think such evil things.... Thus they are made into a deeper darkness, for in horrid pride they have turned back further from you, from you who are "the true light which enlightens every man that comes into this world."[2]

"Let them perish before your face." The Augustinian will is grounded in equal parts on its role in protecting an omnipotent God from evil, its role in judgments of individual responsibility, *and* its role in the bullying of opponents (such as Manichaeans and pagans) who point to alternative ways of interpreting the experience of division. Might it have been possible for Augustine to appreciate the indispensability of the will to his faith and then to soften its punitive character by emphasizing the uncertainty of his own interpretation? Perhaps. But Augustine refuses such a combination. He emphasizes the mysterious character of the will while asserting its primacy with fervor. He eventually lands on a mix of ecclesiastical discipline and divine grace to civilize a will that is otherwise unruly. The severity of the divine punishments he imagines — including the threat of a "second" death for those who willfully rebel against faith in his God — reveals how precarious and bellicose the idea of free will is in Augustinian Christianity.

3. In Augustinian Christianity disciplinary practices and the exercise of the will are combined. The confession instantiates this combination. By the time of the Enlightenment — to abbreviate radically — disciplinary practices and the exercise of the will become separated more acutely, partly because of mysteries clinging to the idea of the will. Beccaria, for example, first elevates the will above human knowledge of it and then becomes an advocate of disciplinary punishment for crime. Since God is the only one qualified to read the tangled text of the will, the intentions and motives of offenders are to be judged by him alone:

> If he has established eternal punishments for anyone who disobeys His omnipotence, what insect will dare to supplement divine justice? What insect will wish to avenge the Being who is sufficient unto Himself..., Who alone among all beings acts without being acted upon? The one Who cannot receive impressions of pleasure and pain from objects...?

> The seriousness of sin depends upon the unfathomable malice of the human heart, and finite beings cannot know this without revelation. How, then, can a standard for punishing crimes be drawn from this?[3]

Is Beccaria an early secularist in the domain of punishment and the will? Beccaria converts punishment grounded in desert into corporeal disciplines designed to subdue perpetrators and to deter others from copying them. Capital punishment now becomes dispensable. It does not deter those who kill out of rage or those who do so out of revenge. And it hardens the hearts of offenders already deeply disaffected from society by demonstrating to them how profoundly the law is founded on a "war" of the well connected against the deeply aggrieved. Besides, for Beccaria, the attempt by humans to punish crime in proportion to the degree of evil in the will is futile. By placing the Christian will on ice, he explores one route open to secularism: to separate punishment from just desert. But his perspective becomes a minority report within a secularism that seeks to preserve the relation between punishment and desert. Beccaria is not, however, a gentle soul in the mold of Jesus. He apportions the harshness of the punishment to the extent to which the crime offends the social order.

> The most powerful restraint against crime is not the terrible but fleeting spectacle of a villain's death, but the faint and prolonged example of a man, who deprived of his liberty, has become a beast of burden, repaying the society he has offended with his labors. Each of us reflects, "I myself shall be reduced to such a condition of prolonged wretchedness if I commit similar misdeeds." This thought is effective because it occurs quite frequently, and it is more powerful than the idea of death, which men always see in the hazy distance.[4]

Beccaria's focus upon the effects of repetitive discipline on the mind takes him to the edge of concluding that the will itself is not a master faculty, grounded in the supersensible realm, but a complex corporeal/cultural formation that bears the imprint of the particular cultural experiences from which it is crafted. His disciplinary conception of society points toward such an insight, while the confidence with which he apportions penalties to crimes in the interests of deterrence and reform verges on the fantastic. In general, retributionists who place a timeless will at the center of freedom, responsibility, and punishment are inclined to assert overweaning confidence in their ability to ascertain the right proportion between offense and penalty; and those who elevate social causality above attributions of willful responsibility often express a corresponding confidence in the ability to devise disciplinary systems geared to the degree of protection, deterrence, and reform desired. Each party joins confidence in the precision of its own perspective to a dismissal of the other's ability to establish the proportionality it seeks. Each, thereby, is insightful about the other and blind about itself.

4. The will and capital punishment soon combine in a new way in that side of the Enlightenment which seeks to rework Christianity in order to save it in the Newtonian age. Kant, who paves the way for future efforts to retain the will in both theological and secular discourses, insists that the will is central to freedom, morality, and responsibility. Its very primacy expresses the priority of the supersensible over the sensible in human life. What is the "root" of the will?

> [It] cannot be less than something that elevates man above himself as a part of the world of sense, something which connects him with an order of things which only the understanding can think and which has under it the entire world of sense. . . . For it is then not to be wondered at that man, as belonging to two worlds, must regard his own being in relation to his second and higher vocation with reverence, and the laws of this vocation with the deepest respect.[5]

To make this conception credible, Kant must resolve the antinomy between Newtonian causation and free will. And, as we shall see in chapter 7, he must also address a deep "propensity" to evil *within* the will as he conceives it. He eventually concludes, with Augustine, that often enough the willful agent cannot pull itself out of evil by its own exertions alone. But, in the face of these difficulties, he still insists upon a retributive model of punishment. He does so even in those difficult cases where children appear to be so depraved by adverse life experiences that they are widely held "to be born villains and incapable of any improvement of character."[6] For Kant knows that any compromise in his doctrine of freedom and responsibility would eventually jeopardize the two-world metaphysic housing his conception of the will.

So Kant ignores these background uncertainties in his own conception when he engages the issue of capital punishment. A crime *deserves* punishment because one who commits it acts against the moral law every ordinary individual is able to recognize and obey; capital punishment for murder flows from the imperative to make the level of punishment proportionate to the will's contradiction of its own essence.

> Accordingly, whatever undeserved evil you inflict upon another within the people, that you inflict upon yourself. If you insult him, you insult yourself; if you steal from him, you steal from yourself; if you strike him, you strike yourself; if you kill him, you kill yourself. . . . If . . . he has committed murder he must *die*. Here there is no substitute that will satisfy justice. There is no *similarity* between life, however wretched it

may be, and death, hence no likeness between the crime and the retribution unless death is judicially carried out upon the wrongdoer, although it must still be freed from any mistreatment that could make the humanity in the person suffering it into something abominable.[7]

A Triumph of the Will in the domain of death. Retribution becomes a moral obligation. Note how gentle and painless the image of capital punishment has become by comparison to the judgment of Beccaria. The offender is to be killed by the state because he brings death upon himself by his murderous act; but this dead man with a beating heart must be treated decently right up to the point of gentle termination because he remains a *person,* a rational agent of free will situated between two worlds. Punishment now becomes purged of the drive to spectacular revenge the sovereign power had only recently invested in it. Bells chime and trumpets sound. Freedom, desert, and punishment are fused through the medium of the will.

But wait a minute. How do those inhabited by this pure will so often develop a "propensity" to will evil maxims they are unable to overcome by themselves? How could "radical evil" (consenting to sensual desires that go against the moral law) be such a *regular* effect of action emanating from "the will"? Could the eruption of violence sometimes be an effect *within the organization of the will itself* of childhood terrors and abuses undergone while the will was being formed and shaped? Kant almost concedes such a possibility, but he recovers in time to reconcentrate all responsibility within the will. For to accept that dangerous thesis *might be to admit worldly, sensuous elements into the very structure of the will.* It would jeopardize the priority of the supersensible realm Kant has worked so hard to save after the advent of Newtonianism. And yet—for Kant himself the source of the will's own tendency to perversity eventually becomes a profound and unanswerable question. He cannot explain with confidence "within the limits of reason alone" how it occurs, even though his inability to do so threatens to recoil back upon the integrity of the will.

Does Kant rescue purity of the will by sacrificing those whose brutal life experiences might otherwise be interpreted to expose instability and cruelty in that conception? He does, at least, insist that the presumption of "free causality" requires the assumption that even the most "depraved" children commit evil deeds as a "consequence of freely assumed evil."[8] The Kantian will, as we shall see more closely in chapter 7, encounters the same paradoxes that introduced perplexity into the Augustinian conception. But Augustine, recall, refused to sanction capital punishment. How do you retain confidence in the morality of retribution, just measure, and capital punishment after these difficulties have been admitted? Kant does not return to this issue. But, to put the point as bluntly as Kant presents the imperative to capital punishment, once you encounter these complexities in the Kantian will, you are pressed either to *forget* them to vindicate capital punishment or to replace a *Kantian* justification of it with another.

5. Neither free will nor scientific determinism, according to Nietzsche, can stabilize itself in the domain of human action, crime, and punishment. Nature does not correspond perfectly, even in appearance, to Newtonian causality. And the assumption of free will consists of an uncertain projection into the soul often infused with an underground drive to vengeance. Each of the preceding perspectives is now challenged.

> Our usual imprecise mode of observation takes a group of phenomena as one and calls it a fact: between this fact and another fact it imagines in addition an empty space, it *isolates* every fact. In reality, however, all our doing and knowing is not a succession of facts and empty spaces but a continuous flux. Now, belief in freedom of the will is incompatible precisely with the idea of a continuous, homogeneous, undivided, indivisible flowing: it presupposes that *every individual act is isolate and divisible*. . . . Through words and concepts we are still continually misled into imagining things being simpler than they are, separate from one another, indivisible, each existing in and for itself. A philosophical mythology lies concealed in *language* which breaks out again every moment, however careful one may be otherwise. Belief in freedom of the will—that is to say in *identical* facts and in *isolated* facts—has in language its constant evangelist and advocate.[9]

Kant and Beccaria are unconscious evangelists of language, the first on behalf of purity of will and the second on behalf of the transparency of causal relations. The rest of us, including Nietzsche, are evangelists of language as well, though we do possess the capacity to tame those evangelical tendencies. Forgive us, for we know not what we do in the realm of punishment.

Nietzsche has a grudging respect for Jesus, who, he thinks, died on the cross too early to develop the deepest implications of his own thinking. Nietzsche himself struggles to find ways to loosen the hold of the two dominant models of punishment. Such is the ethical task of the immoralist. He eventually *recovers* an alternative conception of the will. But this will is implicated in the messiness of corporeality and culture rather than elevated above them. The Nietzschean will becomes a complex cultural/corporeal formation; the elements from which it is formed turn out to be too disparate, variable, and finely grained to be captured entirely either by the crude categories of Newtonian explanation or the discrete idea of a free will. Responsibility now becomes a social practice that is both indispensable and inherently problematic. An element of tragedy attaches to it. To extrapolate beyond Nietzsche, you might say that punishment against crimes already committed may be needed to protect the community, to deter others, and even sometimes to restore to society those who have committed crimes against it. But since the tangled question of desert is fraught with uncertainty, and since judgments about the will of oneself and others are haunted by undecidability, the territory of criminal responsibility is now recognized to be one in which a subterranean injustice seeps into the practice of justice. Here Nietzsche merges with some currents within Christianity, though the parties draw from different sources in reaching a similar position. For a culture generally participates in engendering the violences it opposes. Surely, these considerations militate against capital punishment. Nor can justice and punishment confidently be left to a god, in Nietzsche's view. For it is his subtraction of a god from the self and the world that encourages him to engage the labyrinth of the will and the cruelties attached to the morality of retribution. Our hallowed conceptions of agency, explanation, and punishment are human, all too human. So says Nietzsche—while acknowledging the contestability of the assumptions through which *this* judgment is formed.

If you suspect a visceral drive to revenge infiltrates into the very conceptions of will, freedom, responsibility, and punishment that define this culture, you may be in a better position to fish more of that revenge out when called upon to judge in concrete cases. Generosity and forgiveness now become invested with new energy. To overcome resentment against the absence of fit between the clarity justice seeks and the opacity of the cases actually before us is to fold *generosity* into assessments of the responsibility of others, *hesitation* into cultural explanations of violent conduct, and *forbearance* into the practice of punishment. As I read Nietzsche in writings subsequent to *Human All Too Human,* the practice of judgment cannot be eliminated. But it might be rendered less all too human by those who experimentally apply Beccarian-like tactics *to themselves* to subdue the ressentiment that so readily enters into sacred and secular conceptions of will, freedom, explanation, and punishment. I draw from Nietzsche and Jesus the idea that responsibility is an indispensable and problematic social practice. An ethos in which generosity and forgiveness play a significant role involves work on multiple layers of the self and the culture to diminish cultural resentment and to engage more positively the instability of our fundamental categories of freedom and responsibility. Such an ethos, as we shall see in chapter 6, requires relational arts of the self and micropolitics to sustain itself.

Capital Punishment and Forgetting

With the advent of *Dead Man Walking,* first a book and then a 1996 film by the same title, capital punishment returns as an intense topic of cultural debate.[10] The recent upsurge of state executions excites horror in some, a sense of vindication in others, a strange recollection of uncertainty in many, and a differential mix of these feelings in most. But, for the most part, the labyrinthine history of the will, responsibility, and punishment we have reviewed is squeezed out of the discussion. Most parties treat these to be the pillars of "our Judeo-Christian tradition" rather than paradigmatic sites of uncertainty and instability within it.

Dead Man Walking offers a cultural barometer of sorts in this domain. Do "we" have the right to kill those who murder? The book brings out superbly the awful suffering on death row, and it effectively dramatizes several considerations against state execution. Thus (a) this ultimate act of finality might (and often does) condemn innocent people to death, and the mistake cannot be taken back if new evidence of innocence is found; (b) we never know for certain whether even a hardened criminal might reform in the future; (c) if murder is wrong, so is killing by the state, which sends a message of revenge to hardened criminals and hardens the hearts of citizens; (d) many condemned killers have life histories filled with abuse, violence, deprivation, and neglect, and these circumstances cry out against the death penalty; (e) relatives of the deceased, who (often) press for execution to gain relief from the loss they have suffered, seldom actually experience that much relief after the execution. During a time when the feelings of the aggrieved play such a prominent role in the sentencing of murderers, this last experience is particularly pertinent.

Consider Vernon Harvey, who could not wait for his daughter's ruthless murderer to "fry." He is talking to Prejean, the "sob sister" who opposes capital punishment and has nonetheless become a confidante of sorts a few years after the execution of "Willie":

> "Know what they should've done with Willie?" he says. "They should've strapped him in that chair, counted to ten, then at the count of nine taken him out of the chair and let him sit in his cell for a day or two and then strapped him in the chair again. It was too easy for him. He went too quick."

He says he's been thinking of a much more effective way.... "What we do is fry the bastards on prime-time TV, that's what we oughta do. Show them dying in the electric chair, say, at eight at night, and see if that doesn't give second thoughts to anybody thinking of murder.... We oughta do to them exactly what they did to their victim. Willie should've been stabbed seventeen times, that's what we oughta do to them."[11]

Harvey's rage has not diminished; "this chapter" has not been "closed" by Willie's execution as he had anticipated. So he fumbles for an act of revenge proportionate to the pain he suffers. And the language of "oughta" suggests that he seeks to enclose these feelings in a moral perspective. His rage and his morality become mixed together, understandably so.

Prejean summarizes her conversation with Harvey on another occasion while he is convalescing in a hospital: "He just can't get over Faith's death, he says. It happened six years ago but for him it's like yesterday, and I realize that now, with Robert Willie dead, he doesn't have an object for his rage. He's been deprived of that, too."[12] Harvey is not unique. The promise of relief through revenge often exceeds the experience of it after the unrepeatable deed has been done. If only murderers could be executed several times, or, lacking that, if the single act of execution were rendered more slow, agonizing, and public. Would crucifixion work? What about burning in oil? In the current political context the public demand to vindicate grieving family members through punishment combines with the unstated impossibility of satisfying that desire fully to place opponents of the death penalty in a position of permanent defensiveness. The very act of opposition seems to reveal that we do not care much about mothers, children, lovers, and spouses devastated by the murder of their loved ones.

Prejean poses these issues effectively, then. But a couple of counterdispositions also slip quietly into the book and the film. First, the basic categories through which we judge murderers and assess penalties are themselves treated as untouchable. The harsh childhood of a killer, for instance, is taken to "mitigate" the crime or to provide "extenuating" circumstances; these experiences are not treated as violences that enter into the very crystallization of the perpetrator's will. Such a reflection would throw our most cherished concepts of crime and punishment into uncertainty. It would insinuate culture, with its global divisions along the lines of class, race, and gender and its more finely grained and specific effects on the life of each particular individual, into the very practices of action, judgment, and punishment. Many supporters of the death penalty would rather sacrifice the lives of killers than sacrifice the purity of the concepts through which they are judged and sentenced. And even opponents hesitate to subject the categories to critical review.

Second, as the film reveals, the suspense intensifies pressure upon the condemned man, his loved ones and supporters, the family of the victim, and engaged spectators as the execution clock ticks away and pleas for reversal or delay are rejected. At the end, when the penalty is executed, a certain relief or release accompanies its finality, even among many who resist the death penalty. A decision has been executed, as well as a human. A guttural element of authority attaches itself to the act through its very irreversibility. The uncertainty surrounding the right of the state to kill a killer — an uncertainty circulating within many of us as well as between us — becomes muted. We can now turn to other things. At least those not intimately involved in that particular case can. And the suffering of those most closely connected to the executed man? Or those who have just witnessed the execution of one who killed someone they love? These both recede from the public eye. Two elements deposited in the authoritative background of capital punishment — cultural forgetting of the instability haunting categories of punishment and the strange sense of release attending the finality of execution — work upon one another, each adding a note of silence to the other.

Forgetfulness with respect to the unstable history of the will is lodged in the tangled relations among social science, court decisions, journalistic reporting, electoral campaigns, jury selection, and jury deliberations. These practices form a set of intertexts. Consider the domain of social science. In *Crime and Human Nature: The Definitive Study of the Causes of Crime,* James Q. Wilson and Richard J. Herrnstein work hard to align the dominant cultural mood with respect to punishment to the model of explanation they accept as social scientists.[13] To accomplish this feat the social *explanation* of crime in the interests of deterrence and prevention must be rendered compatible with *retribution* in punishment. To accomplish this effect, they adopt a compatibilist account of social causation and will formation.

> Scientific explanations of criminal behavior do, in fact, undermine a view of criminal responsibility based on freedom of action. And . . . this book has taken pains to show that much, if not all, criminal behavior can be traced to antecedent conditions. Yet we view legal punishment as essential, a virtual corollary of the theory of criminal behavior upon which the book is built. . . . An act deserves punishment, according to the principle of equity, if it was committed without certain explicit *excusing conditions*. . . . For the purposes of the law behavior is considered "free" if not subject to those excusing conditions. One such condition is insanity, but there are others, such as duress, provocation,

> entrapment, mistake and accident.... By proving that excusing condi-
> tions are absent and then punishing, the criminal justice system sharply
> outlines for its citizens the choice between crime and non crime.... To
> the extent such excusing conditions can be demonstrated, punishment
> should be mitigated or totally suspended.[14]

That's it! The definitive 639-page study on crime and punishment con-
denses the most momentous and perplexing issue into one fuzzy paragraph.
Though people's lives hang in the balance, no uncertainty is allowed to
find explicit expression. These experts on punishment press Beccaria and
Kant together while forgetting the troubles that haunt each theory on its own
terms. Deterrence and retribution are both deemed legitimate because, some-
how, the people demand the compatibility of will and social causation.
How is this sleight of hand accomplished? In a society riven by class and
race divisions, "the will" is first moved from a position above culture to a
place within it (the site of "free" acts). But then deadly dispositions within
culture that deviate from an accepted standard of normal conduct are judged
to be deserving of retribution by quietly treating them *as if* they were the
product of the free will of the agent prior to acculturation. That relieves the
culture of apparent implication in the wills it helps to organize and the acts
it punishes. The authors can count on most readers sliding over this shift
because they never truly endorsed the relocation of the will inside culture
in the first place. The authors are the ones pressed to do that, in the interests of fostering a science of criminality.

But what has retribution now become? If the difference between "will"
and "excuse" has now become the difference between motives "society"
places beyond appeal and those "it" allows to excuse, ameliorate, or attenuate responsibility, retribution now slides from an act of equitable compen-
sation tied to an unstable doctrine of the will to an act of revenge tied to
the level of outrage felt by normal people. Can Wilson and Herrnstein, for
instance, reiterate Kant's claim that the killer has willed his own execution
by murdering another? They cannot. They can only draw implicit sustenance
from a broader cultural belief in a model of retribution their own theory calls
into question. They get away with this ruse to the extent that the earlier
model of the will and retribution was itself fueled by a drive to revenge. A
compatibilist doctrine of will and causality now becomes translated into
compatibility between the level of punitive action and the vengeful mood
of dominant constituencies. Execution no longer punishes murderers according to a standard they themselves are reputed to have willed (the Kantian
ideal of retribution); it enacts the desire for revenge that, understandably
enough, follows acts of murder. The pretense to give a definitive *account*

of the compatibility between deterrence and retribution devolves into repetition of a cultural *demand* that they be brought into correspondence. In the world of Wilson and Hernnstein no perplexity or uncertainty is allowed to surface with respect to the most fundamental issues, even though the signs of both keep seeping through their prose.

The U.S. Supreme Court joins the cultural cascade of forgetting in the way it front-loads murder cases. The most consequential way it does so, perhaps, is its determination that only those who are "death qualified" can serve as jurors in cases where the death penalty is at issue. This injunction disqualifies at least 20 percent of potential jurors from the start. It also affects the way the prosecution and the defense proceed in making their cases before a death-qualified jury, for death-qualified juries are demographically distinctive. "They are more likely to be male, to be white, to be well off financially, to be Republican, and to be Protestant or Catholic" than the general population.[15] With such a jury in place, a defense lawyer would be foolish to pose difficult questions about attributions of the will. Few jurors are apt to pick such a theme up during jury deliberation, and most will be hostile to its articulation. A prosecutor, on the other hand, is encouraged to use problematic conceptions of responsibility and the will as a whip to beat down the defense during the sentencing hearing. In such a constrained context—repeatedly set before the public as a trial by peers who embody "the conscience of the community"—cultural immunity against public excavation of self-doubts about the relations among will, action, responsibility, and retribution is assured from the start. The following interrogation by a prosecutor against a social worker who has presented mitigating considerations in a murder case is doubtless repeated in capital sentencing hearings daily:

Q: Do you believe in the Christian principle of free moral agency? Do you believe that God gave us the capacity to choose right from wrong?

A: Yes, that can happen if one has a nurturing environment that would support that capacity and allow it to be used.

Q: Do you believe that Almighty God gave us the capacity to know right from wrong?

A: Almighty God gave us the potential...

Q: How do you explain why some people who come from bad homes do well in life?

A: We all have different innate endowments and ability to tolerate frustration. One can't just look at people and know who will turn out good and who will turn out bad...

Q: Are you saying that people are not responsible for what they do?

A: What William Brooks did was the product of interaction between himself and his environment...

Q: Can someone be just plain mean?

A: No, not without reason. Children aren't born mean. Children are responsive to their environment.[16]

Austin Sarat shows how the hegemony of this legal discourse steers public attention away from structural modes of violence not readily reducible to the actions of individuals and toward violences that appear to be so reducible. Those who die through the systemic denial of effective health care are ignored to focus limited resources of public attention on those who die through individual acts of murder. I would underline another element within this politics of displacement. In such a predetermined context of legal argument, the prosecutor appears to be a clear thinker with coherent categories, while the social worker emerges as a fuzzy idealist trying to force two opposing conceptions of the world into one story line. The first agent appears to embody the clarity of "our culture," while the second struggles to twist that clarity to save the life of a defendant. But in fact *our* culture is marked by fundamental instability in its basic categories of responsibility and punishment, and it is administered by legal/political practices that translate this instability into a vengeful model of responsibility. To say some people are "just plain mean" is to infantilize the judgment of criminal cases by purging the image of the will of those mysteries and ambiguities that haunt it. Dominant practices of social science, court decision, jury selection and deliberation, prosecutorial presentation, media reporting, and citizen predisposition coalesce to organize this politics of displacement. Capital punishment sacrifices the lives of killers to reassure a culture that would otherwise be perplexed and troubled by the constitutive uncertainty haunting some of its most cherished categories of self-interpretation.

Death and the Death Penalty

Powerful cultural demands to protect categorical integrity foster political pressure for the death penalty, even when a politics of cultural forgetting is needed to satisfy those demands. That is one theme. These demands establish an authoritative set of intertexts in which legal practice, journalism, social science, and public opinion support one another. And they infiltrate into the judgment of opponents of the death penalty as well as its supporters. But how could this be? The categories, according to the story I have told, have been unstable since their inception, and yet sentiment about the death penalty changes century by century and decade by decade. It seems to me that two major shifts in contemporary life combine with a couple of more specific changes to intensify contemporary support for the death penalty. The profound shifts include the *globalization* of so many aspects of life in a world organized politically around the presumption of sovereign nation-states and the radical acceleration of *tempo* in several domains of life. The specific changes revolve around the concentration of an African American underclass in inner cities, where the most publicized acts of violence occur.

The globalization of economic life compromises the nation-state as the highest site of citizen sovereignty. According to the logic of democratic sovereignty, *I* am free when I can choose among several life options in a variety of domains; *we* are free when the state is formally accountable to us through elections and can act to protect both its standing in the world and the institutional conditions of nationhood. But the globalization of economic life disrupts the experience of a sovereign democratic state by imposing a variety of visible effects on the state that it is compelled to adjust to in one way or another. The state can most easily respond to many of these by shifting their most onerous burdens to its least powerful constituencies. The tendency to shift burdens to the most vulnerable constituencies is accentuated by the widespread tendency to blame the state for the limits it faces while celebrating the market as a potential site of freedom. That combination, in turn, further depletes the sense of efficacy attributed to the one agency whose actions are accountable in principle to citizens. It deflates again our sense of collective freedom. A compensatory expression of state efficacy and accountability is thereby needed.

Under these circumstances signs of state inadequacy in other domains become transfigured into dramatic displays of state power in the realm of criminal punishment. "We" are free because the state acts impressively in the domain of crime even as its power over the market is limited. Once the state has been constrained from two sides in its effort to address the social conditions of criminality, spectacular acts of state vengeance are wheeled in to compensate for the deficit. That is why the most fervent defenders of the death penalty are so often also defenders of absolute state sovereignty in foreign relations and the minimization of state practices of social welfare. The state becomes a theater of punitive power to retain its appearance of sovereignty and accountability under otherwise unfavorable conditions.

The capacity to execute, like the ability to wage a drug war, is a visible and awesome state power, one able to divert attention from the state's limited efficacy in other domains. The failure of capital punishment, from the vantage point of deterrence, then, is trumped by its success in symbolizing the state as a potent agent of public revenge. The perverse equation is that *we* feel freer as a public under unfavorable conditions of citizen confidence and state efficacy when the primary unit of democratic accountability displays the power to wreak revenge against those it targets as the most visible threats to personal freedom. These internal and external limits to state power then work in rough coordination with the refusal by suburban dwellers to address the conditions of life in the inner cities. The high visibility of black violence in the inner city adds another potent element to the mix, then, making capital punishment the one act that can represent the power of the state while protecting collective unwillingness to invest in extensive programs of job creation, education, and urban renewal.

These pressures combine with the accentuation of tempo in population migration, cultural communication, military mobility, tourism, and entertainment. With the acceleration of tempo in so many domains of life, more people more often encounter ideas and relationships that jostle and disturb cherished aspects of their own identities. Christians encounter diverse theistic and nontheistic faiths; established ethnic groups encounter strange new ethnicities; heterosexuals encounter gays and lesbians who have come out of the closet; males encounter feminists who call into question traits of masculinity previously marked as natural; and so on. The acceleration of tempo renders it more difficult to confirm the natural or transcendental character of what you are, and the tactical advantage such confirmation traditionally carries with it in the domain of moral judgment now becomes jeopardized. What you *are* in the domains of gender, ethnicity, religion, sensuality, and so on no longer so easily becomes translated into a set of moral commands you and everyone else are obligated to *obey*. You are placed under pressure to desanctify elements of your own subjectivity even as they help to define who you are.[17]

The unstable practice of individual responsibility becomes even more difficult to fix under these conditions, for now the persistent instabilities inside are activated by contact with alternative interpretations outside. This categorical insecurity presses a variety of constituencies to insist more fervently upon fundamentalizing traditional dictates of morality, responsibility, normality, and punishment. For how can those constituencies on the margin of economic success and educational attainment receive recognition for their insecure achievements and self-restraint unless those who break the code are held entirely responsible for their failures?[18] This may be why many in this culture who support the death penalty aggressively also insist with equal fervency upon the imperative of heterosexuality, the civilizational authority of Christianity, the irresponsibility of welfare recipients, the vacuity of liberalism, and the nihilism of deconstruction.

Under such conditions, the death penalty performs a set of intercoded functions. It first confirms through its rhetoric of retribution a conception of will and responsibility by which a variety of insecure constituencies ratify desert for the precarious social standing they have attained and the difficult self-restraint they exercise at work, in the home, and on the street. It then allows selective release from this difficult logic of self-restraint by allowing vicarious participation in the legal killing of murderers. Finally, it deflects attention from the state's failure to respond to other grievances of those same constituencies and to the larger contexts in which both their grievances and criminal violence are set. Execution becomes simultaneously a theatrical demonstration of state power (amid a general sense of state inefficacy), a violent vindication of individual responsibility (amid life in interdependent institutional complexes subjected to uncertain coordination), a momentary release from the dictates of self-restraint (in a world where its meticulous practice in other domains is demanded), and an opportunity to express strains of fascination and deniable identification with outcasts whose acts of violence might be taken to repudiate this hierarchy of power, responsibility, and restraint. The very aura of finality that accompanies state executions helps to silence questions about the categories of will and responsibility that vindicate the actions.

Capital punishment thus becomes a major front in cultural war. It mobilizes political divisions between one set of partisans who seek to return to a world in which the responsible individual, retributive punishment, the market economy, the sovereign state, and the nation are said to have coalesced and another set who seek to respond in more generous ways to new experiences of the cultural contingency of identity, the pluralization of culture, the problematic character of traditional conceptions of agency and responsibility, and the ambivalent place of the state in the new world order.

The propagators of cultural war augment the first set of dispositions by attacking carriers of the second set of questions. The politics of forgetting is crucial to their success. We have already seen how William Bennett, in *The De-Valuing of America*, links a variety of right-wing campaigns in education, media programming, and drug wars to the more general "fight for our culture and our children." Let's revisit the Larry King interview with Bennett we examined in chapter 4. There we saw how Bennett's freelancing sought to intensify and activate visceral attachments to a vindictive nation. Here we can see how Bennett also activates *support* for the state as the collective embodiment of vindictive morality. During a call from a listener supporting his drug war, Bennett is pressed to up the ante: "Why build prisons? Get tough like [Saudi] Arabia. Behead the damned drug dealers. We're just too damned soft." Bennett responds:

> "One of the things that I think is a problem is that we are not doing enough that is morally proportional to the nature of the offense. I mean, what the caller suggests is morally plausible. Legally, it's difficult."
>
> I could see King's eyes light up. He asked for a clarification. "Behead?"
>
> "Yeah. Morally, I don't have any problem with it." . . .
>
> "Somebody selling drugs to a kid?" I said. "Morally I don't have any problem with that at all. I mean, ask most Americans if they saw somebody out on the streets selling drugs to their kid what they would feel morally justified in doing—tear them limb from limb. . . .
>
> "What we need to do is find some constitutional and legally permissible way to do what this caller suggests, not literally to behead, but to make the punishment fit the crime. And the crime is horrible." During the program I strongly rejected the calls for drug legalization and endorsed capital punishment for major drug sellers.[19]

Bennett's rhetoric is potent. He unites in one act of identification the theatricality of the state power to kill, forgetfulness of instability in our culture's categories of will and punishment, and the promise to make state punishment "morally proportional" to the criminal acts it punishes. The enunciations of "morally," "morally proportional," "morally plausible," and "feel morally justified" do a lot of work. They invest outrage and vengeance in the blue-chip stock of morality, covertly emptying the latter of restraint and modesty until it becomes a container into which intense energies of revenge through state action can be poured. "Morally proportional" retains the appearance of equivalence between responsibility and punishment, but that uneasy equation now quietly becomes translated into the proportionality between the intensity of public outrage and the amount of agony to be endured by state targets of punishment. The state is now called upon to embody morality as revenge, and this equation itself functions to compensate for the reduction of state efficacy and accountability in other domains.

Bennett *converts* the liberal ripostes he calls forth into energies of cultural war against liberalism. Thus: "Many of the elites ridiculed my opinion. But it resonated with the American people because they knew what drugs were doing, and they wanted a morally proportionate response."[20] Why are these "elites" targets? Because so many hold "our Judeo-Christian tradition" in "contempt" and are "so riven with relativism that they doubt the preferability of civilization to savagery."[21] What is the "morally proportionate" response? One that meets every act of criminal violence with an overwhelming act of state violence. *That* proportionality, again, preserves the state as the consummate instrument of punitive power and obscures its contemporary ineptness as an agent of education and social welfare.

The End of Capital Punishment

While I both oppose the death penalty and admire Jack Kevorkian as a (marred) hero, I imagine that many reverse this combination. They are committed to the death penalty and oppose the right of the terminally ill to doctor-assisted suicide. Why? Perhaps fervent opposition to the right of others to die sometimes also expresses existential resentment against the obdurate fact of death, while calling upon the state to impose the "death penalty" against murderers expresses, at a visceral level, the wish to push the very thought *of the death of the innocent as far away from oneself as possible.* This combination concentrates our attention on death as penalty and pulls it away from death as event. State refusal of the right to die and its support of capital punishment may thereby combine to obscure the character of death as inevitable *event* in favor of it as *penalty.* Some elements in the Christian tradition support such a combination, though others, flowing above all from the sayings of Jesus, work strongly against it. Augustine concluded, for instance, that the first two humans deserved to die because of their sin. Could the combination of intense support for the death penalty and fervent opposition to the right to die even express in some cases covert resentment against the very idea of a Creator who would allow death in the first place? It is hard to say. At any rate, to blame God overtly for mortality is too disturbing for most. And to blame the world for it is pointless. Two of the most eligible constituencies upon whom to project existential resentment for the obdurate fact of death, then, are those who "deserve to die" and those who insist upon "the right to die."

This interpretation, along with others of its type, has no certainty attached to it. Moreover, it is not only contestable, the intensive proto-thoughts to which it points subsist on a field that may not *in principle* be subject to precise representation. The point of interpretation at this juncture, then, is ambiguous. Its abbreviations and exaggerations seek to make contact with an intensive and obscure field of visceral thoughts that have profound effects on the ethos of public life. It cannot represent that field exactly as it was prior to interpretation; it can only hope to hit close enough to spur experimental action on intercultural sensibilities in a domain that carries profound consequences for the politics of life and death.

Even under these limiting conditions the interpretation may make more contact with some dispositions in favor of the death penalty than with others. It may miss those who support capital punishment primarily out of frustration with high rates of crime. Or what about Sister Helen Prejean? She opposes the death penalty and may well oppose doctor-assisted death, too, on the grounds that only God has sufficient wisdom to govern the most fundamental issues of life and death. I am willing to wager, however, that if she resists doctor-assisted suicide, she does not insist upon a law forbidding that decision by others for themselves under protected circumstances. She evinces too much respect both for the judgments of the living with respect to themselves and the contestability of every fundamental faith, including her own, for that. Correspondingly, those of us who support the right to doctor-assisted death must work to ensure that those who resist it for themselves receive institutional protection when they are in the most vulnerable circumstances. Finally, what about the person who supports both capital punishment and the right to doctor-assisted suicide with appropriate procedural protections? It would be interesting to meet her.

Capital punishment has now become a weapon of cultural war on several levels: it coarsens broad sections of the population, preparing them to accept punitive campaigns against a variety of disturbing constituencies; it foments political divisions favorable to the right; it fosters the politics of forgetting by translating "moral proportionality" from an uncertain attempt to match penalty to crime into a politically potent equation between the level of social resentment felt by disaffected constituencies and the level of violence taken by the state against convicted murderers; it displays the state as an awesome theater of force in one domain during a time when its effective accountability is otherwise shaky; and it organizes a set of cultural anxieties about the relation of life to death.

Sister Helen Prejean and Albert Camus have faith that if only more people saw what actually happens on death row and at executions they would reconsider their abstract commitment to capital punishment. Camus dramatizes how the death penalty, often represented publicly as a brief, surgical event, actually involves a long, arduous "premeditation" and "organization," which is in itself "a source of moral sufferings more terrible than death"; how it engenders a "devastating, degrading fear that is imposed on the condemned for months or years"; how futile appeals for official reprieve create a "horror parcelled out to the man who is condemned to death." So, by the time a captive of the state has reached the time of execution, "he is no longer a man but a thing waiting to be handled by the executioners. He is kept as if he were inert matter, but still has a consciousness which is his chief enemy"; and "he travels along in the intricate machinery that determines his very gesture and eventually hands him over to those who will lay him down on the killing machine."[22] Prejean exhibits the essence of this state utopia of violence in a phrase: "I can hear the words San Quentin guards used to yell when a death-row inmate was let out of his cell: 'Dead man walking.'"[23]

In the light of evidence from Vernon Harvey and William Bennett, though, the situation may be more complex. It may well be that capital punishment   exalted in public rhetoric by some as "noble" and hidden behind closed doors in practice—both diverts the eyes of humanists from its degrading effects and incites those who feed upon the state's role in inflicting degradation upon available targets. To satisfy *this* latter demand for "proportionality" is what it takes to save "our" nation, according to some. The imagination of an absolute power delivering a defeated and silenced enemy to a vengeful public focuses upon the long-term suffering of "mad-dog" killers who await their execution. But it may also include somewhere within its compass a punitive fantasy about liberals, secularists, and deconstructionists. The immediate prey of state execution pay a heavy price for their secondary status as surrogates for a larger enemy that cannot be reached so directly. But then the stakes in the war for "our culture" are high. Liberal and deconstructive elites (these two warring factions within the democratic left are treated as allies by many on the democratic right) might play into this social logic of capital punishment when they focus merely on its cruelties.

Under these circumstances, familiar critiques of capital punishment, taken alone, are insufficient. They may even contribute something to the politics of resentment they strive to surmount. That, anyway, is the hypothesis entertained here. To the extent it is true, it remains pertinent to show the less intense devotees of capital punishment how the politics of cultural forgetting proceeds in this domain, how support for capital punishment grows out of that politics, how such a practice imposes immense degradations on its prey while they are on death row and during the moments of execution, and how it diverts the state from other projects needed to sustain the general conditions of democratic pluralism. But these engagements are insufficient and even liable to backfire unless they are linked to a broader, even more difficult agenda. To engage capital punishment at its cultural source we require interpretations that expose the deep sources of that intense social resentment in circulation today, and we need to probe more carefully the politics by which it so readily becomes shifted onto the most vulnerable constituencies. It then becomes incumbent upon us, first, to teach each other how to translate *existential* dimensions of resentment (including resentment over the fact of mortality) into the reaffirmation of life itself. And, second, to join political movements that seek to address those economic, educational, and social circumstances that encourage so many to resent their place in a democratic culture. When we engage each of these dimensions in relation to the others, we might begin to reduce the huge fund of cultural resentment invested in capital punishment.[24]

6

An Ethos of Engagement

The Limits of Individualism

Why would an omniscient, omnipotent, salvational God allow evil in the world? No one has ever answered that question without remainders, doubts, and uncertainties clinging to the answer. Even Augustine, who draws the will into philosophical discourse first and foremost to protect his God from responsibility for evil, found the labyrinth opened by this question to be too involuted for a mere human to navigate with confidence. Paul Ricoeur, a devout twentieth-century Christian, concludes that the Augustinian account of the origins and responsibility for evil must be rewritten if Christianity is to transcend the most punitive dispositions inscribed in its history.[1] Epicurus, writing before the advent of Christianity, found the demand that life continue after death to be part of the problem. Much evil in the world could be curtailed, he thought, if people would come to terms more calmly and affirmatively with the contingency of life.

> Get used to believing that death is nothing to us. For all good and evil lies in sensation and death is the end of all sensation. Therefore, a right understanding that death is nothing to us makes the mortality of life enjoyable, not by adding to it limitless duration, but by taking away the yearning for immortality.... But the wise man neither looks for the escape from life, nor for its cessation.... And just as men do not seek simply and only the largest portion of good but the pleasantest, so the wise seek to enjoy the time which is most pleasant and not merely that which is the longest.[2]

Most secularists find it unnecessary or unwise to discuss publicly the issues of mortality and its relation to evil. George Kateb, however, is both a self-described secularist and convinced that it is important to rethink the problem of evil. Kateb is closer to Epicurus, perhaps, than to Augustine. But unlike both of them, he has witnessed the great political evils of the twentieth century—the holocaust of Hitler, the exorbitant sacrifices of human life by Stalin, Mao, and Pol Pot—and he is alert to the incredible violence accompanying the American enslavement of Africans. Kateb is therefore impelled to enter the labyrinth opened up by the question of evil, particularly by evil in politics.

I find Kateb's account to be insightful, partly because of the cautious way in which the presumptions governing it are advanced. I also find it to be too unpolitical an account of political evil, unpolitical to some degree in its comprehension but even more so in its mode of response. Evil, Kateb says, is "the deliberate infliction (or sponsorship or knowing allowance) for *almost* any reason whatever, of suffering of great intensity."[3] *Political* evil is the infliction by governments or movements of intense suffering. It is most extreme when it inflicts suffering on "a large scale." Political evil is not the same as oppression or despotism, though the latter two can slide into the former. What, then, fosters political evil on a large scale?

The answer does not reside principally in the contrariness of the human will. The key sources of political evil reside cumulatively in the abstract character of political calculation and action, in the ability of leaders to distance themselves from the violences they command, in the difficulty those commanded to violence have in publicizing the concrete suffering they impose on others while carrying out orders, and in powerful tendencies among leaders and subjects to invest this or that collective identity (a nation, a state, a collective movement) with sanctity through dualistic ideologies. "Political commitments transform human beings, making them capable of acting more terribly (in methodical, detached, even self-sacrificing ways) than wickedness ever could."[4] And most political theorists "in the canon" exacerbate these tendencies: in their desire to fashion a legitimate collective identity, they invest the idea of collectivity with far too much sanctity, freedom, unity, and morality. Leaders of states and political theorists "are constantly taking *an invented group reality* for *a natural reality* and allowing it to impose itself, to dictate a logic or pattern that must complete itself."[5]

The strengths of Kateb's analysis are apparent. Group identities do tend toward closure, dogmatism, and dualism. Political action is often abstract in conception and execution. This latter tendency becomes accentuated today when the consumer/citizen/viewer of a CNN battle report targets the enemy through the eye of the sovereign, as a sleek plane on the TV screen locks an abstract target onto *its* radar screen, and as the hit is verified through a flash of light on both screens. In this scenario the commander, the pilot, the camera, the reporter, and the citizen all assume the same angle of vision: each views "the target" through the abstract eye of the sovereign on an attack mission. Generalization of this line of vision mobilizes collective celebration of abstract violence while screening out the complexities that engendered the war and the intense suffering of target "populations." The abstract character of politics and war is conducive to evil, then. But, still, the very pertinence of Kateb's account of political abstraction may point to a defect in his analysis.

In *his* passion to emphasize the artificial, inflated, ideological character of group identity, Kateb is tempted to contrast it to the ordinary, self-correcting perception of the concrete individual. Kateb sometimes writes as if individual identity is concrete and natural, while group identity is abstract and invented. You can hear this tendency in his warning against "taking an invented group reality for a natural reality," a phrase in which the natural reality is implied rather than named. Kateb knows better, but still this tendency comes into play when he is motivated to distinguish between the abstract character of the state and the concrete world of "the individual."

Unfortunately, such a contrast may contain its own tendencies to foster evil and to conceal it from those implicated in it. First, the formation and maintenance of the modern individual requires as many supporting institutional conditions as the formation of an organic collectivity; and second, the contemporary individual's participation in the world of consumption, entertainment, news, politics, and war renders much of its everyday experience as abstract as that of political leaders and "the nation." There are six degrees of separation between the individual eating a tender pork chop and the pig. There is the life of the pig in the feeding pen, the terror it faces just before execution, the act of killing, the cutting and seasoning of the meat, its preparation and cooking, and its presentation on the plate. And the individual who eats a nice red apple with no worms or marks on it is screened from perception of the pesticides that give cancer to apple pickers and pollute the environment. The invented life of the regular, everyday individual is abstract in ways that invite comparison to the world of collective unities.

Kateb resists "dualism" on the grounds that it provokes the categorical divisions between us and them through which evil occurs. But he repeatedly risks installing another fateful dualism of his own in his essay on political evil: that of a natural distinction between the concrete individual and the invented group. He comes close, he even draws upon that dualism to locate the worst evils in the abstractions of state and collective politics. But he never quite completes the maneuver. Reluctantly and against the grain of "On Political Evil," Kateb eventually acknowledges the *necessity* of group identity to life:

> I cannot imagine human life without some measure of group identity, but I also cannot imagine a comparatively decent life (at least internationally) unless group identity is mitigated considerably by the doctrine of individual human rights.[6]

I suppose something that is necessary hovers between the natural and the invented. But the very way Kateb acknowledges the necessity of group identity limits his ability to engage politics as one affirmative way to identify and resist the politics of evil. Kateb (almost) acknowledges the participation of the modern individual in abstract perception, passion, judgment, and action through its layered implications in modern institutional life. But he then slides back to a conception of the ordinary, concrete, individual when it comes to thinking about evil, the state, and politics. He appreciates the role individual rights play in resisting evil, but he evinces little appreciation of how the politics of rights can *also* be a vehicle of arbitrary violence against constituencies explicitly or implicitly located below the standard of the normal or regular individual. Thus "homosexuality"—conceived as an illness, a moral defect, or both—was defined at least until the 1970s in this culture to fall below the threshold of an individual right; the (still precarious) shift in its place on the register of justice has resulted from robust political movements to reconstitute established cultural norms of sexuality. A political movement was necessary in this case to place a new right on the register of individual rights. The evil it remedies was (and is) palpable and painful for a large number of people, but the new right itself is not simply derivable from a fixed set of principles. It is a political invention, requiring, as we shall see soon, a whole lot of micropolitical preparation. Similarly, the "right to die" was a nonstarter in this predominantly Christian culture until a social movement inspired by Jack Kevorkian and ratified by a series of juries in Michigan moved it onto the register of debate over rights. In these two cases, and in numerous others as well, what counts as falling within the province of the individual shifts through political activity. That which previously fell below the threshold of rights sometimes becomes one through the confluence of a political initiative and the cultivation of critical responsiveness to the initiative by others. These collective modes of politics both expose the dense, relational character of "the individual" and show how an established practice of individual rights can inadvertently sanctify injurious exclusions even while it protects important prerogatives.

It is not that Kateb is entirely unaware of these issues; it is more, perhaps, that he finds too many dangers attached to acknowledgment of the indispensability of politics to their definition and response. Kateb's drive to the solidity of the individual — to the one whose perception is its own, whose joys and pains are palpable, whose skin cannot be worn by another, and who ultimately cannot assign another to die for it — enables him to illuminate shadows in the politics of evil. But a dualistic drive to ground evil primarily in the abstractions of collective politics diminishes Kateb's appreciation of how the ordinary individual and the institutional practice of rights can themselves participate in it.

Perhaps it is possible to retain something from Kateb while modifying the minimalist ideal of politics and public life in which his account is set. The drive to wholeness, let us say, becomes most destructive when you both obsessively interpret the cultural identity you participate in to be the best available *copy* of a *true model* and place that model above the threshold of *legitimate interrogation in politics*. When these demands become overweaning, they foster resentment against those innumerable identities that deviate from the putative model and whose very multiplicity may suggest the absence of a final model of identity through which to measure good and bad copies. Now the quest for wholeness becomes the treatment of the identities you embody (or profess to embody) in the domains of nationhood, gender performance, sensual affiliation, religious faith, and so forth as the best copies of a final model. And a whole set of alter-identities must now be treated as bad copies to secure this privileged standing.[7] The fight against the violence of identity now involves modifying the cultural sensibility in which these experiences of identity and difference are set.

The imagination of wholeness can attach itself anywhere. In the canon of Western political theory, this imaginary is discernible in Augustine's plea for unity of the individual will (to be approximated only if and as the divided will becomes *obedient* to the will of God) and in his dim memory of a time of human wholeness before the first sin; in Rousseau's imagination of a general will that is "constant, unalterable and pure"; in Hegel's aspiration to a realized state. In contemporary life it readily becomes attached to ideals of a rational consensus, maternal versions of feminism, images of the nation, fundamentalist presentations of religion, and, as we saw in chapter 4, some models of the regular individual.

The imagination of wholeness readily attaches itself to the nation whenever the state is established as a central agency of collective action and freedom. Take, for instance, the nineteenth-century "America" Tocqueville registers. Tocqueville celebrates local democracy, an independent judiciary, separation of church and state, a modicum of individuality, and an independent press. But he also recalls longingly the (putative) unity provided by the aristocracy in Europe. And he insists that the diversity of democracy itself must be contained within a Christian "civilization" burned deeply into the religious convictions, social mores, cultural imagination, and principles of reason of the American people. In the Tocquevillian imagination the mores of a *nation* are burned into the imagination and reason of the *individual*.

> What keeps a great number of citizens under the same government is much less a reasoned desire to remain united than the instinctive and, in a sense, involuntary accord which springs from like feelings and similar opinions...; only when certain men consider a great many questions from the same point of view and have the same opinions on a great many subjects and when the same events give rise to like thoughts and impressions is there a society....Although there are many sects among the Anglo-Americans, they all look at religion from the same point of view.[8]

"Involuntary accord," "like feelings," "similar opinions," "same point of view," "like thoughts and impressions," and (elsewhere on the same page) "a single nation." While some variations across localities and individuals are possible and even admirable, each member of the nation is to be inhabited by the same general mores and to draw upon the same basic god.[9]

The higher accord upon which Tocquevillian civilization rests involves a common commitment to Christianity (as opposed to non-Christian faiths) and an agricultural way of life (as opposed to nomadic ways of being). Tocqueville concedes that the quest for the civilizational wholeness he admires necessarily engenders violence against "wandering nomads" who occupied America before Europeans arrived. For they lack the Christian faith and mastery over nature essential to a democratic civilization.

Tocqueville's appreciation of the relation between mores and the possibility of pluralism is profound. For mores, as he understood so well when thinking about diversity within the parameters of Christianity, can function not only as national unifiers but also as cultural membranes that promote attachments and forbearances across numerous lines of difference. It is when Tocqueville's imagination reaches the limits of Christianity that he loses sight of the role mores can play in promoting positive connections across multiple lines of difference. He fails to appreciate how the collective evil of the Euro-American holocaust against millions of Amerindians is partly anchored in the pursuit of a democratic nation of Christian universalism, and he thus fails to mine elements within Christianity itself that resist such a politics of territorial universalization.

Less virulent effects of this same imaginary are discernible in his orientation to women, the Irish, slaves, atheists, and wayward Frenchmen who run off to the wilderness with Indian women. Indeed, in Tocquevillian America the figure of the restless, materialistic, selfish atheist forms an internal corollary to those mobile, external nomads. The internal nomads forfeit effective eligibility for political office or leadership because of their inveterate tendencies to amorality and unreliability. For atheists forfeit contact with the essential source of morality that binds a democratic nation together. So Tocqueville's positive valorizations of locality, plurality, and a small federal government are set in a frame that engenders a whole series of injuries to constituencies and localities that exceed it. My sense is that only to the degree that a positive ethos of engagement is negotiated between constituencies of numerous types honoring diverse gods and moral sources does it become possible to redress the deepest injuries of Tocquevillian civilization. Tocqueville himself, with his grasp of the visceral register of intersubjectivity and his appreciation of plurality within Christianity, prepares us to explore such an alternative.

Relational Arts and Micropolitics

If the imagination of wholeness flows easily into a variety of containers, and if it readily spawns arbitrary violence, by what means can it be modulated and chastened? I will address this question first by locating a key source of evil in the politics of identity\difference relations themselves and then by responding in two stages to the problem so posed. The agenda is to situate ethical arts of the self and particular constituencies into a larger political culture in which an ethos of engagement is negotiated between interdependent partisans honoring a diverse set of moral sources.

Every individual simultaneously (a) crystallizes a particular (perhaps unique) combination of identities made available by the institutionally established fund of possibilities, (b) contains differences that mark it as deviating from social norms in particular ways, and (c) embodies fugitive currents of energy and possibility exceeding the cultural fund of identities and differences through which it is organized. The value of the language of identity and difference is that it already mediates among the terms of the individual, the constituency, and the state. Thus if you "are," say, Indian, female, gay, Catholic, and a citizen of the United States today, each of these collective identities participates in your constitution as an individual. Indeed, each exists at the (often) dissonant conjunction between the institutional recognition bestowed upon it and the self-identification it projects to others. Some of the identifications through which you are socially recognized will probably require political work to enable you to get on in life without intense suffering.

It may be that contingencies in the identities that constitute us are potentially more widely discernible today than heretofore because of the accentuated tempo of life and the rapid movement of populations and cultural communication across territorial borders. But this does not automatically make the task of forging a generous ethos of engagement easier. It may make it more arduous, as those who imagine the possibility of wholeness are pressed to work harder to secure that appearance. For cultivation of generosity between interdependent constituencies often involves the difficult work of desanctifying some elements in the identity of each. Identity requires difference to be: differences provide it with the shadings and contrasts that animate it. But when the imagination of wholeness captures a constituency, some of those very differences are experienced as the defective cause of its own lack of wholeness.

It is not that others never really pose a real threat to your life or your possibilities of being. They do. It is, rather, that some threats to that identity are manufactured by your own imagination of a wholeness that is unattainable. When the imagination of wholeness is attenuated the prospects improve both to allay some of those threats and to forge more affirmative relations with constituencies who differ from it. The paradoxical element circulating through relations of identity\difference, then, is that every identity needs a set of differences through which to define itself, while its imagination of wholeness can also translate that affirmative condition of possibility into a primordial threat. This paradoxical element can be negotiated when both parties work on themselves to diminish or redirect the drive to wholeness. One source of political evil is thereby attenuated. To note one example, if men first constitute "women" as sources of nurturance from which to develop their own capacities for agency and then define them only as spectators and/or objects through which to confirm that agency, then any other sign of agency by women will be received as a threat to masculine integrity. Here work on established practices of masculinity becomes necessary. Or take another even more poignant condition. If and when heterosexual desire and consummation of pleasure are organized around the repudiation of homosexual unions, the very maintenance of the former pleasures engenders a punitive orientation to public displays of same-sex desire. Considerable work on the character of heterosexual desire will now be needed to redress the mode of suffering it now produces. Failure to do that work tempts those whose desire is bound up with such punitiveness to pretend that the future of civilization and morality themselves require these punitive practices.

Identity\difference relations are endlessly complex. Maybe you (as individual, group, class, or nation) convert a range of differences into otherness to fix blame for the unexpected sense of uncertainty or incompleteness you feel. Or, perhaps, the appearance of wholeness in some models with whom you identify drives you to try to replace them to acquire the prize they seem to possess. Or your public self-identification as gay or atheistic may pose a threat to the insistent demand for wholeness by a subset of heterosexuals or monotheists. Constituencies in which the theme of a primordial "lack" or "alienation" is central are highly susceptible to the first two political operations. And any constituency striving to place a new identity on the register of legitimacy is potentially susceptible to the third.

How to participate in the pleasures and efficacies of identity without succumbing to the evils those pleasures and efficacies can generate? How to enjoy the manifold desires, capabilities, and grace of identity without becoming the target of aggression from those whose quest for wholeness renders you threatening? There may be no foolproof answer to such questions, and not just because they are posed abstractly. For the difficulty is lodged inside the very structure of identity\difference relations. But there are ethical dispositions and political orientations that can make a significant difference. The responses pursued here are set in a tragic sensibility in which the ambiguity of identity both fosters the dangers and provides significant resources to struggle against them.

Nietzsche and Foucault provide promising resources, though the sustenance I draw from each does not correspond entirely to his intentions. Both Nietzsche and Foucault pursue relational arts of the self as an ethical strategy. Self-artistry does not aim—as several Kantian and neo-Kantian critics persist in claiming—at creating a self-indulgent self. That interpretation fails to discern the connection between self-artistry, the desanctification of critical elements in your own subjectivity, and cultivation of forbearance and generosity in relations with other constituencies. The problem with the neo-Kantian critique is that it slides over the ubiquitous role that arts of the self do and must play in ethical and political life. And it ignores, as we shall see in chapter 7, Kant's own emphasis upon the importance of "gymnastics" to the moral life.

The craftsmanship involved in the self-artistry endorsed here is modest and experimental, and the modifications to be crafted vary with the settings and distinctive materializations already in place. The goal is to work demurely on a relational self that has already been formed, recrafting vengeful, anxious, or stingy contingencies that have become entrenched and forging them into a distinctive form you can admire without having to treat it as a true copy of a universal model. Working on yourself in relation to the cultural differences through which you have acquired definition. Doing so to render yourself more open to responsive engagement with alternative faiths, sensualities, gender practices, ethnicities, and so on. Doing so to render yourself better able to listen to new and surprising movements in the politics of becoming without encasing them immediately in preset judgments that sanctify the universality or naturalness of what you already are. Self-artistry is not a "subjectivist" practice, then, if that means simply expressing what you already are or, more dramatically, treating what you purport to be as the universal standard to which everyone else must conform. Such artistry, rather, involves *the selective desanctification of elements in your own identity.* And it is often spurred into action by specific movements in the politics of becoming that impinge upon you, by movements that purport to show how implicit assumptions of naturalness or universality in elements of your identity often impose otherwise unnecessary injuries upon others. The most admirable arts of the self cultivate the capacity for critical responsiveness in a world in which the politics of becoming periodically poses surprises to the self-identifications of established constituencies.

I acknowledge that my inflection of this artistry depends significantly on the particular metaphysical faith in which it is set. The artistry commended by Augustine diverges from that commended by Kant, and that commended by Foucault differs in some ways from both of these practitioners. What I want to concentrate on now is how the metaphysical register of politics itself is sometimes susceptible to movement by such arts. The following example displays such a ripening.

Suppose you habitually assume that death must come when God or nature brings it. A new political movement by those who claim the right to doctor-assisted death when people are in severe pain or terminally ill shocks you to the core. You concur with those critics who accuse the doctors of death of cruelty to the dying and a lack of respect for the fundamental design of being. But later, when the shock of the new demand wears away a little, your concern for the suffering of the dying in a world of high-tech medical care opens a window to exploration of other possibilities. *One part of your subjectivity now begins to work on other parts.* In this case your concern for those who writhe in agony as they approach death may work on contestable assumptions about divinity or nature already burned into your being. But how to proceed? Cautiously. Perhaps you attend a film in which the prolonged suffering of a dying person becomes palpable. Or you talk with friends who have gone through this arduous experience with parents who pleaded for help to end their suffering. Next you expose yourself to a larger variety of understandings of divinity and nature than you had previously entertained. These two activities in tandem may enable you to appreciate more vividly the significant shifts in such conceptions that have already swept across Western history. So perhaps the current organization of your instincts in this domain is not the last word after all. Then you reencounter the high-tech world of medical care, reliving as you do distressing images of your father struggling with pain when he died of pancreatic cancer. You now visualize more starkly how contemporary medical practice often splits into distinct parts elements heretofore taken to constitute the unity of death itself. The brain may die while the heart still beats. Or the possibility of participating in cultural life may disappear while other signs of life persist. Or intense pain may make the end of life intolerable to bear. Through the conjunction of these diverse modalities of intervention, changes in the thinking behind your thoughts may now begin to form. Some elements in your experience of nature and morality may now clash more actively with others. Or perhaps you still find your previous conception of nature to be persuasive. But uncertainties and paradoxes attached to it combine with a more intensive appreciation of contemporary dilemmas of medical care to encourage you to try to desanctify that interpretation to a greater degree. You continue to affirm, say, a teleological conception of nature in which the meaning of death is set, but now you acknowledge how this judgment may be more contestable than you had previously appreciated. And you begin to feel this uncertainty more intensely as a conflict within yourself. You even begin to wonder whether your previous refusal to allow others to die as they determine (when such determinations are possible) might have contained a desire to preserve a reassuring interpretation of the wholeness of nature even more than a concern for their dignity or well-being. What was heretofore nonnegotiable may now gradually become rethinkable. You now register more actively the importance of giving presumptive respect to the judgment of the sufferer in this domain, even when the cultivation of critical responsiveness to them disturbs your own conception of nature, death, or divinity. Eventually, through personal communications and public engagements, you bring these considerations to others with whom you are associated, seeking to spur them to similar bouts of reappraisal.

You have now worked artfully on yourself in a modest but politically salient way. And the ethical effects of that work now inform the micropolitics in which you participate. The key thing, the thing that makes this an example of self-artistry in the interests of critical responsiveness rather than *merely* reformation of an old pile of arguments, is that it involves movement back and forth between registers of subjectivity: working now on thought-imbued feelings, then on thought-imbued intensities below the reach of feeling, now on received images of death and suffering, again on intensive memories of suffering, and then on entrenched concepts of divinity, identity, ethics, and nature. You move back and forth across these zones because each infiltrates into the others. You allow work done on each to flow into the others, without being in complete control of the relays. That's why you proceed cautiously, reviewing the effects of previous experiments before going on. In doing so, you may now appreciate more palpably how judgment occurs on several registers, and how much more there is to thinking than argument. You don't control the process entirely. That is one of the disturbing things about arts of the self, as well as one of their incitements. Besides, you had less control over those modes of subjectivity and intersubjectivity already installed in you. You experiment for ethical reasons upon multiple zones of your subjectivity and our intersubjectivities. Thinking becomes engaged at multiple levels. Some thoughts now may become more mobile partly because a set of intensive proto-thoughts behind them have been nudged. Since thinking operates on several registers of being, and because each register is invested with a set of feelings or intensities, to change your thinking is to modify to some degree the sensibility in which it is set. To change your sensibility in turn is to allow you to give more weight to minor feelings and arguments whose importance were heretofore minimized.

Who knows what new possibilities of being will be opened by this modest shift? Or what effects you now may have on the relational experience of others in your school, army, office, church, corporation, neighborhood, or family? These are the enchantments and risks of micropolitics. Neither can be avoided entirely. For we often work on ourselves without attending closely to the process; and we are regularly worked upon at multiple levels by the numerous institutional complexes in which we participate. Such techniques can be more or less artful, and more or less intensive. But they are not eliminable as long as the living think and participate in institutional life.

What is an art of the self from one perspective is micropolitics from another. The films, family memories, social movements, dietary regimens, marches, dream work, medical techniques, gossip, medications, curriculum organization, talk shows, identity performances, material disciplines and rewards, sermons, leadership techniques, and rituals you draw upon tactically to work upon the self are, from another angle, micropolitical practices that regularly impinge upon us individually and associationally. Arts of the self and micropolitics are two sides of the same coin. Micropolitics can function to stabilize an existing set of identities. It can also usher a new identity or right into being, such as, in the case we have reviewed, the right to die. If the right to die becomes installed as a fervent demand by a significant constellation, they will work to encase it in institutional practices such as court decisions, medical practices, legislative enactments, living wills, family obligations, and insurance policies. The political project will now be to devise procedural protections against the misuse of this institutionally entrenched right rather than to prohibit it to guard a contestable conception of nature or God from performative assault by those who do not endorse it. The very introduction of such a new right helps us to see more clearly how the appeal to a principle of respect for life or the rights of the individual is very often insufficient to the ethical issues at stake.

Self-artistry affects the ethical sensibility of individuals in their relations to others; micropolitics helps to shape an intersubjective ethos of politics. Consider some macropolitical proposals: "Let's allow gays in the military." "Let's grant individuals the right to doctor-assisted suicide." "Let's get rid of the property tax and give everyone an equal education." "Let's save the rain forests in North America." None of these proposals, enunciated by a court, a parliament, or executive decree, is either likely to be made or to get very far unless and until micropolitical receptivity to it has been nurtured across several registers and constituencies. If you think of public proposals and legal enactments as the molarpolitics of public officials, much of its preparation occurs through the molecular movements of micropolitics. William Bennett, Sister Helen Prejean, and Gilles Deleuze all understand this.

Even though micropolitics works at the level of detail, desire, feeling, perception, and sensibility, that does not mean it is "any less coextensive with the entire social field than molar organization."[10] Such an assumption entails the most elemental mistake. For micropolitics is both subjective and intersubjective. It flows through and across clubs, families, neighborhoods, regions, armies, TV constituencies, Internet networks, and religious associations, even as it operates at different levels than macropolitics. Detailed studies of parallels, differences, and connections between micropolitics and microeconomics in specific domains would be invaluable. For merit pay schemes and official organization of professional judgment surely participate in both. At any rate, politics becomes most intensive and most fateful at those junctures where micropolitics and macropolitics intersect.

There is no guarantee that artful selves and experimenting constituencies will always succeed in the experiments they undertake. And — it *almost* goes without saying — in a highly stratified society many individuals and constituencies are in an unfavorable position to pursue such experimentation. This latter fact, however, can easily be exaggerated.[11] And it does not diminish the importance of such work on the part of those who do find themselves in a favorable position. It increases it. Charges of "elitism" delivered at this juncture by advocates of morality as command function to reinstate the authority of the neo-Kantian model of morality by diversion rather than by demonstration of its superiority. For, first, even Kant himself finally found morality to be bound up with relational arts of the self. And, second, most advocates of multidimensional pluralism also favor a reduction in economic inequality. Indeed, many of us think multidimensional pluralism and economic justice set essential conditions of possibility for each other, and some have offered specific proposals to reduce inequality.[12] Part of the issue, then, is whether micropolitics and relational arts can play a role in promoting such an objective or are facile indulgences that divert people from obedience to moral injunctions already intact. One consideration that might throw light on this question is the judgment, already supported in chapters 4 and 5 of this study, that in the United States during the past few decades liberal visions of secular justice have ceded much of the terrain of micropolitics to the Christian right while focusing on moral principle and state macropolitics.

The goal of self as modest artist of itself needs be neither to *discover* a true self underneath those sedimented layers nor to *create* the self anew entirely by oneself. The contestable metaphysic in which my appreciation of these arts is valorized, at least, is defined in resistance to both of these models. One of the most compelling objectives of self-artistry, within this problematic, is to fend off the drive to evil installed in the imagination of wholeness already circulating through many individuals and collectivities. It is to become a self you can respect without having to elevate what you have become into a true copy of an intrinsic model. It is to *become* who you are, without resenting the world too much either for your inability to change some entrenched, unappealing dimensions of yourself or for failing to discover an intrinsic model that automatically elevates you into one of its very best copies. It is to become a being who rises above the twin evils of ressentiment and transcendental egoism.

A comparison with Augustinian arts might clarify things further. Augustinian arts are perpetual and reverential, as in the confessional to be enacted daily. They aim at cultivating love of God and enhancing obedience to his directives, by preparing the self to receive a grace that may or may not be given. The arts valorized here are periodic and set above all in political contexts in which new challenges to the universality of one's own identity periodically emerge. The occasion for them often arises in specific political contexts, as when, say, a new and surprising movement in the domain of race, gender, work, faith, dying, or sensual affiliation disturbs dimensions of your identity. Under these conditions self-artistry might desanctify elements in your identity enough to allow you to listen more attentively to a new and disruptive claim. Moreover, the highest aim of self-artistry projected here is not obedience; it is cultivation of political virtues such as critical responsiveness, agonistic respect, and studied indifference in relations between interdependent constituencies. There are significant moments, nonetheless, when the ends pursued here connect with those flowing from the Augustinian perspective, moments when the Augustinian love of divinity makes contact with critical responsiveness to difference. These are lines of connection across difference to be cultivated and appreciated.

Some who disavow the ideals of community and hierarchy in the name of pluralism may think that relieves them from practicing relational arts. Only community and obedience, they may feel, require such arts. Let us call this version of pluralism "Madisonian," setting aside the virtues Madison himself promulgated. Madisonians often think that because they aim at neither national religious sanctification nor secular community they have little need for micropolitics in political life. They think that since they don't ask too much of politics, not much need be asked of those who participate in it. Self-interest regulated by well-designed institutional balances and a few moral compunctions are enough. Or, in another version, self-reliance punctuated by obedience to moral principle will suffice. What a laugh. Such laissez-faire economists of political life underplay the extent to which institutional practices not only regulate people but help to shape and constitute them. They also underestimate the tolerances within a Madisonian system of balances for violence. The official and unofficial American carnage against Amerindians, decades of state-sanctioned violence against organized labor, and the micropolitical conditioning of McCarthyism all occurred within the institutional frame of Madisonianism. Such pluralists—to be admired for the appreciation of diversity they muster—underestimate the virtues needed to nurture and maintain a responsive and expansive culture of pluralism. Perhaps they should consult someone like Norbert Elias, for instance, on how a dense set of micropractices already composes the unconscious orientations to nature and civilization in which we participate today. How, say, the introduction of napkins, tablecloths, separate dishes, and knives and forks into the routines of eating in the late Middle Ages significantly modified the instinctive register of social behavior and changed operative orientations to nature.[13]

Even if Madisonian pluralism were sufficient to contemporary life—which it is not—micropolitical networks would still be needed to foster the virtues appropriate to it. Thus, for example, when gay activists press against Mayor Giuliani's program to close down public spaces of routine gay association in New York City, they are fighting to maintain space in which men and women outside the dominant heterosexual matrix can mingle in contexts devoid of shame or secrecy, in which unorthodox sexual communities can organize into a political force, in which resistance to cultural heteronormativity can find visible places of public expression, and in which pressure on the state to find a cure for AIDS can be intensified.[14] These struggles are micropolitical in initiative and energy, even as they flow into the macropolitical realm. By deflating or ignoring the role that such networks play, Madisonian pluralists cede too much cultural ground to conservative commanders of community.

Consider Rousseau in this connection. In *The Government of Poland,* Rousseau institutionalizes disciplines that would bind an entire "people" to the nation.[15] His presentations of national modes of dress, severe limits on immigration and foreign contact, public festivals, citizen military service, national rewards for public merit, public pledges, and so forth all serve this function. He knows that such disciplines condition character as well as regulate it. Public repetition of a pledge of allegiance in patriotic contexts enters into the psychic life of the participants (even if not always with the exact effect intended), and a national style of dress combined with the minimization of foreign contact makes others seem strange when contact does occur. The Rousseauian nation is an artifact of intensive institutional disciplines bolstered and supported by publicly sanctioned work by citizens on each other. My version of relational arts, however, transposes them into arts appropriate to a pluralist and pluralizing culture. The goal is to cultivate pluralist virtues, and to incorporate them into institutional design and political habit. The global movement to press universities in several countries to divest endowment funds from South Africa during the period of apartheid, for instance, not only had direct effects on the conduct of the South African state, it also helped a lot of people rise above treating their own state as the final site of political allegiance and action. It helped to open up new sites of action available to cross-national, nonstatist movements seeking to modify the behavior of states. Similarly, the recent effort to authorize homosexuality in the military would release those in same-sex relations from the unique burden of keeping those relations private or even secret; it would also apply institutional pressure upon straights in the military to work on themselves to affirm the legitimacy of gay desire.

An Ethos of Engagement

The following formulation by Foucault spurs my thinking on the complex relations, first, between symbolic systems and tactics of the self and, second, between the politics of self-artistry and a larger ethos of politics:

> It is not enough to say the subject is constituted in a symbolic system. It is not just in the play of symbols that the subject is constituted. It is constituted in real practices — historically analyzable practices. There is a technology of the constitution of the self which cuts across symbolic systems while using them.[16]

Foucault's early accounts of disciplinary society locate sites where institutional techniques and symbolic systems intersect. His later inquests into arts of the self, individually and in concert, suggest how we might exert positive effects on ourselves and others at precisely these points. The irony of Foucauldian arts is that you enact disciplines on yourself in part to temper the demand to impose harsh disciplines and punishments upon others in the name of sanctifying generally what you are or purport to be. Such arts seek to subvert transcendental egoism. They work in tandem with political mobilizations to modify racial, religious, gender, sexual, national, or ethnic identities that punish difference in the pursuit of wholeness. These are ethico-political arts, then. Once you address the complex connections among disciplines, institutions, and identities it becomes clear how important it is sometimes to politicize the identity\difference relations in which we are set. Let us now imagine, then, a positive ethos of politics appropriate to a pluralist culture, presupposing a culture in which public elections occur regularly and cultural diversity has a foothold. The focus is not on institutional design but on intercultural virtues that enliven and inform institutional life.

If you define democracy only as mode of *rule* or *governance,* where elected representatives legislate, execute, and enforce general policies, and where the debate is whether officials should represent the electorate (the idealist view) or be insulated from it in order to govern rationally (the realist view), then the democratic state can readily become a mode of collective action inconsonant with individual and constituency freedoms. This is the durable insight in the political minimalism of George Kateb. In fact, in Rousseauian and neo-Hegelian traditions — where citizens seek a general will or a unified nation-state — democratic governance readily degenerates into the organization of unity through the demoralization of otherness. These forms readily become vehicles for consolidation of violence against the internal other (those within the state who deviate from the nation or general will), the interior other (that in the self which differs from its socially constituted identity), and the external other (those outside the state who threaten the self-confidence of its identity).

When you imagine democracy not only as a particular organization of governance, but also as a distinctive culture in which constituencies have a significant hand in modeling and moving the identities that constitute them, then negotiation of a democratic ethos of engagement becomes very pertinent. First, when a positive ethos of engagement between multiple constituencies is operative, *productive tension* is maintained between governance of a populace through established standards and the periodic interruption by social movements of modes of governance because of the suffering or exclusions they embody. This is the first productive ambivalence in a democratic ethos, then. But, second, such an ethos itself is forged by negotiation between a variety of constituencies honoring different moral sources, rather than engendered as the unified product of a nation in which all legitimate participants honor the same moral source. No single God, primordial contract, fixed conception of rationality, settled conception of self-interest, unified principle of justice, or practice of communicative consensus sits at the apex or base of an ethos of engagement. It is negotiated between numerous interdependent constituencies divided along multiple dimensions. It becomes possible as a political achievement when many have come to appreciate the contestability of the source of morality they honor the most. And when a large number in the first category have overcome resentment of this condition of being.

Multidimensional plurality is necessary but insufficient to these interfaith negotiations. It is when the relations "between" resonate with reciprocal appreciation of elements of contestability in the fundamentals of each party that positive possibilities begin to glow. A generous ethos of engagement between partisans honoring different moral sources expands room for diversity to be, even as it engenders its owns limits, sacrifices, and exclusions. It limits the prerogatives, for instance, of religious, gender, sexual, ethnic, and national constituencies who feel aggrieved unless the culture in which they participate sanctifies as imperative for everyone the particular organization of being they embody (or purport to embody). It does not stop such constituencies from living within the orbit of such assumptions; it does stop them from placing such assumptions at the authoritative center of political culture.

The greatest danger adhering to such an ethos is that its initial signs of success will spur into being virulent movements to restore a national wholeness that never really existed in the way represented. But this risk is worth running. For the corollary virtue of a generous ethos of engagement is that it can support a more multifarious pluralism than otherwise available: a *pluralism* in which multiple possibilities of connection open up across several lines of difference because more of the parties involved appreciate the profound contestability of the faiths they honor the most, and a *democracy* in which limits are set to the probable intensity of conflict between contending parties because more partisans acknowledge their own ambiguous implication in many of the differences they engage.

An ethos of engagement among multiple constituencies honoring different moral sources, then, is both likely to generate reactive drives to wholeness and to spawn cultural resources through which to soften and contain such movements. It is the ways in which it turns back its most dangerous possibilities that make it promising and enchanting. Negotiation of an ethos of engagement provides the best alternative to both a secularism in which partisans pretend to leave their basic presumptions at home when they enter public life and a republican nation governed by a single conception of the common good. As negotiation of such an ethos proceeds, its effects infiltrate into the shape of military bureaucracy, marriage practices, patterns of immigration, school curricula, the organization of health care, child-rearing practices, political campaigns, local meetings, and interstate relations. The diversity of religious faith, gender practice, and sensual affiliation can then be enhanced in each domain.

Widespread appreciation of the constitutive ambiguity of identity can provide a spur to the cultivation of respect between constituencies bound together in relations of interdependence and strife. For a constituency identity is formed from numerous materials: by the organization into settled form of fleeting possibilities within it, by organization of that (within and without) that varies from itself into defined modes of difference, and by reception and resistance to the identifications projected upon it by alternative constituencies.

In identity\difference relations subcurrents of empathy emerging from fugitive signs of difference, resistance, and incompleteness in each identity already flow across the membranes of separation. When the comparative contingency of what you are is contemplated, or, at least, the contestability of the assumptions that would universalize you are addressed, these currents are invested with considerably more legitimacy. The irony, which Nietzsche, Foucault, and Emmanuel Levinas (in different ways) understand, is that those moralities that insist upon grounding themselves in a universal matrix of reason, the fixed commands of a single god, the intrinsic identity of the regular individual, or the higher unity of a harmonious community risk losing touch with some fugitive sources within and between from which agonistic empathy for difference is cultivated.[17] They can reduce that risk while retaining their faith, however, by acknowledging the distance between the end they pursue and their actual approximation of it to date. That might open them up, for instance, to cultivate relations of agonistic respect and critical responsiveness to the type of perspective advanced here. Empathy, pathos, and humor flow more readily across lines of difference if and when such reciprocal acknowledgments are made.

Attachment across the space of distance insinuates forbearance into strife and generosity into interdependence. It does so without exerting incredible pressure on either party to become what the other already is. Attachment across distance now becomes possible because neither party is hell-bent on achieving universality or wholeness by erasing the distance between it and the other. Atheists and theists, for instance, can now smile together on occasion as each encounters moments of difference within itself from itself. When such an ethos of engagement is operative, cushions of generosity and forbearance form between contending identities so that the collisions between them become less bellicose. But, of course, such an ethos is never sufficiently in place. It is always in need of repair or revivification along one dimension or another as new and surprising issues are pressed upon it. It recurrently encounters new questions as to what limits must be set with respect to this new challenge or that new claimant to a place of legitimacy. Its partisans acknowledge that it does not have recourse in advance to a set of criteria sufficient to resolve those spiritual questions. For such an ethos is a political formation or cultural artifact much more than a derivation, discovery, or set of implications drawn from a few general premises.

It is possible to read Nietzsche—the arch-adversary of democracy as a Rousseauian mode of *self-rule* and carrier of nostalgia for an aristocratic ethos—to be an involuntary contributor to the ethos of democracy needed in the late-modern age.[18] Nietzsche's arch-adversary in late-nineteenth-century Europe was the culture of Christianity, wherever that culture achieved sufficient hegemony to overwhelm every contending pattern of spirituality. But he also felt a certain pathos for his favorite adversary. Not because he hoped to convert its adherents to his philosophy, though such a possibility was held open for some by this ironic evangelist of metaphysical atheism. But, first, because the culture of Christianity helped him to sharpen his critical faculties, and, second, because its authoritative embodiment of a way to read and respond to the mysteries of existence helped to illuminate the alternative path he charted with respect to mystery and opacity. For, much more than most versions of secularism, Christianity honors a role for mystery, paradox, and existential struggle in life. So Nietzsche admired Christianity as an agonistic partner while dissenting radically from the model of salvation that motivates many of its partisans. Consider his invitation for a "spiritualization of enmity" between these contending orientations to the paradoxes of being:

> The Church has at all times desired the destruction of its enemies: we, we immoralists and anti-Christians, see that it is to our advantage that the Church exists.... In politics, too, enmity has become much more spiritual—much more prudent, much more thoughtful, much more *forbearing*.... We adopt the same attitude toward the "enemy within"; there too we have spiritualized enmity, there too we have grasped its *value*. One is *fruitful* only at the cost of being rich in contradictions; one remains *young* only on condition the soul does not relax, does not long for peace.[19]

I concur with Nietzsche here, with some crucial qualifications. Don't long for peace. It is for that reason to "our" advantage that Christianity exists. That is, its existence helps us to cultivate nontheistic *gratitude* for the ambiguity of being through both selective indebtedness and selective contrast to Christian practices. Christianity provides an invaluable spur to us, even while we resist drives by a significant minority of Christians to constitute us as irreverent, amoral, a-theists—irreverent because we do not bow before the God they worship, amoral because we do not endorse the fundamental source of morality they identify, and a-theistic because we do not "affirm anything." Adding "Judeo" in front of "Christian" is welcome because it pluralizes things somewhat. But it does not go nearly far enough. And besides, one suspects that while many Christians now find Judaism to offer a valuable diversification of religious experience, a significant minority still quietly take the prefix "Judeo" to signify the archaic predecessor to the real thing.

What would help the most is cultivation by a variety of monotheists and secularists of agonistic respect for minorities who draw ethical inspiration from alternative sources, including nontheistic and asecular sources. Nietzsche concludes that only a noble few will ever be prepared to spiritualize enmity in this way. He may exaggerate a significant truth. It *is* unlikely that such a relational orientation will form the ecumenical ethos of a pluralistic democracy as such. We may never live in a world in which an overwhelming majority of "Christians," "pagans," "Jews," "secularists," "Muslims," and "atheists"—to list a few types along merely one dimension—fold the spiritualization of enmity into their intra- and intercultural relations. Yet what is fascinating about the history of Christianity is that it has periodically made profound adjustments to new developments that recast its claims to authority and universality. Nietzsche's statement that the church has "at all times desired the destruction of its enemies" is a coarse exaggeration. The advent of secularism in modern life provides one example of a radical change in relations between Christianity and the states in which it is set. So do the emergence of Protestantism and the post-World War II shift in relations between Christianity and Judaism. Moreover, against Nietzsche's expectations, and moving below the radar screen of secular conceptions of public life, a postsecular ethos of public engagement between diverse spiritualities has already made considerable advances in several places. These events combine to suggest both that Christian culture has harbored harsh and fateful resistances to the acceptance of diversity and that its potential for adaptability and flexibility in this respect is greater than Nietzsche's polemic acknowledges.

A generous ethos of engagement need not be shared by each and every constituency to the same degree to play a positive role in politics. More significant yet, such an ethos is unlikely to find active expression anywhere today unless it establishes an active presence in democratic states. Finally, unless such a reciprocal ethos of engagement between diverse spiritualities acquires significant presence in formal democracies, democracy itself will be more stingy, dogmatic, and exclusionary than it has to be. An aristocratic world of "nobility" (both Tocqueville and Nietzsche would agree) cannot be reinstated today—if it ever really existed; and Nietzsche's compensatory ideal of nobility for a few diverse spirits above and beyond the reach of "herd" politics is not sustainable either.[20] Today, the possibility of a spiritualization of difference and collaboration among multiple constituencies is greatest in those pluralistic democracies where such practices already have some leverage. It is a regulative ideal appropriate to contemporary democracy.

One can think of instances in the politics of gender, sexuality, class, religion, ethnicity, and generation where tinges and touches of such an ethos are already discernible. Let's focus for a moment now, though, on the place of the atheist in contemporary political culture. The historic, American/Christian/Tocquevillian constitution of "the atheist" as amoral, selfish, restless, materialistic, and morally unreliable requires reconfiguration if an ethos of engagement among multiple constituencies is to function well. For Tocqueville's nineteenth-century dictum that a professed atheist could not be elected to public office in America still holds. No public advocate of atheism, to my knowledge, currently holds a major public office in the United States. And Bertrand Russell couldn't even get a temporary academic appointment confirmed in the America of the 1940s. What is most pertinent about this example, though, is its disclosure of how the quest for public universality by some partisans of monotheism and the drive by many secularists to make faith irrelevant to public life combine to rule out the distinctive contributions public atheists might make to public life.

What contributions to a public ethos of engagement might public atheists make in such a situation? Well, a political movement that translates the assigned marks of atheism into cultivation of nontheistic gratitude for the ambiguity of being opens up some possibilities. Such an orientation recasts the categories of restlessness and materialism through which atheists are often defined. In a world in which the quest for wholeness can foster evil unless tempered by other forces, a certain amount of restlessness becomes salutary. Also, public elaboration of a nontheistic metaphysic of the infrasensible and the sensible might challenge other perspectives to reconsider their own thin renderings of the sensible and to engage more explicitly challenges to the metaphysic of the supersensible. Nontheists are in a favorable position to explore sources of care for the plurivocity of being overlooked or undervalued in other traditions.

So you refigure atheism modestly while asserting its positivity more actively. You become an ironic evangelist of metaphysical atheism, leaving the door open to receptivity or even conversion by others without insisting that your orientation provides the only possible opening to ethical dignity. You say, "If you can't come to terms with atheism, at least let others help your kids overcome this disability." Such nontheists inflect in a particular way, then, a larger cultural need to craft an ethos of engagement among a variety of constituencies honoring different moral sources. Doing so by actively endorsing a nontheistic, asecular source of ethical inspiration. Connecting nontheistic gratitude for existence to selective currents in other traditions without reducing it entirely to any theism or secularism currently in circulation.

Of course, this is not the only public philosophy available to those who accept the indefinite designation "atheistic." Moreover, nontheistic gratitude for the protean abundance of being does not *erase* the self-interests, insecurities, passions, and interpretive priorities of those who do subscribe to it; at its best it enters into these modalities, adjusting and modulating them. The projection of such a perspective into public discourse begins, though, to *enact politically* a new public identity out of a historical pile of cultural marginalizations and uncertain tolerances. The success of such an intervention, certainly, depends at least as much upon the critical responsiveness of others as it does upon the initiatives of its pastors. But if and as it moves from a nonplace below the threshold of viable public participation to a place on the register of public life, it jostles and disrupts established debates over the model of public life and the sources of imperfections in it. It reopens the question of public ethos during a time when the need to re-think this question is unmatched by the level of creativity brought to the assignment.

The ethical refiguration of atheism discloses a few chinks in the armor of dominant moral theories. For secular theories of justice or rights and na-tional theories of democratic unity tend to obscure the ambiguous *politics of becoming* by which a new entity is propelled into being out of injury, energy, and difference. They therefore obscure how inadvertent exclusions and violences can be ensconced within an established constellation of legiti-mate identities and honored rights. These partisans seem to us—with our valorization of the fundamental mobility of being—to underplay how a new, unexpected movement can expose modes of suffering and injury hereto-fore located below the radar of public discourse. Sometimes the politics of becoming exposes how a list of basic rights that recently seemed complete harbored obscure and inadvertent exclusions inside the sweep of its formu-lations. Our discussion of "the right to die" supports such a reading.

When atheism crosses that invisible line of separation between legiti-mate and illegitimate perspectives in public life, it becomes possible to ren-der critical engagements among theists, nontheists, secularists, and atheists more "prudent," "thoughtful," "forbearing," and "fruitful." A series of inter-dependencies and affinities among contending spiritualities now becomes more palpable. You now exercise forbearance toward adversaries who help to crystallize your spiritual identity even while deflating claims some advance to completeness. You invite them to reciprocate. You might do so, partly from attachment to the ambiguity of being, partly through appreciation of the role distance between you and others plays in opening space for new candidates to lobby for a place on the cultural register of being, partly out of respect for the way the periodic introduction of new identities broadens your own experience of relational interdependence, partly out of gratitude toward the difference *of* the other in helping you to crystallize what you are, partly through encountering traces of the other *in* your identity, and partly out of prudence in a world in which you seldom know now which allies you will need in the future. An ethos of engagement is crafted from diverse materials, and each constituency deploys them in somewhat differ-ent ways. Such an ethos draws strength from its lack of purity. Again, it does not rise above partisan identities, interests, interpretations, and anxi-eties; it enters into them and the cultural relations they enable. It is less tight, unified, formal, and complete than some conceptions of public life demand; it is more resilient, generous, dense, and susceptible to modification for that reason.

The spiritualization of enmity among multiple constituencies forms a cardinal virtue in a vibrant ethos of engagement. It incorporates into a general ethos intercultural appreciation of the fact that no partisan orientation to the fundaments of being has yet established itself with certainty. To the degree such an ethos is absent, formal democracy gives off the odor of stagnation or the offensive smell of stinginess and dogmatism. A positive ethos of engagement exposes and fights against violences grounded in the pursuit of wholeness, when that pursuit becomes too insistent in its institutional definition of others. It thereby provides an excellent antidote to evil in contemporary politics.

In pressing this comparative case I nonetheless remain wary of claiming too much. First, such an ethos, as an irregular, haphazard modus vivendi limited significantly by the structures of inequality in which its negotiations occur, will itself engender surprising and unexpected injuries. Its compensatory virtue here is its ability to foster critical responsiveness to the politics of becoming through which such surprises can be addressed. Second, because such a cobbled ethos plays a mediating role within the play of self-interest, partisan interpretation, competition over resources, and contention over power, it might break down under pressure from these forces. I can invoke no metaphysical guarantee to ward off that possibility. This imaginary stands up well, then, when placed into competition with other contemporary models of public life. It looks puny when set against the awesome contingency of the human condition. The issue is whether this *latter comparison* is to be invoked to support the quest for a whole, secure, centered, transcendental way of being or to support work on ourselves, privately and publicly, to participate in an ethos of engagement that rises above the demands for wholeness and purity in public life.

7

A Critique of Pure Politics

"Don't pick your nose and eat it." Who would want to in the first place? It is disgusting. You break one taboo about the relation of the bodily inside to the outside when you pick your nose (though everybody seems to do it); another more visceral one when you eat the proceeds. That turns the stomach of anyone watching, at least in this culture. The stomach is one of the body's centers of culturally infused thought and feeling. When it is pierced by a sharp feeling of rage, or overcome by dread, or filled with disgust, it sends messages to the major brains, sometimes turning them around or overwhelming them. Disgust is a thought imbued feeling, then, and it also has effects on other registers of thought and judgment. It is thought-imbued in that it responds acutely to some events and activities while remaining quiescent before others; and these thoughts are bathed in an intense feeling that can unsettle or overwhelm those sunk in it. A feeling of disgust can make you retch, even against your will. So, disgust, while it is indispensable to life and ethical judgment, sometimes breeds ethical thoughtlessness. When overcome by disgust, for instance, you might become thoughtless about the feelings of those who disgust you. And thoughtless people readily become crude or ruthless. We saw in chapter 1 how the secular presentation of public space encourages it to ignore or degrade the visceral register of subjectivity and intersubjectivity. This tendency, in turn, as we saw in chapter 6, encourages its supporters to underplay the importance of self-artistry and micropolitics in ethico-political life. We now need to take another step down this trail, focusing on *feelings* that are thought-imbued. Our intention is to appreciate the role that the cultivation of sensibility plays in intellectual, ethical, and political life. That concern eventually carries us into the territory of metaphysical orientations that devalue the significance of sensibility.

Snot is matter out of place. It can unsettle everyone in the vicinity. So does menstrual blood for the Maori, according to Mary Douglas: "The Maoris regard menstrual blood as a sort of human being *manque*. If the blood had not flowed it would have become a person, so it has the impossible status of a dead person that has never lived."[1] A dead person who never lived is too much to take. So menstrual blood—a condition of life—becomes a pollution assaulting the dignity of life. Does it remind people of the bodily messiness and ambiguity from which human life emerges, and in which feeling, thinking, action, and judging are set? Does the sight of snot or menstrual blood jeopardize purity in those concepts of the soul, personhood, identity, morality, reason, and politics widely taken to elevate us above animality? Does a certain civilizational disgust for ambiguity and messiness in the very categories of morality have deleterious effects on the possibilities for generosity in relations among diverse constituencies? This question is difficult to address. For the feeling of disgust may already find expression in the way the question is posed and the categories through which it is engaged. Perhaps an engagement with two thinkers in the West who seek purity in different domains may help us to address the issue. To put the goal of purity itself up for reconsideration, we will engage Immanuel Kant on the nature of morality, the will, and the senses. And then, after exploring how Hannah Arendt contests the purity of these Kantian categories, we will ask whether the quest for purity returns in her thinking about the political. Our attention will be drawn to the role that disgust and taste play for each, and, correspondingly, the role each plays when you endorse the ethical importance of the visceral register of subjectivity and intersubjectivity. So, once more with feeling.

The Kantian Metaphysic of Pure Morality

"It is . . . of great consequence to ethics in general to avoid admitting, so long as it is possible, of anything morally intermediate, whether in actions (adiophora) or in human characters; for with such ambiguity all maxims are in danger of forfeiting their precision and stability."[2] Purity and danger. The moral life must be pure if it is to be stable. It must be precise if it is to be pure. "Pure practical reason," according to Kant, governs morality. It is pure when it is uncontaminated by sensible desire or inclination. Indeed, everything must be done to protect the moral will from such contamination. For the *motivation* to duty becomes uncertain when it is infiltrated by sensible desire, and what *counts* as duty becomes culturally variable when inclination is allowed to enter into its determination. It is through practical reason that we are impelled to "postulate" ourselves to be free, while speculative reason—the reason through which we examine the appearances of nature—only indicates freedom as a possibility. The capacity for freedom, in turn, shows human beings to be poised between two worlds, the Newtonian world of causal laws in which human sensibility and inclination are set and the supersensible world of moral freedom.

The most famous Kantian antinomy, perhaps, is that posed by the coexistence of these two realms the sensible and supersensible worlds—each of which is undeniable and neither of which appears to be compatible with the other. The Kantian solution, of course, is to conclude that the world of causality is the world as it appears to us in our spectatorial capacity while practical reason informs and properly governs the world of action. "Consequently, if we wish still to save it [freedom], no other course remains than to ascribe the existence of a thing so far as it is determinable in time, and accordingly its causality under the law of natural necessity, merely to appearance, and to attribute freedom to the same being as a thing in itself."[3] This conclusion protects the compatibility of the two realms by creating an abyss between them, with neither in its purity containing elements found in the other. Yet morality will be ineffective unless the moral will can intervene in the sensible world. So practical reason must be given the capacity to govern the world of sensibility.

The first result of the Kantian quest for moral purity, then, is a two-world metaphysic. The second is the demand that the first world be able to intervene in the second. The third is that the world of sensible desire and inclination be treated as something that, though innocent and worthy of satisfaction in itself, must be *sacrificed* whenever it comes into conflict with the moral law. Kantian morality is a morality in which the sacrifice of desire takes priority over the cultivation of desire, even though the latter does occur. The fourth result is a morality in which only human beings—those beings who alone participate in both worlds—receive intrinsic value. Animals and ecosystems of the earth are not valued either in themselves or as parts of an interdependent world in which we are implicated up to our necks and above.

> There is a judgment that even the commonest understanding cannot escape when it meditates about the existence of things in the world and of the world itself. It is the judgment that all these diverse creatures would exist for nothing if they did not include human beings (or some king of rational beings), no matter how artfully devised these creatures

may be, and how diversely, coherently, and purposively interrelated. . . .
In other words, it is the judgment that without man all of creation
would be a mere wasteland, gratuitous and without a final purpose.[4]

Once the two realms have been separated and recombined in the name
of morality and freedom, a series of new difficulties emerge. For while Kant
seeks to retain the purity of practical reason, he soon finds himself struggling
to ward off the threat of admixture and ambiguity *within* the practice of
freedom. The Kantian antinomy between the sensible and the supersensible
returns as a tension within the practice of freedom itself. In *Fallen Freedom:
Kant on Radical Evil and Moral Regeneration,* Gordon E. Michalson traces
the aporias internal to freedom that grip Kantianism.[5] This struggle becomes
most sustained in *Religion within the Limits of Reason Alone,* where Kant
engages the specter of "radical moral evil." To summarize briefly, radical
moral evil is not first and foremost a set of horribly violent acts, such as tor-
turing children or committing genocide; it is the "propensity of the will" to
allow itself to be governed by maxims that derive from the inclinations.
Radical moral evil is common, even prevalent in human life.

> Now if a propensity to this does lie in human nature, there is in man a
> natural propensity to evil; and since this very propensity must in the
> end be sought in a will which is free, and can therefore be imputed, it
> is morally evil. This evil is *radical,* because it corrupts the ground of all
> maxims; it is, moreover, as natural propensity, *inextirpable* by human
> powers, since extirpation could occur only through good maxims, and
> cannot take place when the ultimate subjective ground of all maxims is
> postulated as corrupt; yet at the same time it must be possible to *over-
> come* it, since it is found in man, a being whose actions are free.[6]

Radical moral evil must "in the end" be sought in the will, for the will,
the source of moral purity above sensibility, also has within itself a propensity
that "corrupts the *ground* of all maxims." This propensity is "inextirpable"
by human powers alone and yet it must be "possible to overcome it." These
formulations reflect something closer to constitutive tensions in the Kantian
system than antinomies Kant states and resolves: the will is the site of morality but something in its relation with the senses corrupts it within itself; it
must be capable of freeing itself from this contamination, but, still, because
of the depths of corruption to which it can fall, it may not be able to do so
by itself alone. If the propensity to evil is located in the will itself—in its
internal propensity to succumb to inclination rather than to sacrifice inclination to morality when necessary—this means that the will is not merely the
site of freedom as obedience to moral law. It is also the site of freedom as
a wildness or "perversity" (as Kant puts it) with respect to moral action.

The element of wildness hovers in that nano-instant between willing and nilling. From one side, this picture of the will is reassuring. It means that the will is unshackled, free to obey or to disobey the moral law. But from another side the element of wildness in freedom is disturbing to Kantianism. Wildness becomes a danger to the providential character of the entire two-world system. Kant does everything he can to contain this wildness. But the moral will now becomes more treacherous and less pure than the first picture of it in *The Critique of Practical Reason* suggests. Kant, the philosopher of the Enlightenment, now slides close to Augustine, the philosopher of original sin. Michalson puts the connection this way:

> The parallel between radical evil and original sin is very real. In both cases, we are dealing with a debility that is brought upon us through our own act of will rather than through mere ignorance or lack of information. In neither case is moral evil a problem arising out of an insufficient data base, or even out of unfortunate environmental circumstances. Likewise we are dealing in both cases with a debility that produces a fundamental alteration in our basic condition. . . . Finally, in the case of both radical evil and original sin the debility in question is defined in such a way as to make it evidently impossible to save or renew ourselves through our own efforts.[7]

Kant explores a couple of explanations of perversion of the will. One of them locates the deepest propensity for evil in trying, dependent experiences of childhood before reason matures.[8] But such an explanation, while it may appear plausible, would confound the entire Kantian system if accepted: it would entangle the sensible world in the very organization of the will, giving the will a cultural and personal variability disrupting the two-world metaphysic and morality as free obedience to a law; moreover, it might implicate the Kantian God himself (who exists merely as a postulate, of course) in the origin of evil, drawing Kant closer to the tragic tradition he strives to overcome. So Kant concludes that the "rational origin of this perversion of will whereby it makes lower incentives supreme among its maxims, remains inscrutable to us."[9] Such a finding coheres with Kant's claim that the supersensible world is presupposed but not known, and it protects his governing thesis of the will as source of action in the last instance. The will is free; it has a propensity for evil; the source of this propensity is inscrutable; we are nonetheless responsible for it.

This new combination generates further difficulties, for Kant is now moved to draw upon grace to help the will pull itself out of its propensity to evil. It is incorrect ("from within the limits of reason alone"), Kant insists, to attribute grace dogmatically to God. That would be to pretend to know more about Being in itself (the intelligible realm inscrutable to us) than we can. But we can still "hope" for grace because it is needed to maintain the integrity of morality, and because the integrity of morality is something we cannot avoid incorporating into our subjective presumptions. The first move is to insist that in every human, however depraved, "it must indeed be presupposed...that a seed of goodness remains in its entire purity."[10] That is the seed to work on. Kant then cites the Christian religion that has guided, but not entirely governed, his moral thought all along:

> But in the moral religion (and of the public religions which have ever existed, the Christian alone is moral) it is a basic principle that each must do as much as lies in his power to become a better man, and that only when he has not buried his inborn talent (Luke XIX, 12–16) but has made use of his original predisposition to good in order to become a better man, can he hope that what is not within his power will be supplied through cooperation from above.[11]

Kant cannot follow strictly the Augustinian doctrine of grace, but he cannot entirely remove the will from the province of grace either. So cautious sentences appear. Formulations that at first appear simply as limits upon reason with respect to grace may be read after plumbing the predicament of the Kantian will as solicitation of a hope for grace that stretches beyond the limits of reason alone. Thus: "Hence we can admit a work of grace as something incomprehensible, but we cannot adopt it into our maxims either for theoretical or practical use."[12] When you recall how inscrutable the Ideas of reason are, even though we regularly draw sustenance from them, and how entrenched the propensity to evil can become within the will, even though the will is the site of pure morality and freedom, it may be plausible to inflect this formulation in favor of a hope for grace because it is needed to sustain the integrity of morality along with a refusal to incorporate that hope into one's own practical maxims because the source from which it may emanate is inscrutable to reason. Otherwise why would Kant address grace at all? From the perspective of morality alone, it is both impossible to adopt grace as a maxim and imperative to hope it is available to a will caught in the propensity to perversity.

Why so much caution here? Well, if grace becomes folded into Kantian morality as hope, another quandary becomes intense. The Kantian system is built around human autonomy. Autonomy, though, is now threatened from one side by a deep propensity to evil installed in the will and from another through hope for a grace that helps to elevate the will by compromising its autonomy. Autonomy—the free obedience to moral law—finds its purity compromised in the very process of forming and maintaining itself.

The tensions we have identified destabilize the Kantian system by folding a series of admixtures and ambiguities into it. Rather than pursue these tensions further here, though, I will challenge the preliminary demand that puts this quest for purity into play. Doing so may help to determine whether these are tensions that morality itself must negotiate or impurities particular to the Kantian system. Let me put the issue in the form of a question: What makes Kant so certain that morality must assume the form of a *law* we are obligated to obey? Why not pursue a practice of ethical life in which the equation between morality and law is relieved? The importance of these questions becomes apparent when one sees how Kant's two-world metaphysic, the demand to protect the will from contamination by sensible desire, and the pressure to reduce evil to an evil propensity of the will are all bound up with the insistence that morality must take the form of obedience to a law located above the sensible realm.[13]

Morality as obedience to law is, according to Kant, neither a thesis we "postulate" nor one shown to be "presupposed" by other things we must accept as indubitable. Nor is it a thesis Kant argues for extensively by comparison to alternative conceptions of ethical life. The latter sort of argument does occur, with Epicurus and Spinoza providing his favorite targets. But these arguments occur mostly after the key equation has been secured. The rendering of morality as law provides Kant with an initial, indubitable point of reference from which other presuppositions, postulates, and arguments proceed. Morality as law is neither a presupposition nor an interpretation of experience; it is, rather, a *recognition* everybody already bestows upon moral life by participating in it. In Kant's presentation a mere "as it were" stands between that equation and its status as an effect "of pure reason."

> For whatever needs to draw the evidence of its reality from experience must depend for the ground of its possibility on principles of experience; by its very notion, however, pure yet practical reason cannot be held to be dependent in this way. Moreover, the moral law is given, as an apodictically certain fact, as it were, of pure reason. . . . Thus the objective reality of the moral law can be proved through no deduction, through no exertion of the theoretical, speculative, or empirically supported reason; and even if one were willing to renounce its apodictic certainty, it could not be confirmed by any experience and thus proved a posteriori. Nevertheless, it is firmly established of itself.[14]

Something given by pure reason "as an apodictically certain fact" is rendered immune from legitimate contestation. It would be mad to deny it. Indeed, Kant thinks that anyone foolish enough to deny the equation of morality with law would quickly fall into self-contradiction. How will you explain the self-blame or self-loathing that arises in your breast when you act immorally? How will you either account for responsibility or eliminate its attribution from your moral judgment? Still, the quandaries and sacrifices haunting Kantian morality may encourage some to experiment with a contending conception, placing its quandaries into competition with those in the Kantian system. For within the Kantian demand to apodicticize the equation between morality and law there is also an insistence that the moral law be simple, fixed, and clear.

> That is to say, what duty is, is plain of itself to everyone, but what is to bring true, lasting advantage to our whole existence is veiled in impenetrable obscurity, and prudence is required to adapt the practical rule based upon it. . . . But the moral law commands the most unhesitating obedience from everyone; consequently the decision as to what is to be done in accordance with it must not be so difficult that even the commonest and most unpracticed understanding without any worldly prudence should go wrong in making it.[15]

Even a child understands moral directives in a Kantian world. But *if* you suspect, against Kant, as it were, that the supersensible realm is a dangerous fiction; also, that ethical life is simultaneously complex, fragile, and indispensable to civilized life; besides, that it assumes the form of care for being first and responsibility and obligation next; moreover, that some of its most important perplexities arise when new, unexpected issues, events, or identities are propelled into being; furthermore, that this preparation to respond generously to new events involves *experimental work upon the sensible organization of the will* already installed between and within us through our previous history of transactions; and, finally, that ethical life must contend with the persistent gap between the reach and scope of responsibility and the self's limited capacities for action at any particular moment—*then* you may be motivated to contest this "recognition" of morality as law with its presumption in favor of simplicity and "unpracticed understanding."

Epicurus, Spinoza, Nietzsche, and Freud are four thinkers, stretched across twenty-four centuries, who challenge the apodictic certainty of morality as law. The last three acknowledge the cultural force of that idea enough to interpret it as a powerful, secondary formation repeatedly mistaken for a primary recognition. Each, however, challenges the Augustinian/Kantian tradition of morality, construing it to be a tradition deeply inscribed in Western religious/secular practices after the advent of the monotheisms of the Book rather than an apodictic certainty installed in the supersensible dimension itself. Each speaks, moreover, to that uncertain moment in Kant when he speculates about the effects upon the adult will of difficult, dependent childhood experiences.

Spinoza, to take just one example, refabulates the story of Genesis as one in which childlike beings are issued a prudential warning from the God: "Thus the command given to Adam consisted solely in this, that God revealed to Adam that eating of the fruit brought about death; as he reveals to us through our natural faculties, that poison is deadly."[16] Adam and Eve receive the God's prudential warning as a command; they translate the former into the latter *retrospectively,* as it were, under the influence of the hallucinatory state induced by the poison and the simple categories available to them. They then interpret the bad effects they experience from eating the poison fruit, after the fact again, as *punishment* for disobeying a divine command. Morality is thereby misrecognized as law. Because "the multitude" is "incapable of grasping sublime conceptions," this retrospective reading becomes lodged in Scripture, even though it misrepresents the most profound element in ethics.[17] Spinoza's allegory locates the false equation between morality and law into those childhood experiences prior to reason upon which Kant tentatively speculates. Jean Piaget's experiments investigating the moral experience of young children lend support to such an interpretation. The twin ideas of law and the simplicity of morality may come into being at the same time in the same way; they are then consolidated in adult life through a culture pervaded by Christian conceptions of law, will, freedom, responsibility, and punishment.[18]

Spinoza's story, setting up complex, later variations by Nietzsche and Freud, suggests that to grow up ethically is to outgrow the Kantian interpretation of morality as law. Even though you may endorse a reworked idea of "law" as, first, summary precepts of conduct that generally work in familiar contexts; second, those dimensions in the ethic you cultivate affirmed as incorrigible obligations because they are so fundamental to it; and third, that irreducible and yet mobile element of "madness" or implacability that haunts action as the factors shaping it regularly exceed your operative ability to articulate them. Stuart Hampshire, inspired in part by Spinoza, expresses such a perspective when he says, "More of human conduct than we had thought and aspects of it that we had not expected may be outside the possible control of practical action; less of human conduct than we had thought may flow from an unalterable natural endowment."[19] Now the moral law becomes a secondary formation you may sometimes find it ethically important to modify by tactical means.

How does Kant protect the apodicticity of morality as law from such an alternative reading? He refers to difficulties you fall into if his equation is denied. But since his doctrine has its own tensions and quandaries, such references do not suffice to still dissent unless and until they are joined to a more fundamental brief on behalf of the initial equation. So in the *Critique of Judgment* Kant presents the "common sense" with which "we" recognize beauty and from which judgments of beauty are communicable to others. Universal judgments of natural beauty are important because they provide promising signs of a teleology extending beyond the necessary appearance of nature as a system of Newtonian laws.[20] Such a subjective apprehension of teleology supports the demand of morality that its dictates be realizable in the last instance, and it gives us a sign that the world itself is congenial to the ideas of morality. The Kantian common sense, of course, does not correspond to the opinions or prejudices of ordinary people; such prejudices are far too sensual and variable to play the juridical role assigned to common sense. Nor is it statable in concepts or established by means of a transcendental argument. Rather, aesthetic common sense manifests a spontaneous accord between the faculties of understanding and imagination. You might say that the aesthetic common sense *enables* universal judgments of beauty while its manifestation in these judgments *supports* that Kantian faith in an implicit accord of the faculties crucial to the credibility of his two-world metaphysic.[21]

Gilles Deleuze suggests that Kant locates an analogous common sense within morality itself.

> Kant often reminds us that the moral law has no need at all for subtle arguments, but rests on the most . . . common use of reason. . . . We must therefore speak of a moral common sense. . . . Moral common sense is the accord of the understanding with reason, under the legislation of reason itself. We rediscover here the idea of a good nature of the faculties and of a harmony determined in conformity with a particular interest of reason.[22]

Now a fundamental way in which Nietzsche and Deleuze dissent from Kant is in the contention that thinking itself is both located within the sensible world and dependent upon a profound element of *discordance* between the faculties. It is in and through such discordances that new ideas become possible. They contest the Kantian idea of common sense all the way down, in the interests of thinking and ethics alike. An ethic of cultivation must be attentive to the judgment of familiar cases in familiar contexts, and, in my judgment, Deleuze does not pay enough attention to the question of how to honor this responsibility while attending to other considerations in tension with it. But an ethic of cultivation must also attend, as we saw in chapter 2, to the politics of becoming, to that politics by which old rules, laws, and identities are disturbed as new possibilities of life are propelled into being. Such a double attentiveness subtracts simplicity from ethics; it folds ambiguity and complexity into its very core while calling into question the sufficiency of morality as law to the politics of becoming. Once this contestation is pursued, as it is by Deleuze most persistently in chapter 3 of *Difference and Repetition,*[23] the Kantian attempt to solidify the apodicticity of moral law through common sense becomes open to critical interrogation. From this alternative perspective Kant can now be interpreted first to project persisting elements of a Christian culture into a "common sense" projected as a constitutive universal and then to invoke this projected accord of the faculties to justify a Christian-inspired rendering of the moral life. Common sense is projected as an unschematized universal; it then functions to place beyond critical review a particular interpretation of morality. To criticize this projection is to add an interrogation of the Kantian *recognition* of morality to those critiques of Kantian transcendental *arguments* already highly advanced in contemporary literature.

The Kantian image of common sense can be brought into rough correlation with a particular *velocity* of cultural life. That image attained great plausibility in the early-modern period, the period of the enlightenment, when the tempo of life was both more rapid than during the preceding medieval era and less rapid than today. In medieval life, before the corrosive power of nominalist theology had reached its peak, the culture of Christianity was lodged in a slow, expressive world of divine harmonies; since the signs of harmony were everywhere in the world there was not so much need for an internal common sense to guarantee it. Common sense in the Kantian sense becomes important with the increase of pace and tempo in early modernity, when the prose of the world retreats, as it were, into the interior of each Christian/Kantian self. The Kantian substitute of a necessary, subjective presupposition of the teleology of nature for the old "dogmatic" teleological model symbolizes this shift perfectly. But by late modernity, when the movement of people, ideas, cultures, decisions, military weapons, and commodities accelerates to a yet higher level of velocity, the Kantian idea of common sense may lose its temporal condition of automatic plausibility. Everything now moves faster and there is not enough time to install the same common sense into everyone inhabiting the same space. Now contending drives to *fundamentalize* "common sense" or to *pluralize* it escalate into a series of cultural wars. This historical effect means that the status Kant bestowed upon common sense is placed in jeopardy from all sides. The Kantian common sense might be reimposed by force, or treated as one image of moral life in competition with others, or sublimated into something new, but it can no longer be experienced generally as a spontaneous accord of the faculties. Today whenever such a spontaneous universal is invoked it arouses suspicion in some, nostalgia in others, insistence in still others, and an ambiguous mixture of these sentiments in many. Its invocation as a universal constitutes a call to cultural war more than recognition of a universal mode of judgment through which to resolve cultural issues.

To challenge the Kantian idea of common sense is both to call into question the apodicticity of morality as law and to disrupt (rather than to "disprove") the metaphysical idea of an inscrutable supersensible realm expressed through free obedience to the law. When that challenge is issued, a secondary dimension within Kant can be expanded. For Kant, while giving primacy to the timeless will, nonetheless insisted upon the pertinence to moral life of what might be called, in honor of Michel Foucault, relational arts of the self. Such work on the *sensibility* of the self might appear problematic within Kantian philosophy, since the sensible world appears under the control of Newtonian laws and the manifestation of the supersensible in practical reason rises above the reach of such strategems. But Kant repeatedly both invokes these tactics and confines their status. "Ethical gymnastics, therefore, consists only in combatting natural impulses sufficiently to be able to master them when a situation comes up in which they threaten morality; hence it makes one valiant and cheerful in the consciousness of one's restored freedom."[24] Disciplines applied by the self to the self can refine crude desires and render implacable desires more responsive to the moral will. Nonetheless, the most fundamental moral change always occurs as "a change of heart" within the will itself; and the will, in its timelessness, remains above the reach of those temporal tactics by which the sensible is modified.

Within the Spinozian/Nietzschean/Foucauldian/Deleuzian and Hampshirite problematics, however, the will itself is conceived as a complex cultural/corporeal formation, mostly formed as a "second nature" before the self has reached the age at which it might act reflectively upon itself. Arts of the self, then, are applied to this formation by the self to modify modestly the sensibility of the self. These tactics are best practiced in an experimental and cautious way. Experimental because they often reach into infrasensible modes of thought/disposition not fully available to consciousness. Cautious for the same reason.

There is no a priori guarantee you will succeed in your objective each time you apply arts of the self, just as there is no such guarantee, as we have seen, in the Kantian world of freedom of the will. But there are stratagems available, as we saw in chapter 6. As you proceed, you may find cautious intervention into the thought-imbued feelings of the stomach to be as important as work on the images of the brain. For, we now know, the stomach has a simple cortical organization of its own. This infrasensible center stores thought-imbued feelings of sadness, anxiety, happiness, disgust, anger, and revenge to be activated under particular circumstances, as when, for example, an intense feeling of disgust rises up when you observe someone picking his nose and eating it. Or when you observe public signs of a practice of sexuality that disturbs the sense of naturalness sedimented into your own. The stomach forms a significant site in the complex formation of your subjectivity, then, and in cultural patterns of intersubjectivity. Sometimes it expresses concordance with several brains in the head and sometimes discordance with them. Nietzsche knew this before recent experimental study confirmed it, saying simply enough, "We think with our stomachs."

Such tactics by the self upon itself—and larger cultural assemblages upon themselves—are experimental because the infrasensible, intersubjective organization of thought, images, feelings, desires, passions, and concepts is only partly and precariously susceptible to *direct* overview and control. The infrasensible, as I call it to recall some dimensions of the Kantian supersensible while veering sharply from others, is, like its predecessor, "inscrutable" beyond a certain point. Some of its subjective and intersubjective patterns subsist and insist; they have significant effects upon the world of complex, conscious intersubjective judgments without being reproduced in their entirety by that world.[25]

Joseph LeDoux, whose work on the amygdala mustered our attention in the first chapter, lists several systems that interact in the formation of complex judgments and emotions. Let us say, for starters, that the amygdala organizes thought-imbued *intensities* below the level of conscious judgment and feeling; that the cortical organization of the stomach houses several thought-imbued *feelings* of disgust, fear, love, rage, and the like; and that higher brains such as the hippocampus and the prefrontal cortex organize *conceptually sophisticated translations of these* intensities and feelings while also remaining in regular communications with the other cortical centers. Thus

> when the amygdala detects danger, it sends messages to the hypothalamus, which in turn sends messages to the pituitary gland, and the result is the release of a hormone called ACTH. ACTH flows through the blood to the adrenal gland to cause the release of steroid hormone. In addition . . . the steroid hormone flows through the blood into the brain, where it binds to receptors in the hippocampus, amygdala, prefrontal cortex and other regions.[26]

Without the amygdala and the stomach, neither unconscious intensity nor conscious intensity of feeling would reach the higher brains. Without the higher brains—interacting with each other, with these two systems, and independently with the world—you would not have the capacity for complex thought and judgment. The less complex somatic systems provide much of the intensity and part of the direction for action. But sometimes when the higher brains register intensities and feelings flowing from the first two systems, their own capacity for thoughtfulness and receptivity to difference becomes overwhelmed. To take an extreme instance, the hippocampus, which helps to regulate the amygdala, will break down if the stress signals coming to it from the latter remain too intense for too long. And so on and on, through endless circuits of parallelism, complementarity, intersection, and restraint.

The brain network is a rhizome, as Deleuze and Guattari already see, operating on several registers, each with its own internal capacities, speeds, and relays with other brains.[27] When nervous cultural unitarians insist that the organization of political action in concert would be impossible in a rhizomatic culture, they might learn a few things by examining how their own brains work.

Micropolitics and relational self-artistry shuffle back and forth among intensities, feelings, images, smells, and concepts, modifying some of them and the relays connecting them, opening up, thereby, the possibility of new thinking and alterations of sensibility. If LeDoux's guess is correct, you seldom have much direct effect on intensities installed in the amygdala, but you can have effects on a variety of systems that draw from it while regulating and monitoring it. Anyway, there is never a vacuum in those domains where the arts of the self do their work. The cultures in which we participate regularly work on these fronts. And today, the cultural right works more actively on several of them than any other group through its organization of TV evangelical programs, talk shows, authoritative patterns of gossip, authoritative patterns of narrative, and so forth. Liberals and the left have ceded too much of this territory to the right.

We sometimes need to work on preconscious modes of intensity and thought-imbued feelings built into the stomach. Doing so to untie knots in our thinking, or to desanctify elements of our own identity so as to cultivate the capacity to listen more attentively to unexpected voices in the politics of becoming.[28] Since the multiple brains in each human have a complex social structure, with numerous sites existing in domestic, foreign, and warlike relations, you work on several registers of subjectivity and intersubjectivity in relation to each other. You sometimes work on corporealized patterns of cultural appraisal, reviewing periodically the effects of that work upon your explicit articulations. In the light of that review, you might renew your previous effort or pursue another strategy, all the while keeping one eye on a larger ethical agenda: the expansion of little spaces of joy and generosity already there so as to cultivate the spirit needed to respond creatively and generously to political movements of identity that cast universal pretensions of this or that aspect of your own identity into doubt.[29]

To honor relational arts in this way is to challenge a pure morality of law derived from a supersensible realm; it is also to rewrite the ideology of sacrifice such a model of morality enjoins upon the sensible realm. Such tactics, on my reading, reach no point at which they give way to a supersensible realm; neither are they reducible to a crude behaviorism that shapes subintelligent dispositions entirely by simple strategies of reinforcement. The ethical gymnastics of the self and the culture, already given limited acknowledgment by Kant, become endowed with more nobility if the Kantian realm of the supersensible is subtracted from your metaphysical picture. For now it is no longer feasible to treat "the sensible" as simply dumb, or automatic, or equipped with only slight capacities for sublimation and augmentation. The sensible and the infrasensible are domains in which we think, within which intensities of cultural appraisal are stored, and through which we value and devalue.

Nothing said here, however, *disproves* the Kantian metaphysic of the supersensible and the sensible. Rather, it brings out the profound contestability of that doctrine, pressing its supporters to acknowledge their inability to represent the unchallenged character of morality itself and, perhaps, to reconsider those crude renderings of the sensible upon which much of the credibility of the idea of supersensible rests. It thus endows an ethic of cultivation with more complexity and credibility than is often acknowledged by Kantian and neo-Kantian philosophies.

The Purity of Politics

We have identified an irreducible element of wildness in the Kantian will. It must be there for radical evil to be lodged in a propensity of the will rather than outside it. But Kant wants desperately to nullify the dangerous effects of an unruliness he cannot eliminate. That's why this devotee of moral purity calls the element of wildness "perversity." Other things in his characterization of the supersensible and sensible realms move in the direction of minimization too. For the sensible is the realm of appearance as lawful *regularity* and the supersensible is properly the source of morality as lawful *obedience*. When you address the relation of speculative reason to the sensible and of practical reason to the supersensible, the Kantian world becomes doubled over in regularity.

Hannah Arendt responds to the element of wildness in an un-Kantian way. She could easily include Kant when she says that "professional thinkers, whether philosophers or scientists, have not been 'pleased with freedom' and its ineluctable randomness; they have been unwilling to pay the price of contingency for the questionable gift of spontaneity, of being able to do what could also be left undone."[30] Arendt resists the Kantian morality of law; she prizes the element of opacity, division, and wildness in the will; and she resists any metaphysic that gives singular priority to foundational authority, law, regularity, routine, or the unworldly. Arendt, indeed, is impressed by the extent to which the morality of law proved to be impotent under the onslaught of totalitarianism; she is even, perhaps, wary of the degree to which the vaunted simplicity of Kantian morality carries with it a disposition to obedience and thoughtlessness that might spawn acquiescence in the face of a fascist takeover of the state. Arendt worries about the underside of moral purity.

Arendt, by comparison to Kant, is a philosopher of *births and beginnings* as new and surprising events are propelled into the world; of *action* as a mode of politics in which people enact something new exceeding the intentions of the participants prior to their mutual engagement; of *gratitude for being and the appreciation of cultural plurality* as crucial conditions of ethical thoughtfulness in political conduct;[31] and of *publicity, promising, forgiveness and augmentation* as ways to build islands of stability, trust, and responsibility into a world ungoverned by a set of preordained moral laws.[32]

But while Arendt dissolves the purity of morality into a solution of politics, she is sorely tempted to reinstate a corollary model of purity inside the political "realm" itself. To consider Arendt in relation to Kant is to probe again the temptation to purity, the extent to which it is avoidable, and alternative ways in which it might be negotiated. We will focus on three closely interwoven issues: Arendt's bracketing of "the social question" in relation to her opposition to the nation; her depreciation of "the body" in thinking, ethics, and politics; and the restrictive spaces of political action she admires.

Arendt resists all modes of politics organized around the general will, sovereignty, or the nation. These ideals, she insists, engender a politics that suffocates diversity and drowns out the capacity for political action in concert. They reduce politics either to administration or to the thoughtless pressure of social movements. Among other things, they jeopardize the only sort of legitimacy political governance can attain in the modern age. For today to appeal to one universal moral source to justify governance over a plurality of people is to ensure that a whole series of constituencies will be assaulted, suppressed, or excluded; the "we" of governance emerges, then, out of a series of promises across plurality that enable action in concert to occur and stable arrangements to persist.

Arendt's avoidance of the nation is admirable, and, as became clear in chapters 3, 4, and 5, I endorse a version of it. Nonetheless, her avoidance of the social question is often set in the context of resisting the nation. The social question speaks above all to the drive to escape poverty. But it might also involve questions about the organization of work, the governance of the household, the organization of gender and sensual relations, or the sedimentation of an ethos into corporeal sensibilities. Arendt typically links the social question to the urgencies of mass politics. Questions of economy and identity, when urgently felt, draw the multitude into politics, as they did for the "first time" in the French Revolution. "And this multitude, appearing for the first time in broad daylight, was actually the multitude of the poor and the downtrodden, who every century before had hidden in darkness and shame." It becomes a paradigm of the multitude as such.

> What from then on has been irrevocable, and what the agents and spectators of the revolution immediately recognized as such, was that the public realm—reserved as far as memory could reach, to those who *were free*, namely carefree of all the worries that are connected with life's necessity, with bodily needs—should offer its space and its light to this immense majority who are not free because they are driven by bodily needs.[33]

Several Arendtian themes and anxieties are discernible in this formulation. First, Arendt knows that the emergence of the masses into politics is irrevocable; this knowledge informs the melancholy that permeates her writing about modern democratic politics. Second, the eruption of the social question into "broad daylight" introduces a compulsory mood into politics that threatens to overwhelm its deliberative and creative possibilities. Third, this "immense majority who are not free" is translated by the last line into the present tense, signaling again Arendt's recognition that a force has been unleashed that cannot be pushed back into the private realm combined with the sense that nothing very good can come from it. And fourth, Arendt closely connects the social question—poverty—to "bodily needs," to that domain of the automatic and the moody structurally resistant to political elaboration and refinement.

Arendt is alert in a salutary way to how corruptions of the rich and the high readily incite corollary violences and brutalities by the lowly. "Wherever society was permitted to overgrow, and eventually to absorb the political realm, it imposed its own mores and 'moral' standards, the intrigues and perfidies of high society, to which the lower strata responded by violence and brutality."[34] And she makes suggestive points when she compares tendencies on the left to idealize the motives and nobility of the poor with her judgment that "abundance and endless consumption are the ideals of the poor" and that the oppressive experience of poverty is likely to lead to a politics of demand and condemnation of difference rather than self-restraint and free action in concert.

But Arendt is also caught in a dilemma underarticulated in her work. Some of the issues she seeks to insulate from the political realm become by that very means resources through which nationalizing elites can mobilize disaffected constituencies on behalf of the drive to *renationalize* the state. If, for example, many of those chafing under job insecurity and authoritarianism at work are also white, Christian males, failure on the part of nonnationalists to engage the social question sets this constituency up for mobilization by the right to restore a nation of ethnic purity, masculine superiority, and religious unity.[35] The Arendtian exclusion of the social question thus fosters a political result she herself resists. Arendt acknowledges how Indians and slaves were excluded from the founding of the American Republic. But now the dynamics of early American exclusions and entitlements intersect with contemporary effects of the social question upon working-class males of European descent to produce the very effect Arendt wants to avoid (almost) the most: implacable pressure to renationalize the state to restore a putative unity it never really had and to return to the center of power constituencies that never actually occupied it. Arendtians must reconfigure their understanding of the relation between "the social question" and "the political" to better resist these compensatory drives to (re)nationalize the state.

Arendt, however, does not read the danger this way. "Nothing, we might say today, could be more obsolete than to attempt to liberate mankind from poverty by political means; nothing could be more futile and more dangerous."[36] Arendt here binds "liberation" to the social question by restricting her attention to a "Marxist" engagement with that question. But there are approaches that proceed against poverty and job insecurity without binding either pursuit to liberation. The two are bound together by Arendt, perhaps, to use the impossibility of the latter to discredit the credibility of the former. Against Arendt's formulation it must be said that nothing could be more dangerous and futile from the standpoint of a politics seeking to move beyond the nation than to try to bracket the social question from politics. This also means that the Arendtian ideal of politics in small islands of action, such as the Soviet Councils, the localities of early America, and syndicalist organizations must be diversified much further too. The state itself must be embraced as *one* indispensable site of politics, a site containing its share of dangers but also the site most capable of supporting general conditions for the cultural plurality Arendt admires. Indeed, to the extent the social question and the body are purged together from Arendtian plurality, that plurality becomes bleached and aristocratic, expunging modes of ethical cultivation and dimensions of diversity that might otherwise enrich and fortify it.

The masses, Arendt says, are governed by interests or moods whenever they exist in need and remain outside the small precincts of political discussion. Moods and interests are thereby resistant to the type of public discussion that might elevate and refine them. Opinions alone can be discussed and elevated because they are "carefree." There are other things Arendt says that implicitly qualify this disjunction between mood and opinion. But the consideration that presses Arendt to join interests and moods so ponderously to imperative need while linking opinions so lightly to carefree engagement is above all her rendering of the body in relation to thinking, judgment, action, freedom, and politics. Here is a dramatic formulation that binds those elements together:

> The most powerful necessity of which we are aware in self introspection is the life process which permeates our bodies and keeps them in a constant state of change whose movements are automatic, independent of our activities and irresistible—i.e., of an overwhelming urgency. The less we are doing ourselves, the less active we are, the more forcefully will this biological process assert itself, impose its inherent necessity upon us, and overawe us with the fateful automatism of sheer happening that underlies all human history.[17]

It is a mistake to say, then, that Arendt "forgets the body" or "fails to recognize its importance." It is the way she remembers it that requires revision and augmentation. Here Arendt takes one large step in the right direction ("The less we are doing ourselves, the less active we are, the more forcefully will this biological process assert itself"), but then almost cancels its positive effect with another step in the wrong direction. To invoke terms introduced earlier, she implicitly treats all subsystems below the highest levels of conceptual organization to be sunk in a "fateful automatism" that does not even describe the amygdala perfectly. She then declines to come to terms reflectively enough with the regular effects that culturally organized, thought-imbued intensities and feelings have on the *active world of intersubjective thought and political action*. It is sometimes wise to seek to rise above such intensities and feelings. But it is foolish to refuse to draw sustenance from these registers or to address the micropolitics by which thought-imbued feelings of anxiety, disgust, resentment, responsiveness, and generosity enter into patterns of ethical judgment. Arendt does not appreciate sufficiently the profound importance of arts of the self and of micropolitics to the quality of ethical life.

Arendt does not seem to me always to follow her own most programmatic statements in this domain. But such a perspective, *if* relentlessly pursued, not only removes diverse dimensions of life from the politics of enactment such as diet, gender identity, the organization of sensuality, health, the cultural organization of dying, and the cultivation of critical responsiveness. It also places profoundly important dimensions of ethical life beyond the reach of practical action. In general, the Arendtian duality between active thinking and corporeal automatism obscures the extent to which numerous dimensions of corporeality are always already *objects* of extensive political action as well as protean *sources* from which new possibilities of thinking and being might be cast into the world of public appearance.

If Arendt rejects the Kantian "supersensible"—and her repudiation of Kant's conception of morality does not suffice to make me certain of that—and if she then consolidates his dull presentation of sensibility, there remains little space in the Arendtian world for selves to work upon each other to render themselves more responsive to the fundamental contingency of things and less resentful about the human condition as she understands it. Arendt, in effect, cedes micropolitics and arts of the self to the very forces her politics would otherwise resist. The body is more profound and multiplicitous than the soul. But it all sounds too much like humming to her.

In her published lectures on Kant, Arendt works upon the Kantian idea of "common sense," to render it suitable for a philosophy of judgment she can endorse. It never becomes entirely clear (to me) where Arendt stands on the Kantian relation between common sense and the supersensible. For him the judgment of beauty, refracted through a common "taste," both manifests a free accord of the faculties and intimates something fundamental about the form of nature beyond the mechanistic appearance it necessarily presents to our understanding. Arendt focuses upon the way common sense mediates the experiences of taste and smell.

> Hence we may be tempted to conclude that the faculty of judgment is wrongly derived from this sense. Kant being aware of all of the implications of this derivation, remains convinced that it is a correct one. And the most plausible thing in his favor is his observation, entirely correct, that the true opposite of the Beautiful is not the Ugly, but "that which excites *disgust*."[38]

Once more with feeling. . . . I think both Arendt and Kant are right. Disgust does play a role of significance in the ethics of the self and the ethos of a culture. But disgust, on my reading, is reducible neither to the manifestation of a spontaneous accord of the faculties nor to a brute datum of the body. It is a complex corporeo-cultural code of feeling scripted into the cortical organization of the stomach and the brain. Moreover, since disgust, if strong enough to turn the stomach, can readily foster thoughtlessness, its subjective and intersubjective organization has profound effects on political and ethical life. Sometimes a culturally formed feeling of disgust becomes ripe material to work on by experimental methods, say, when a heterodox practice of sexuality disgusts you by threatening the claim to natural superiority of your own sensual disposition. Or when "the Jew" offends your pursuit of national purity even as you endorse equal respect for "persons." Or when a previously conquered indigenous people occupying the same territory as you practices a model of responsibility at odds with the one burned deeply into your stomach and brain. The predicament for Arendt is this: either acknowledge that disgust is a (sometimes) movable feeling of appraisal and thus affirm the ethico-political importance of arts of the self or deny both claims and leave little space to cultivate the positive sensibility she admires in politics. For Arendt herself seeks to enhance that love of the world which, when we are fortunate, is already there to some degree. Of course Arendt believes the sensibility she admires emerges most vibrantly within politics itself, when the conditions are right. And there is much to her point. But a preliminary condition for the salutary effect of publicity upon politics is lacking if too many parties are viscerally predisposed to thoughtlessness on the most important corporeo-cultural issues of the day.

Tactics to modify the infrasensible register of subjectivity and intersubjectivity must be experimental because, since you seldom know exactly how the initial feeling became installed and since you typically lack direct control over triggering scripts in the amygdala, stomach, and elsewhere, you don't quite know in advance how the tactics you adopt will act upon the existing shape and intensity of your sensibility. So you act cautiously and experimentally on those intensities, images, feelings, and concepts that curtail the capacity for responsiveness or thoughtfulness in this or that domain. Surely some dimensions in Arendt's thought press in the direction of such tactics, for she herself emphasizes the connection between thoughtlessness and the "banality of evil." And yet her portrayal of corporeality drives a wedge between its complexity and those tactics that might modify the sensibility within which thoughtfulness and thoughtlessness are set.

Arendt is admirable in her resistance to the Kantian purification of morality and in her linkage of ethics to a love of the world. Her appreciation of how the new comes into being is impressive and her refusal to buy into disenchanted interpretations of the world is admirable. But her intercoded orientations to the social question, the body, and spaces of political action tend to relocate the quest for purity in the domain of politics. Her rendering of the body is the pivot upon which the other two dispositions turn. But the body contains a relatively mobile, stratified, unfinished set of sites *from* which new energies and surprising experiments emerge and *upon* which multiple cultural scripts are unevenly and imperfectly written. The Arendtian politics of action will thus be enriched immeasurably when corporeo-cultural scripts become issues of political engagement.

Deep Pluralism

Kant's drive to moral purity is bound up with his attempt to refigure the Christian two-world metaphysic in the wake of a Newtonian revolution that placed traditional versions of Christianity in jeopardy. And Arendt? Does this twentieth-century inhabitant of a post-Newtonian world endorse a two-world metaphysic? Or is she a charter member of that large and growing club in the *academy* that purports to move "beyond metaphysics," or to be "postmetaphysical," or "political, not metaphysical," or "postfoundational"?[39] It is hard to say, though some of her most sympathetic interpreters place her in the postmetaphysical camp.[40] I want to suggest, however, that the experiment to reach beyond metaphysics—often celebrated today by academics who purport to be practical and pragmatic in politics—has failed both theoretically and practically. It has failed theoretically because of the constitutive ambiguity in the term *metaphysics* itself, signaling both that which is most fundamental to a perspective and that which goes beyond the physical, the sensible, or the realm of appearance. It is thus always possible, by reference to one term or the other, to show how others remain entangled in metaphysical issues they pretend to leave behind. Indeed, a whole academic mill grinds out such charges and countercharges on a regular basis, with several grinders then implying that they have now washed their own hands clean of metaphysics or, at least, "controversial" metaphysical assumptions.

Moreover, academics are pretty much the only people in politics who effect the postmetaphysical pretense in the name of practicality. Most other participants either explicitly adopt a religious version of a two-world metaphysic, implicitly express it in their drives to practicality, find themselves caught in a struggle between two or three such perspectives, or strive to develop an alternative to dominant perspectives as they address the adverse effects upon themselves and others of the identities commonly projected upon them.

It seems to me that an overt metaphysical/religious pluralism in public life provides one key to forging a positive ethos of engagement out of the multidimensional plurality of contemporary life. In such a culture, participants are called upon neither to leave their metaphysical baggage at home when they participate in various publics nor to adopt an overarching faith acknowledged by all parties who strive to promote the common good. Rather, a deep plurality of religious/metaphysical perspectives is incorporated into public discourses.

Politics does not now become reducible to metaphysical debate (although someone may well concoct such a reduction to knock it down again), and often enough this dimension can be placed in abeyance to defuse a political debate or negotiate a difficult settlement. But it is often pertinent to place such questions on the register of public debate when issues appear such as the right to die, abortion, gender politics, the legitimate range of sensual diversity, the character of responsibility, the appropriate responses to criminality, the project of becoming a nation, or the comparative value of an ethic of cultivation. For in these domains today some parties to the debate *already* assert a general metaphysical orientation as if it were unquestionable, while a variety of liberals and secularists hesitate to contest the certainty of these assumptions actively. Indeed, today the power of the metaphysical politics of William Bennett, Pauline Hanson, and others to shift the terms of debate toward the right depends to a significant degree upon the failure of many who resist them to contest the metaphysical orthodoxies they invoke.

Incorporating deep plurality into existing political pluralism is consonant with democracy if and when an ethos of engagement is negotiated between numerous constituencies honoring different assumptions and moral sources. The negotiation of such an ethos, in turn, depends upon reciprocal acknowledgment by a significant set of partisans of the uncertainty and profound contestability of the metaphysical suppositions and moral sources they honor the most. Such acknowledgment does not take these debates off the public register; rather, it increases their salience. First, such debates increase the chances of more partisans coming to terms with those elements of comparative contestability in their own perspectives, rather than treating this domain as one either irrelevant to practical issues or unsusceptible to reconsideration. Indeed, those two views complement and reinforce one another, for they combine to pull the metaphysical dimension out of public discussion. Second, public debate over such presumptions in the context of specific issues can often be productive. Others may pose questions or alternatives that press you to clarify your thinking, or to modify it. Or a new line of thought may open up paths previously unexplored by any party. Or you may find heretofore overlooked points of connection between subthemes in your perspective and central themes in the perspective of others. Or some dramatic issue that plagues you may assume a different appearance, replete with new possibilities of response.

The profound contestability of deep judgments, then, is quite compatible with appreciation of ways in which debate, deliberation, and arts of the self can have profound effects upon judgment. Everyone can point to some conversion experience, replete with the intensities that made it compelling and the new thoughts that enabled its consolidation. Such experiences are unlikely to disappear in the future. But it also seems unlikely that a universal conversion experience will emerge that reduces the range of viable cultural alternatives to one. At least it has not happened yet; and vigilant attempts to generate singularity in this domain have so far fostered totalistic societies. Indeed, such a consensual condition is even more unlikely today than in the past because of the acceleration of mobility and speed in so many domains of life. Nor does it seem likely, at least to me, that the post-metaphysical pretense will persist much longer. The most noble aspiration, then, is to pursue an ethos of engagement among numerous constituencies in a world of deep, multidimensional plurality. That aspiration, in turn, is bound to the hope that many will come to appreciate the need for general practices of economic and educational inclusion that support the conditions of multidimensional pluralism. Such inclusive practices are far more likely to emerge from a pluralist ethos of forbearance and generosity in which many have a stake than from anywhere else. The problem is that the ethos of plurality and the politics of economic inclusion each set conditions of possibility for the other; neither advances very far until the other makes progress.

If and as a democratic ethos of engagement across multidimensional lines of difference and collaboration is negotiated, the contestable metaphysic of the infrasensible and the sensible can make a positive contribution to it. When this fundamental orientation is joined to a sensibility that *affirms* the ambiguity of being and the deep contingency of things it supports an intra-cultural ethos of agonistic respect among contending constituencies and critical responsiveness to the politics of becoming. It thereby makes contact with some contemporary movements within religions of the Book and secularism proceeding toward a similar place from different starting points. It also brings distinctive considerations to bear upon those ubiquitous arts of the self, turning them toward cultivation of critical responsiveness to the politics of becoming in a pluralistic world moving at a faster pace than heretofore. Because its ethic is organized around cultivation of care for the plurivocity of being, it brings distinctive energies to an ethos of engagement among diverse constituencies. Moreover, the very character of its assumptions encourages its partisans not only to thematize the element of surprise in political life but also to emphasize the comparative contestability of diverse orientations in this domain, including its own. Finally, though the hopes and aspirations it supports occasionally stretch far beyond the realities of actually existing politics, this feature provides yet another point of connection between it and other regulative ideals of politics. Besides, nothing is more unrealistic today than to insist upon the incontrovertibility of a particular metaphysical faith or to pretend to bypass this dimension of politics altogether.

If we participate increasingly in a world in which a variety of fundamental perspectives gain a significant presence in cultural life while no party has so far shown its perspective to be undeniable, reciprocal acknowledgment of this condition can widen the politics of forbearance, generosity, and selective collaboration between interdependent partisans. Murmurs of progress toward such a deep pluralism are audible in several quarters of contemporary life. Such murmurs may be silenced. We have already seen how the drive to conquer plurality and pluralization proceeds. But they might also resonate more widely as the positive effects of cultural negotiations among a plurality of constituencies become more deeply inscribed in our sensibilities. No definite effect, of course, can be assured in a world where the ethical dimension of political life is both indispensable and fragile. That's politics.

Notes

Introduction

1. Reprinted in Bertrand Russell, *Why I Am Not a Christian* (London: George Allen & Unwin, 1957), appendix titled "How Bertrand Russell Was Prevented from Teaching at the College of the City of New York," 182.

2. The judge, quoted in ibid., 192. Following is a small sample of the outrages against civilization the judge cited: "It is not necessary to detail here the filth which is contained in the books. It is sufficient to record the following. From *Education and the Modern World,* pages 119 and 120: 'I am sure that university life would be better, both intellectually and morally, if most university students had temporary childless marriages. This would afford a solution to the sexual urge neither restless nor surreptitious, neither mercenary nor casual, of such a nature that it need not take up time which ought to be given to work'" (199). And, finally, "While this court could not interfere with any action of the board insofar as a pure question of 'valid' academic freedom is concerned, it will not tolerate academic freedom being used as a cloak to promote the popularization in the minds of adolescents of acts forbidden by the Penal Law" (202).

3. Both the quotation from Russell cited by the judge and the statement by the judge are quoted in ibid., 204.

4. Paul Edwards, "Introduction," in Russell, *Why I Am Not a Christian,* viii.

5. In particular, they become burned into that brain called the amygdala, the Latin word for almond, which, in turn, characterizes the shape of this brain at the base of the prefrontal cortex. More about this in chapter 1.

6. It is pertinent here to call attention to a book by Barbara Herrnstein Smith, *Belief and Resistance: Dynamics of Contemporary Intellectual Controversy* (Cambridge: Harvard University Press, 1997). She shows how various performances of the self-performative contradiction depend upon a reworking of key terms until they have

moved away from several meanings invested in their initial presentation and toward a tight network of definitions that capture the unwary in circles. It is a very thoughtful and timely study. I would add that there are times when thought gets caught in paradox. The question then is the mood or temper with which you approach that effect and what you think it may indicate. I pursue this issue in chapter 1.

7. The ethical importance of treating my own perspective as contestable is discussed in the symposium "William Connolly's *The Ethos of Pluralization*," *Philosophy and Social Criticism* (January 1988): 63–102. In this symposium, Donald Moon, Stephen White, and Frederick Dolan offer very thoughtful critiques of *The Ethos of Pluralization* (Minneapolis: University of Minnesota Press, 1995), to which I reply. The issues posed there help to set up the themes of this study.

8. See Jane Bennett, "The Enchantments of Modernity: Paracelsus, Kant and Deleuze," *Cultural Values* (Winter 1997), and "'How Is It, Then, That We Still Remain Barbarians?': Schiller, Foucault, and the Aestheticization of Ethics," *Political Theory* (November 1996).

1. The Conceits of Secularism

1. An excellent version of this story is told by Albert Hirschman in *The Passions and the Interests: Political Arguments for Capitalism Before Its Triumph* (Princeton, N.J.: Princeton University Press, 1977).

2. For an engaging version of this story, see Hans Blumenberg, *The Legitimacy of the Modern Age,* trans. Robert Wallace (Cambridge: MIT Press, 1983). This is an indispensable element in any story I would endorse. One of its effects is to call into question those stories of secularism as a loss of Christian community engendered by the forces of science, capital, and secular morality alone. For movements within Christianity itself also helped to pave the way for this possibility. I pursue some of these themes in *Political Theory and Modernity* (Oxford: Basil Blackwell, 1988; 2d ed. with new epilogue, Ithaca, N.Y.: Cornell University Press, 1993). I will address others shortly.

3. Such a reading is discernible in Foucault's essay "Governmentality," in *The Foucault Effect,* ed. Graham Burchell, Colin Gordon, and Peter Miller (Chicago: University of Chicago Press, 1991), 87–105. A wonderful exploration of Foucault's work by Thomas Dumm, *Michel Foucault and the Politics of Freedom* (Thousand Oaks, Calif.: Sage, 1996), provides several elements in that interpretation.

4. John Rawls, *Political Liberalism* (Cambridge: Harvard University Press, 1993), 151–52. The quotes in the preceding paragraph are from 148.

5. Editorial, *First Things* (January 1997), 27.

6. Alexis de Tocqueville, *Democracy in America,* 2 vols., trans. George Lawrence (New York: Harper & Row, 1969), 292.

7. Ibid., 290–91.

8. Talal Asad, *Genealogies of Religion* (Baltimore: Johns Hopkins University Press, 1993), 63.

9. Friedrich Nietzsche, *The Anti-Christ,* trans. R. J. Hollingdale (New York: Vintage, 1968), 151.

10. See Friedrich Nietzsche, *Twilight of the Idols,* trans. R. J. Hollingdale (New York: Vintage, 1968), 82, and *The Gay Science,* trans. Walter Kaufmann (New York: Vintage, 1974), 274, no. 8. Drawing inspiration from Gilles Deleuze, Brian Massumi

probes the "autonomy of affect" in *Deleuze: A Critical Reader*, ed. Paul Patton (Oxford: Blackwell, 1996). Massumi's rich essay correlates nicely with the above quotations from Nietzsche, and it also gains support from LeDoux's work, to be addressed shortly, on the complex circuits connecting the multiple brains within each individual.

11. Nietzsche, *The Gay Science*, no. 9.

12. Joseph LeDoux, *The Emotional Brain: The Mysterious Underpinnings of Emotional Life* (New York: Simon & Schuster, 1996), 258.

13. Ibid., 303.

14. For a review of how several neo-Kantian secularists reduce "the aestheticization of ethics" to a caricature and a set of thoughtful corrections to these misrepresentations, see Jane Bennett, "'How Is It, Then, That We Still Remain Barbarians?': Schiller, Foucault, and the Aestheticization of Ethics," *Political Theory* (November 1996).

15. I concentrate here on the implications of the Kantian ideal of the university for the organization of public life. Kant himself pursues such implications as he proceeds. For an excellent account that focuses on the university, see Barry Hindess, "Great Expectations: Freedom and Authority in the Idea of a Modern University," *Oxford Literary Review* 17 (1995): 29–51.

16. An excellent reading of Kant's *Conflict of the Faculties* can be found in Ian Hunter, "Conflicting Enlightenments: Kant's True Rational Religion," *Political Theory Newsletter* (December 1995): 20–35. Hunter presented an earlier version of this paper at Johns Hopkins University in 1994, and it became clear to me then that I would need to engage this text. Hunter explores Kant's ambivalence about disciplines of the sensuous self in a subtle way. He also is very clear about the role of rational religion in Kant's version of enlightenment. Finally, he suggests that Thomasius offered a better model for secularism than that presented by Kant and followed by many contemporary secularists.

17. Immanuel Kant, *The Conflict of the Faculties*, trans. Mary J. Gregor (Lincoln: University of Nebraska Press, 1979), 89.

18. Ibid., 81.

19. Ibid., 115–17; emphasis added.

20. The engagement by Jürgen Habermas with Kant's conception of public life is very insightful on these issues. Although I will shortly take issue with the conception of the public sphere in Habermas's *The Structural Transformation of the Public Sphere*, trans. Thomas Burger and Frederick Lawrence (Cambridge: MIT Press, 1989), this book, originally published in 1962, has several admirable traits, including an engagement with Kant that addresses thoughtfully the tension between Kant's conception of moral life and his projected teleology of progress by automatic means in public life.

21. Ibid., 164.

22. Ibid., 175.

23. Ibid., 179.

24. Ibid., 210.

25. Ibid., 215.

26. Thomas Dumm, in *Michel Foucault and the Politics of Freedom*, pursues sensitively the relation between freedom and the organization of political space. See particularly chapter 2, "Freedom and Space."

27. Jürgen Habermas, *Postmetaphysical Thinking*, trans. William M. Hohengarten (Cambridge: MIT Press, 1992), 139–40.

28. I review several of them, as well as some of the elements that might go into such an ethos, in *The Ethos of Pluralization* (Minneapolis: University of Minnesota Press, 1995).

29. Habermas, *Postmetaphysical Thinking,* 32.

30. Habermas makes this move easier for himself by tending to equate all such perspectives with the thought of Theodor Adorno. He sees pessimism built right into Adorno's "negative metaphysics," whereas I see much of Adorno's pessimism to flow from the awful particulars of life under Nazism in a world where even most opponents of Nazism were unable or unwilling to rise above "identitarian thinking." But that is another story. Romand Coles paves the way for it in *Rethinking Generosity: Critical Theory and the Politics of Caritas* (Ithaca, N.Y.: Cornell University Press, 1997).

31. Habermas, *Postmetaphysical Thinking,* 36.

32. Ibid., 41.

33. Gilles Deleuze, *Difference and Repetition,* trans. Paul Patton (New York: Columbia University Press, 1994), 227–28.

34. Further clarifications, responses, and challenges are possible. For example, Barbara Herrnstein Smith, in *Belief and Resistance: Dynamics of Contemporary Intellectual Controversy* (Cambridge: Harvard University Press, 1997), argues that the trap of the performative contradiction is often set by subtle redefinitions of key terms by the critic, pulling discussants away from the multiple, culturally informed uses of those about to be entrapped. It is this translation that does the job, if it remains unnoticed or unchallenged by others. See chapters 6 and 7 of her book for a refined engagement with the vocabularies of critical reason.

35. Habermas, *Postmetaphysical Thinking,* 145.

36. Deleuze, *Difference and Repetition,* 95.

37. For a discussion of the difference, see Jane Bennett, "The Enchantments of Modernity: Paracelsus, Kant and Deleuze," *Cultural Values* (Winter 1997).

38. Kierkegaard: "Or there is the man who says he has faith, but now he wants to make his faith clear to himself; he wants to understand himself in faith. Now the comedy begins again. . . . On the contrary, he has learned to know something different about faith than he believed and has learned to know that he no longer has faith, since he almost knows, as good as knows, to a high degree and exceedingly knows." *Concluding Unscientific Postscript to Philosophical Fragments,* ed. and trans. Howard Hong and Edna Hong (Princeton, N.J.: Princeton University Press, 1992), 211.

39. Deleuze, *Difference and Repetition,* 95.

40. Ibid., 96.

41. My reading, augmentation, and consequent endorsement of Deleuze on this point seems to me to parallel compelling points Judith Butler makes about Foucault on identity in *The Psychic Life of Power* (Stanford, Calif.: Stanford University Press, 1997), chap. 3. She is talking about identity, and I am discussing theistic faith or its denial, but the two logics are close. "For Foucault, the symbolic produces the possibility of its own subversions, and these subversions are unanticipated effects of symbolic interpellations" (98). Later, in chapters 5 and 6, I will explore another element in this picture more extensively, one covered in this chapter under the headings of the visceral and the infrasensible. According to Foucault (and me), the subject does not reside simply in the symbolic, or merely at those moments of subversion within it, though these are extremely important. The most productive and fateful sites are

those points of intersection between the symbolic and tactics or disciplines not entirely reducible to the symbolic. It is at such intersections where disciplinary power operates and where arts of the self do their best work. When Althusser's cop hails a pedestrian, the interpellation is accompanied by the possibility, and sometimes the actuality, of being handcuffed or beaten with a nightstick. It is partly because the latter happens often enough that it enters into your imagination when you are hailed. When a "straight" steps into a gay rights march for the first time, one part of the anxiety may involve the fear of being identified under that label and another part may be bound up with the imagination of becoming an object of violence. To participate may thus be to do some work on the visceral register of subjectivity as well as to support a cause with which you identify.

42. The prefix *theistic* in front of faith and faithlessness is significant. I do not claim that atheism is without an element of faith—it just does not inflect that faith as theistic.

2. Suffering, Justice, and the Politics of Becoming

1. John Caputo, *Against Ethics* (Bloomington: Indiana University Press, 1993), 145.

2. Ibid., 158.

3. Ibid., 203.

4. Ibid., 200.

5. "We cannot just avoid or simply step outside metaphysics, which would mean to step outside the logic and ontologic or our grammar and our intellectual habits." Ibid., 221.

6. Ibid., 222.

7. Ibid., 4.

8. The prefix *meta* "is joined chiefly to verbs and verbal derivatives; the principal notions which it expresses are: sharing; action in common; pursuit or quest; and, especially, change of place, order, condition, or Nature." *OED*.

9. The issues are still more complicated, of course. It is very difficult, some say impossible, to write and speak a European language without invoking implicitly a fundamental order or logic that governs everything. Caputo acknowledges this. He has read his Derrida. But I concur with Nietzsche, Michel Foucault, and Gilles Deleuze that we do possess some resources within these languages to press a positive alternative forward that is not completely captured by the old doctrines. This is a debate I will not pursue further here.

10. Friedrich Nietzsche, *Thus Spoke Zarathustra*, trans. Walter Kaufmann (New York: Penguin, 1978), 200–201.

11. Friedrich Nietzsche, *Beyond Good and Evil*, trans. Marianne Cowan (South Bend, Ind.: Gateway Editions, 1955), 58.

12. Is *gratitude* the right word here? If so, it has to be reworked so that it is not governed by the idea that you are always grateful to some agent(s). But every word Nietzsche tries in this domain has to be reworked to play the role he asks it to play. Wonder, (nontheistic) reverence, awe, affirmation are other possibilities, equally in need of reworking. Is it Nietzsche's fault that the language of the Christian/secular

West is often inadequate to his thought? Reworking familiar terms is part of the ethical project.

13. Friedrich Nietzsche, *Twilight of the Idols,* trans. R. J. Hollingdale (New York: Penguin, 1968), 92. I am grateful to comments by Jill Frank, Mort Schoolman, and George Shulman on this point.

14. Nietzsche, *Beyond Good and Evil,* 151–52.

15. Some themes in the relation of ethics to the politics of becoming cannot be pursued here. For example, "gratitude" is certainly not a sufficient basis of ethics on my reading; it is, rather, an element that must flow through established codes, contracts, identities, interests, and habits of responsiveness if they are to be generous, if care for difference is to find operational expression in them. This chapter is a companion to another essay that sets forth this perspective. See "Beyond Good and Evil: The Ethical Sensibility of Michel Foucault," *Political Theory* (August 1993).

16. I discuss the politics of identity\difference relations in *Identity\Difference: Democratic Negotiations of Political Paradox* (Ithaca, N.Y.: Cornell University Press, 1991). In that book I give more attention to how state and corporate institutions constitute identities. Here the focus is on the politics of social movements by which elements in those identities are modified.

17. Jan Clausen, "My Interesting Condition," *Outlook: National Lesbian and Gay Quarterly* (Winter 1990): 19.

18. Ibid., 20, 21.

19. Arthur Kleinman, *Rethinking Psychiatry: From Cultural Category to Personal Experience* (New York: Free Press, 1991), 7.

20. The following statement by I. Rosenfield, quoted by Kleinman, makes contact with the Nietzschean conception of nature as unfinished. "There are good biological reasons to question the idea of fixed universal categories. In a broad sense they run counter to the principles of Darwinian theory of evolution. Darwin stressed that populations are collections of unique individuals. In the biological world there is no typical plant.... Qualities we associate with human beings and other animals are abstractions invented by us that miss the nature of biological variation." Ibid., 19.

21. For example, a child of a "colored" mother was automatically defined as black, regardless of skin tone, during the period of slavery in America. This protected the sexual rights of slaveholding white fathers over enslaved mothers and exempted them from embarrassment or responsibility for the consequences. This, in turn, supported a double imperative against white women having sex with black men, an injunction still operative to some degree; for that combination would compromise the "purity" of the white race. Sons and daughters of mixed parenthood today still bear the effects of these two legacies. They are presumed "black," unless a whole set of other social factors override that presumption. "Whiteness" is the absence of that which makes you "black."

22. John Rawls, *Political Liberalism* (New York: Columbia University Press, 1993), 51; emphasis added.

23. For a very thoughtful effort to locate Rawls in the tradition of "virtue theories," see Bonnie Honig, *Political Theory and the Displacement of Politics* (Ithaca, N.Y.: Cornell University Press, 1993).

24. "All this presupposes the fundamental ideas of justice as fairness are present in the public culture, or at least implicit in the history of its main institutions and the

traditions of their interpretation." Rawls, *Political Liberalism,* 78. Here is a set of Rawlsian considerations that could be brought to bear against the sufficiency of this implicit/explicit logic, but are not: "a) the evidence . . . bearing on the case is conflicting and complex. . . . b) Even when we agree fully about the kinds of considerations we may disagree about their weight. . . . c) To some extent all our concepts . . . are vague and subject to hard cases. . . . d) To some extent . . . the way we assess evidence . . . is shaped by our total experience, our whole course of life up to now. . . . e) Often there are different kinds of normative considerations . . . on both sides of an issue. . . . f) Finally . . . , any system of social institutions is limited in the values it can admit so that some selections must be made from the full range of moral and political values that might be realized" (56–57). Rawls seems to think these factors enter into reflection by reasonable persons about fundamental doctrines, but not so necessarily or actively into the practice of justice they share while holding a variety of reasonable doctrines.

25. I discuss "fundamentalism in America" in chapter 3 of *The Ethos of Pluralization* (Minneapolis: University of Minnesota Press, 1995). That book, more generally, explores the constitutive tension between pluralism and pluralization and how some of the very conditions of possibility for pluralization also foster pressures toward fundamentalism.

26. Rawls, *Political Liberalism,* 118.

27. Ibid., 122.

28. It actually reinforces the central point. For if you could devise a sufficient *code* in advance to adjudicate between acceptable and unacceptable movements of difference, critical responsiveness would not be required as an ethical counter and supplement to justice. An additional point: in this essay I focus on the relation of "critical responsiveness" to the politics of becoming. I do so because this dimension has been underplayed by both theorists of sufficient justice and defenders of the politics of becoming. But of course agents of *initiation* are crucial to the politics of becoming. You might be on one side of that line in some instances (for example, women involved in feminist initiatives) and on the other side in others (for example, white, Christian, heterosexual women responding to the politics of becoming by African Americans, gays/lesbians, and atheists). Often enough, you will be on both sides to different degrees on the same issue. The politics of becoming probably has a better chance in a culture where most "subject positions" are multiple, and where most people find themselves on the initiating side in some domains and the responsive side in others.

29. Because chapter 6 engages other alternatives, let me anticipate. Participants in an ethos of engagement draw selective aspects of their fundamental doctrines, as needed, into public engagements; they occasionally practice arts of the self and micropolitics on the visceral register of subjectivity and intersubjectivity; they participate in a culture that is more rhizomatic or networked than the centered picture of an overlapping consensus allows; many of them supplement the practices of tolerance and justice with those of agonistic respect, critical responsiveness, and studied indifference; and many honor the politics of becoming while understanding it to stand in a paradoxical relation of tension and interdependence with the politics of being. Or, in more subtle terms, they appreciate the element of becoming already inscribed in being.

30. I criticize Seyla Benhabib's dialectical interpretation of the politics of becoming in *The Ethos of Pluralization,* chap. 6. It now seems to me that I underemphasize

there my own ambivalent relation to the model she develops. I like this rendering better.

31. A Heideggerian would resist this antinomy between being and becoming on the grounds that difference inhabits being as such and that the "oblivion of being" in Western history is bound up with the demand to make Being into a solid ground. Heidegger criticizes the Nietzschean separation between being and becoming, finding it to be connected to Nietzsche's implication in the metaphysical tradition. There is something to Heidegger's point, but I join Nietzsche in finding it economical to bring out the profound ambiguity within Being by setting up a tension between being and becoming in the political domain. Heidegger's way of waiting for the release of being is too unpolitical in my judgment, but Nietzsche's way is not that much better. Neither attends carefully to the politics of becoming. An excellent rendering of the oblivion of being is found in Heidegger's *Identity and Difference,* trans. Joan Stambaugh (New York: Harper & Row, 1969). I also concur that the oblivion of being (difference) is never recuperated directly, but only experienced indirectly through the effects of its movement.

3. Liberalism, Secularism, and the Nation

1. A chimera, according to *Merriam-Webster's Collegiate Dictionary* (10th ed.), is "a fire-breathing she-monster in Greek mythology"; "an imaginary monster compounded of incongruous parts"; and "an illusion or fabrication of the mind." The chimera of the nation, as I will think it, is an illusion that engenders monstrous effects when it is treated as an imperative to pursue or restore.

2. Ernst Renan, "What Is a Nation?" in *The Nationalist Reader,* ed. Moar Chabour and Micheline R. Ishay (New York: Humanities Press, 1995), 148. The essay was originally published in 1882.

3. "It is to the honor of France that she has never tried to attain unity of language by means of coercion. Is it impossible to cherish the same feelings and thoughts and to love the same things in different languages?" Ibid. Renan seems to think it is. And some may think that France, Quebec, and the United States have become more vociferous about the need for a common language today than Renan would have expected. Finally, note the problematic use of "unity" and "same" in this sentence.

4. Ibid., 153.

5. Ibid.

6. John Stuart Mill, *Considerations on Representative Government,* ed. Currin V. Shields (New York: Liberal Arts, 1958), 6. The essay was first published in 1861.

7. Ibid., 35.

8. Ibid., 34.

9. Ibid.

10. "It is not sufficiently considered how little there is in most men's ordinary life to give any largeness either to their conceptions or to their sentiments. Their work is a routine; not a labor of love, but of self-interest...; neither the thing done nor the process of doing it introduces the mind to thoughts or feelings extending beyond individuals; if instructive books are within their reach, there is no stimulus to read them; and in most cases the individuals lack access to any person of cultivation." Ibid., 53. Mill, certainly, wanted to lift ordinary people out of the ruts and harsh rou-

tines of ordinary life. He thought that participation in governance was one way to accomplish that, in combination with reforms in education and the distribution of income. I am with Mill on these points. I even think that cultural elites could teach regular folks a thing or two sometimes, as well as the other way around. But the point here is to underline how prominent patricians are in the Millian language of "minority" and what a major role concern for *this* minority plays in the Millian scheme of proportional representation.

11. Ibid., 59, 59, 32, 24, 7, 63, respectively.

12. Ibid., 230.

13. Ibid., 121; emphasis added.

14. Ibid., 229; emphasis added.

15. Ibid.; emphasis added.

16. For an excellent discussion of the implications of different strategies of mapping, see Michael Shapiro, *Violent Cartographies: Mapping Cultures of War* (Minneapolis: University of Minnesota Press, 1997).

17. Mill, *On Representative Government*, 232.

18. Ibid., 233.

19. Ibid., 234; emphasis added.

20. Ibid.

21. Ibid., 236.

22. I am indebted to Sid Maskit for this point.

23. Consider Deleuze and Félix Guattari on flows, for instance: "But there is no Power regulating the flows themselves. No one dominates the growth of the 'monetary mass,' or money supply. If an image of the master or an idea of the state is projected outward to the limits of the universe, as if something had domination over flows, as well as segments, and in the same manner, the result is a fictitious and ridiculous representation. The stock exchange gives a better image of flows and their quanta than does the State." *A Thousand Plateaus*, trans. Brian Massumi (Minneapolis: University of Minnesota Press, 1987), 226. Deleuze and Guattari are neither indeterminists nor causalists in the traditional sense. Their multicausalism projects a world of multiple, microcausal agents too dense in texture and multiple in shape to be captured entirely by any explanatory theory. They are thus philosophers who do not seek deep *explanations,* but, rather, to find strategic points of *intervention* in institutional complexes. But many critics miss this point, asserting over and over, "Deleuze can't explain this..." "Foucault fails to account for that...," thereby defending a dubious model of explanation by pointing to those who explicitly refuse to try to live up to it.

24. Jean-Jacques Rousseau, *The Government of Poland*, trans. Willmoore Kendall (New York: Dobbs-Merrill, 1972). Rousseau writes about a nation coming into being under adverse conditions of actualization, whereas Mill writes about a people who already take themselves to be a nation.

25. I concur with both Rousseau and Mill in thinking that the reduction of economic inequality sets a precondition for a state that enables all to participate in the general life. The production of a "rabble" closed out of the general life does not, as Hegel suggests, simply produce alienation; it sets up some disaffected constituencies participating in traditional ethnic, religious, and linguistic practices to support movements to renationalize the state. I disagree with Hegel and Mill, who think that a *nation*-state sets a precondition to state action to reduce economic inequality, and with

Hannah Arendt, who thinks that bracketing "the social question" is needed to escape the oppressiveness of nationalism. A rhizomatic pluralism in which an ethos of ago-nistic respect and critical responsiveness between diverse constituencies has been developed provides the best condition for formation of collective assemblages in sup-port of reducing inequality. For a reflection on the paradoxical relation of interde-pendence and tension between reducing inequality and promoting pluralism, see William E. Connolly, *The Ethos of Pluralization* (Minneapolis: University of Minnesota Press, 1995), chaps. 3, 4.

26. It is pertinent to recall that existing inequalities of race and class have arisen in states where the image of the nation has assumed priority for a few centuries and where national calls to redress those inequalities have not been very successful.

27. Critical responsiveness to new constituencies in the process of coming into being is a crucial part of the perspective projected here. I discuss it in chapters 2 and 6 of this study.

28. To rethink pluralism and secularism in an age of the globalization of capital and the acceleration of pace is to set the stage for a reconsideration of existing mod-els of cosmopolitanism too. The Kantian model of cosmopolitanism is poorly suited to the late-modern time. Today we witness the fragile beginnings and future possibility of a more layered cosmopolitanism, one in which citizens participate in cross-national movements above the state as well as movements within it.

29. I discuss the ethos of engagement needed to sustain these multidimensional relations in more detail in chapter 6.

4. Freelancing the Nation

1. Editorial, *Canberra Times,* August 2, 1997. The same paper the next day re-ported how American leaders were trying to promote international pressure to op-pose the Australian experiment. Eventually, the Howard government stopped the ACT from carrying out its experiment.

2. William J. Bennett, *The De-Valuing of America: The Fight for Our Culture and Our Children* (New York: Simon & Schuster, 1992), 25.

3. Bennett quoting and endorsing a statement by Midge Decter in ibid., 258.

4. Ibid., 36, 99.

5. Ibid., 94.

6. Ibid., 36.

7. Ibid., 105.

8. Ibid., 133.

9. Ibid., 118.

10. Ibid., 103.

11. Ibid., 103–4.

12. Ibid., 116.

13. Here is how Bennett puts it: "The reaction was illustrative. Many of the elites ridiculed my opinion. But it resonated with the American people because they knew what drugs were doing, and they wanted a morally proportionate response." Ibid., 116.

14. Slovoj Zizek, *Tarrying with the Negative* (Durham, N.C.: Duke University Press, 1993), 14.

5. The Will, Capital Punishment, and Cultural War

1. Augustine, *The Confessions of St. Augustine,* trans. John K. Ryan (New York: Image, 1960), bk. 8, chap. 9, 196–97.

2. Ibid., bk. 8, chap. 9, 197.

3. Cesare Beccaria, *On Crimes and Punishments,* trans. David Young (New York: Hackett, 1986), 17.

4. Ibid., 49.

5. Immanuel Kant, *Critique of Practical Reason,* trans. Lewis W. Beck (New York: Macmillan, 1993), 90.

6. Ibid., 104.

7. Immanuel Kant, *The Metaphysics of Morals,* trans. Mary Gregor (Cambridge: Cambridge University Press: 1991), 141–42.

8. Kant, *Critique of Practical Reason,* 104–5.

9. Friedrich Nietzsche, *Human All Too Human,* trans. R. J. Hollinger (New York: Cambridge University Press, 1986), 306.

10. Sister Helen Prejean, *Dead Man Walking* (New York: Random House, 1994).

11. Ibid., 235–36.

12. Ibid., 226.

13. James Q. Wilson and Richard J. Herrnstein, *Crime and Human Nature: The Definitive Study of the Causes of Crime* (New York: Simon & Schuster, 1985).

14. Ibid., 505–6.

15. V. P. Hans, "Death by Jury," in Norman J. Finkel, *Commonsense Justice: Jurors' Notions of the Law* (Cambridge: Harvard University Press, 1995), 184.

16. Quoted in Austin Sarat, "Speaking of Death: Narratives of Violence in Capital Trials," in *The Rhetoric of Law,* ed. Austin Sarat and Thomas R. Kearns (Ann Arbor: University of Michigan Press, 1994), 168–69.

17. For an account of the relation between ethics and desanctification of selective elements within one's own subjectivity, see my "The Desanctification of Subjectivity," *Theory & Event* (Winter 1998) (http //muse jhu edu/journals/theory & event/V001.2).

18. Wendy Brown, in a superb chapter in *States of Injury: Power and Freedom in Late-Modernity* (Princeton, N.J.: Princeton University Press, 1995) titled "Wounded Attachments," explores how the attachments people form to destructive modes of their own subjection can foster profound resentments seeking legitimate outlets. "Insofar as what Nietzsche calls slave morality produces identity in relation to power, insofar as identity rooted in this reaction achieves its moral superiority by reproaching power and action themselves as evil, identity... becomes deeply invested in its own impotence, even while it seeks to assuage the pain of its powerlessness through its vengeful moralizing, through its wide distribution of suffering.... Indeed, it is more likely to punish and reproach—'punishment is what revenge calls itself—...' than to find venues of self-affirming action" (71). This book, and in particular that chapter, explores deeply and persistently the psychological and social mechanisms engaged here with respect to capital punishment.

19. William J. Bennett, *The De-Valuing of America: The Fight for Our Culture and Our Children* (New York: Simon & Schuster, 1992), 116.

20. Ibid.

21. Ibid., 173.

22. These quotations occur between pages 199 and 202 of Albert Camus's "Reflection on The Guillotine," in *Resistance, Rebellion and Death,* trans. Justin O'Brien (New York: Vintage, 1960).

23. Prejean, *Dead Man Walkin,* 156.

24. I suppose that Nietzsche can help on the first front, whereas thinkers like Arendt and Foucault might help on the second. The problem, for starters, is that few of us are now prepared to show how each front is entangled in the other and not too many are prepared to listen even if we made progress in the diagnosis. But it remains important to keep trying.

6. An Ethos of Engagement

1. Paul Ricoeur, *The Symbolism of Evil,* trans. Emerson Buchanan (Boston: Beacon, 1967).

2. Epicurus, letter to Menoeceus, in *The Epicurean Philosophers,* ed. John Gaskin (London: Everyman, 1995), 43.

3. George Kateb, *The Inner Ocean: Individualism and Democratic Culture* (Ithaca, N.Y.: Cornell University Press, 1992), 200.

4. Ibid., 205.

5. Ibid., 210; emphasis added.

6. Ibid., 209.

7. In a compelling essay, Paul Patton explores the implications for art of Deleuze's attack on the idea of a model from which good and bad copies are drawn. Once you challenge the threefold metaphysic made up of models, copies, and simulacra, with the last being false copies of the true model, simulacra now become productions to be assessed by considerations other than truth or falsity. Now, "the difference between a simulacrum and what it simulates . . . is of another order altogether. This simulacrum is not in essential respects the same as what it simulates, but different. Although it reproduces the appearance of the original, it does so as an effect." "Anti-Platonism and Art," in *Gilles Deleuze and the Theater of Philosophy: Critical Essays,* ed. Constantin V. Bouundas and Dorothea Olkowski (New York: Routledge, 1994), 154. In the related language of this book, the infrasensible provides energy/thoughts that enter into the organization of appearances, sensibilities, and identities even though the latter never simply copy a model that precedes them. The infrasensible is not shaped like a model.

8. Alexis de Tocqueville, *Democracy in America,* 2 vols., trans. George Lawrence (New York: Doubleday, 1966), 373.

9. In *The Art of Being Free* (Ithaca, N.Y.: Cornell University Press, 1997), Mark Reinhardt does an impressive job of using one strain in Tocqueville against the other, until he comes up with a rendering of post-Tocquevillian freedom and pluralism that is admirable.

10. Gilles Deleuze and Félix Guattari, *A Thousand Plateaus,* trans. Brian Massumi (Minneapolis: University of Minnesota Press, 1987), 214. The best discussion of the promises and dangers of micropolitics is in this chapter, titled "Micropolitics and Segmentarity."

11. The dissertation by Deborah Connolly, "Mothering in the Margins: An Ethnography of Homeless Mothers" (University of California, Santa Cruz, 1997), reveals both how actively many who live in difficult circumstances work on themselves and how difficult it is to induce the desired effects when the contingencies of life press so hard upon you.

12. My attempts are to be found in (with Michael Best) *The Politicized Economy*, 2d ed. (Lexington, Mass.: D. C. Heath, 1982); *Politics and Ambiguity* (Madison: University of Wisconsin Press, 1987), chaps. 2–5; and *The Ethos of Pluralization* (Minneapolis: University of Minnesota Press, 1995), chap. 3.

13. See Norbert Elias, *The Civilizing Process,* trans. Edmund Jephcott (New York: Urizen, 1978), 84–128.

14. For a review of this struggle within both the academy and the city, see Caleb Crain, "Pleasure Principle," *Lingua Franca* (October 1997), 26–37. An excellent paper on this issue was delivered by Michael Warner, "Zones of Privacy, Zones of Theory," at the English Institute, Harvard University, September 24–25, 1998.

15. Jean-Jacques Rousseau, *The Government of Poland,* trans. Willmoore Kendall (New York: Bobbs-Merrill, 1972).

16. Michel Foucault, "On the Genealogy of Ethics: An Overview of Work in Progress," in *The Foucault Reader,* ed. Paul Rabinow (New York: Pantheon, 1984), 369. A fascinating engagement with Foucault and Freud on the relation between the formation of the psyche, institutional power, and identification is pursued in Judith Butler, *The Psychic Life of Power* (Stanford, Calif.: Stanford University Press, 1997).

17. The version of this perspective developed by Emmanuel Levinas is well represented in his *Totality and Infinity,* trans. Alphonso Lingis (Pittsburgh: Duquesne University Press, 1969). The issues involved in a Levinasian ethic are composed compellingly in Simon Critchley, *The Ethics of Deconstruction: Derrida and Levinas* (Oxford: Basil Blackwell, 1992). The recent book by Michael Shapiro, *Violent Cartographies: Mapping Cultures of War* (Minneapolis: University of Minnesota Press, 1997), contains an excellent critical examination of Levinas. Shapiro's discussion of the "ethics of encounter" in chapter 6 overlaps significantly with the orientation to a public ethos of engagement pursued here. He plays up the encounter between cultures that have had minimal contact. An ethos of engagement emerges within cultures in which the terms of prolonged contact between alternative constituencies have reached a preliminary point where several can negotiate with others without one party insisting that the negotiations be governed by the moral source it takes to be universal.

18. Of course some theorists regularly object to such opportunistic appropriations on the grounds that they are untrue to the true Nietzsche or that democracy does not need any help from this undemocratic quarter. For a reply to this type of objection, see William E. Connolly, "Reworking the Democratic Imagination," *Journal of Political Philosophy* (June 1997).

19. Nietzsche, *Twilight of the Idols,* trans. R. J. Hollingdale (Middlesex: Penguin, 1969), 44. I delete the sentence "A new creation in particular, the new *Reich* for instance, has more need of enemies than friends: only in opposition does it become necessary," partly because the terms "friends" and "enemies" are misleading here (after Schmitt) and partly because even when clarified within the broader meaning of the "spiritualization of enmity" the very form the nation-state assumes in the late-modern

age makes the cultivation of this form of enmity particularly dangerous. Nietzsche is wary of the state as "idol." I am wary of the nation. My Nietzsche is not a proto-Schmittian. Indeed, Schmitt's "decisionism" grows out of the insistence that its persistent lack of unity is something that must be remedied by the decisionism of the state.

20. Nietzsche himself argues in the *Gay Science,* trans. Walter Kaufmann (New York: Vintage, 1974), that modern individuals are no longer "stones in an edifice." We are much more like "actors" who expect to have a voice in the cultural parts we are called upon to play. This change in self-conception forms a crucial part of the democratic ethos. But if the old Nietzschean world of aristocratic politics is not reinstatable, the secondary Nietzschean ideal of nobility above politics is not likely to be operationalized either. I argue in chapter 5 of *Identity\Difference: Democratic Negotiations of Political Paradox* (Ithaca, N.Y.: Cornell University Press, 1991) that the space for this Nietzschean world above the "poisonous flies" of politics has been squeezed out by the contemporary acceleration of pace and intensification of organizational life. So I am with Nietzsche on the self as work of art and the spiritualization of enmity and against him when I locate democracy as the place to cultivate these virtues.

7. *A Critique of Pure Politics*

1. Mary Douglas, *Purity and Danger* (London: Routledge & Kegan Paul, 1966), 96.

2. Immanuel Kant, *Religion within the Limits of Reason Alone,* trans. Theodore Greene and Hoyt Hudson (New York: Harper Torchbooks, 1960), 18.

3. Immanuel Kant, *Critique of Practical Reason,* trans. Lewis White Beck (New York: Macmillan, 1993), 99.

4. Immanuel Kant, *Critique of Judgment,* trans. Werner S. Pluhar (Indianapolis: Hackett, 1987), 331, no. 86.

5. Gordon E. Michalson, *Fallen Freedom: Kant on Radical Evil and Moral Regeneration* (New York: Cambridge University Press, 1990).

6. Kant, *Religion within the Limits of Reason Alone,* 32.

7. Michalson, *Fallen Freedom,* 17. For a defense of the will that works within its aporias without succumbing to the Kantian idea of practical reason, see Richard Flathman, *Willful Liberalism: Voluntarism and Individuality in Political Theory and Practice* (Ithaca, N.Y.: Cornell University Press, 1992). Flathman refuses either to seek transparency of will or to treat the opacity of the will as its default. The latter is a source of individuality, one we must prize even as it carries risks and dangers with it.

8. Kant, *Religion within the Limits of Reason Alone,* 38.

9. Ibid.

10. Ibid., 41.

11. Ibid., 47.

12. Ibid., 48.

13. My strategy here is *not* to disprove Kantian theory and then replace it with an alternative without its own tensions and difficulties. Rather, it is to treat Kantian theory as a *problematic,* replete with the tensions and difficulties that flow out of its fundamental pattern of insistences, concepts, and assumptions. By introducing another problematic, with its own set of tensions and difficulties, you open up the terms of debate

and collaboration between the two perspectives. The attempt is to mount a challenge and to issue an invitation, rather than to present a proof after posting a disproof.

14. Kant, *Critique of Practical Reason,* 48–49.

15. Ibid., 38. In *Rethinking Generosity: Critical Theory and the Politics of Caritas* (Ithaca, N.Y.: Cornell University Press, 1997), Romand Coles argues that Kantian morality is cramped in its ability to cultivate a sensibility of generous receptivity to others whose mode of being exceeds the cultural mode of understanding in which we are set. He draws upon Nietzsche and Adorno to develop such a sensibility. I am aided by Coles's reading of Kant and implicated in the ethical sensibility he seeks to develop.

16. Benedict De Spinoza, letter to Blyenbergh (Letter XXX), in *Philosophy of Benedict De Spinoza,* ed. R. H. M. Elwes (New York: Tudor, n.d.), 337.

17. Ibid., 339. Deleuze says, "The evil suffered by a man is always, according to Spinoza, *of the same kind as indigestion, intoxication or poisoning.* And evil done to a man by some thing, or by another man, always operates like a poison, like a toxic or indigestible matter.... We should not think, says Spinoza, that God forbade Adam anything. He simply revealed to him that such a fruit is capable of destroying the body and decomposing his relation.'" Gilles Deleuze, *Expressionism in Philosophy: Spinoza,* trans. Martin Joughin (New York: Zone, 1990), 247–48.

18. Bernard Williams continues this side of the Spinozian tradition when he treats the equation between morality and law to be a "fiction" or "device" that has ambiguous implications for relations between groups. "The device is specially important in helping to mediate between two possibilities in people's relations. One is that of shared deliberative practices, where to a considerable extent people have the same dispositions. ... The other is that in which one group applies force or threats to constrain another. The fiction underlying the blame system helps at its best to make a bridge between these possibilities, by a process of continuous recruitment into a deliberative community. At its worst, it can do many bad things, such as encouraging people to misunderstand their own fear and resentment — sentiments they may quite appropriately feel — as the voice of the Law." *Ethics and the Limits of Philosophy* (Cambridge: Harvard University Press, 1985), 193.

19. Stuart Hampshire, *Thought and Action* (New York: Viking, 1959), 254. Jacques Derrida develops a related idea in *The Gift of Death,* trans. David Wills (Chicago: University of Chicago Press, 1995).

20. "To have a principle that makes it possible to reconcile the mechanical and teleological principles..., then we must posit this further principle in something that lies beyond us.... The only cause that can be assumed (in order to account) for the possibility of organized beings in nature is a cause that acts intentionally, and...the mere mechanism of nature cannot at all suffice to explain these products of nature." Kant, *Critique of Judgment,* 297, 298.

21. Gilles Deleuze, in his incredible little book on the interdependence among the three Critiques, puts the point this way: "Aesthetic common sense does not represent an objective accord of the faculties (that is the subjection of objects to a dominant faculty which would simultaneously determine the role of the other faculties in relation to these objects), but a pure subjective harmony where imagination and understanding are exercised spontaneously, each on its own account. Consequently aesthetic common sense does not complete the two others; *it provides them with a basis or*

makes them possible. A faculty would never take on a legislative and determining role were not all the faculties together in the first place capable of this free subjective harmony." Gilles Deleuze, *Kant's Critical Philosophy,* trans. Hugh Tomlinson and Barbara Habberjam (Minneapolis: University of Minnesota Press, 1984), 49–50.

22. Ibid., 35–36.

23. Gilles Deleuze, *Difference and Repetition,* trans. Paul Patton (New York: Columbia University Press, 1994).

24. Immanuel Kant, *The Metaphysics of Morals,* trans. Mary Gregor (New York: Cambridge University Press, 1991), 274.

25. Perhaps this is a good place to acknowledge the influence that Arthur Kleinman's work on psychiatry has on my thinking. In *Rethinking Psychiatry: From Cultural Category to Personal Experience* (New York: Free Press, 1988), Kleinman shows how attention to cultural differences in suffering increases the need to engage the corporeal effects of cultural practices. This work continues in Kleinman's *Writing at the Margins: Between Anthropology and Medicine* (Berkeley: University of California Press, 1996).

26. Joseph LeDoux, *The Emotional Brain: The Mysterious Underpinnings of Emotional Life* (New York: Simon & Schuster, 1996), 240. LeDoux draws upon experiments by him and others to reconfigure behaviorist, psychoanalytic and computer maps of the brain. His compelling exploration is closer, in my judgment, to philosophical work by Friedrich Nietzsche and Gilles Deleuze than to any other philosophical perspective in the West.

27. Gilles Deleuze and Félix Guattari, *What Is Philosophy?* trans. Hugh Tomlinson and Graham Burchell (New York: Columbia University Press), "Conclusion: From Chaos to Brain."

28. For a refined review of arts of the self and the registers upon which they do their work, see Jane Bennett, *Thoreau's Nature: Ethics, Politics, and the Wild* (Thousand Oaks, Calif.: Sage, 1994): "I describe Thoreau's quest as a series of eight techniques: moving inward, idealizing a friend, keeping quiet, going outside, microvisioning, living doubly, hoeing beans, and eating with care.... Taken as a group they display how Thoreau's art of the self combines bodily discipline with relaxation of intellect, and how it mixes intellectual rigor with flight of fancy" (17).

29. I develop this side of the ethical perspective in question in "Beyond Good and Evil: The Ethical Sensibility of Michel Foucault," *Political Theory* (August 1993): 365–90.

30. Hannah Arendt, *The Life of the Mind,* vol. 2, *Willing* (New York: Harcourt Brace Jovanovich, 1994), 198.

31. In a book that may remain (after all the new studies) the wisest study of Arendt available in English, George Kateb explores the critical role that wonder and gratitude play in the Arendtian sensibility. "Altogether, wonder at and gratitude for Being may help to diminish resentment of the human condition, just as inflamed resentment may close off susceptibility to wonder and gratitude. Where resentment proceeds... alienation ensues and works to block widespread commitment to the world (as culture) and to the life of political action." George Kateb, *Hannah Arendt: Politics, Conscience, Evil* (Totowa, N.J.: Roman & Allanheld, 1984), 268. To take the embodiment of dispositions seriously, though, is to think about how to cultivate the very feelings Kateb honors. He, like Arendt, hesitates to move onto this terrain.

32. Bonnie Honig, in *Political Theory and the Displacement of Politics* (Ithaca, N.Y.: Cornell University Press, 1993), brings out superbly these dimensions in Arendt's work. She also poses some of the reservations I will pursue, "augmenting" Arendt until she has elevated Arendtian politics above them. Here is a summary of how Arendtian bracketing of the social question becomes overdetermined: "Indeed, any reading of Arendt that takes seriously the agonistic, virtuosic, and performative impulses of her politics must, for the sake of that politics, resist the a priori determination of a public-private distinction that is beyond contestation. . . . Arendt secures her public-private distinction with a multi-tiered edifice . . . : 'We hold' vs. 'self-evident truth,' self versus body, male versus female, resistible versus irresistible, courageous versus risk-averse, multiple versus univocal, speech versus silence, active versus passive, open versus closed, power versus violence, necessity versus freedom, action versus behavior, extraordinary versus repetition, light versus dark — in short, public versus private" (119).

33. Hannah Arendt, *On Revolution* (New York: Penguin, 1965), 48.

34. Ibid., 105.

35. As we saw in chapters 3 through 5, the cost of ignoring such undercurrents of resentment is great. I discuss specific ways such currents sometimes find expression in the white working class in *The Ethos of Pluralization,* chap. 3, "Fundamentalism in America."

36. Arendt, *On Revolution,* 114.

37. Ibid., 58.

38. Arendt, *Lectures on Kant's Political Philosophy,* ed. Ronald Beiner (Chicago: University of Chicago Press, 1982), 68. Ronald Beiner, in his interpretive essay, suggests that Kant's analysis of common sense sets a model from which Arendt proceeds. But that seems to commit her to Kant's metaphysic of the supersensible. And Beiner also says, "Arendt does not really face up to this question of the ultimate cognitive status of shared judgments" (115). I suspect that Arendt wants to retain the authority of Kantian judgment while remaining wary of the philosophy that endows it with such authority. But if she repudiates the Kantian philosophy of the supersensible while sliding toward a deaf and dumb model of corporeality there is not much space left to work on the ethical sensibility of the self. Others may doubt that Arendt uses the Kantian theory of judgment as a model at all, reading her engagement primarily as an attempt to understand Kant in preparation for future work never accomplished. I am uncertain. But here is a quotation from *On Revolution* that speaks to that issue: "The same is true with respect to judgment, where we would have to turn to Kant's philosophy, rather than to the men of the revolution, if we wished to learn something about its essential character and amazing range in the realm of human affairs" (229).

39. I do not mean to say, certainly, that everybody is already inhabited by one, clean metaphysical perspective that only needs to be adumbrated. If advocates of a postmetaphysical perspective meant *that* I would have to agree with them. I imagine that most of us much of the time are inhabited by multiple metaphysical perspectives, existing in various relations of mutual tolerance, selective collaboration, and incompatibility. What I do mean to say is that this dimension very often comes into play when specific issues emerge, such as the right to die, responsibility for poverty, punishment for crime, the permissible range of sensual diversity, the sovereignty of the state, and the appropriate relation between indigenous people and those of Euro-

pean descent in a settler society. The differences within and between us on the metaphysical register must often be put into play if the relevant issues are to be considered. *Deep pluralism,* then, refers both to a diversity of religious and metaphysical perspectives and to a diversity of *ways* people of different perspectives and heritages relate to the same state. For a very reflective version of deep pluralism that addresses the role of indigenous peoples within it, see James Tully, *Strange Multiplicity: Constitutionalism in an Age of Diversity* (Cambridge: Cambridge University Press, 1995).

40. In a very thoughtful study of Arendt, Dana Villa says that "her political theory attempts nothing less than the rethinking of action and judgment in light of the collapse of the tradition and the closure of metaphysics (the 'death of God')." *Arendt and Heidegger: The Fate of the Political* (Princeton, N.J.: Princeton University Press, 1996), 157. Villa does not explore Arendt's orientation to the body in the light of his claim that she is postmetaphysical.

Index

academics: and postmetaphysical thinking, 19–20, 184–86; and secularism, 19–20, 29–30, 184–86

amygdala: as intensive brain, 28–29, 175–76, 189

Arendt, Hannah: and corporeality, 181–83; and disgust, 183–84; and freedom, 178; and love of the world, 15, 178; and the multitude, 179–80; and opinion, 181; and the social question, 179–81

arts of the self: and Augustine, 150–51; and ethics, 144, 146–48, 174–75; and Foucault, 145, 153; and Kant, 173–74; and Madisonianism, 151–52; and micropolitics, 148–49, 152, 153; and neo-Kantians, 145; and Rousseau, 152–53; and the symbolic, 153–54, 192–93; and the visceral register, 28, 35–36, 175–77, 183–84

Asad, Talal: on symbolism and technique, 25–26

atheism: and amorality, 67; and the difference within, 43–46; and gratitude for being, 159–60; and Russell, 2–3, 156; and the politics of becoming, 159–60

Augustine: and arts of the self, 150–51; and the will, 116–17

becoming: and ambiguity of being, 196; and dialectical progress, 70–71;

and justice, 62–70; and moral codes, 58–59; and responsiveness, 57–58, 68; paradox of, 58; and pluralism, 184–87; politics of, 51–53, 56–59, 195

Beiner, Ronald: on common sense in Arendt, 205

Bennett, Jane: and arts of the self, 204; and enchantment, 15–16, 190

Bennett, William: and alcohol, 103–4; and capital punishment, 131–33; and cultural war, 11, 100–106, 108–11; and the drug war, 100–106, 108–11; and freelancing, 104–5, 106–7

Blumenberg, Hans: and secularization, 190

Bowie, David: and *The Man Who Fell to Earth*, 81–82

Brown, Wendy: and wounded attachments, 199

Butler, Judith: and subversion of the symbolic, 192

Camus, Albert: and capital punishment, 134–35

capital punishment: and cultural war, 131–32, 134–35; and existential resentment, 135–36; and the right to die, 133–35; and the state, 129–31; and the will, 115–22, 127–28

capitalism: and the nation, 112–13

William E. Connolly teaches political theory at the Johns Hopkins University, where he is professor of political science. His recent books include *The Ethos of Pluralization* (Minnesota, 1995) and *Identity\Difference: Democratic Negotiations of Political Paradox*.